The
EVERYTHING®
Reflexology Book

Dear Reader:

Your interest in reflexology has made this book a reality. My intent is to encourage you to pursue this fantastic healing art in the way that speaks to you. Reflexology is for everyone. The journey of writing my thoughts, feelings, and knowledge about my passion has been a blessed lesson. My belief is we are only just beginning!

Take what you learn in this book and begin your travels into the wonderful world of touch. Explore schools and wellness centers, take classes, and become inspired. Reflexology will delight you as it does me, whether you are having fun or becoming a professional. Enjoy being a giver and you will receive.

Namaste,

Valerie Voner

The EVERYTHING® Series

Editorial

Publishing Director	Gary M. Krebs
Managing Editor	Kate McBride
Copy Chief	Laura MacLaughlin
Acquisitions Editor	Eric M. Hall
Development Editor	Lesley Bolton
Production Editor	Khrysti Nazzaro

Production

Production Director	Susan Beale
Production Manager	Michelle Roy Kelly
Series Designers	Daria Perreault
	Colleen Cunningham
Cover Design	Paul Beatrice
	Frank Rivera
Layout and Graphics	Colleen Cunningham
	Rachael Eiben
	Michelle Roy Kelly
	Daria Perreault
	Erin Ring
Series Cover Artist	Barry Littmann
Interior Illustrator	Chris Dowling

THE
EVERYTHING®
REFLEXOLOGY
BOOK

Manipulate zones in the hands and
feet to relieve stress, improve circulation,
and promote good health

Valerie Voner, C.R.T., C.T.M., R.M.T.

Recommended by:

Adams Media Corporation
Avon, Massachusetts

To Mom, for all your love and faith in me, your encouragement is priceless.
Dad, here is another book for you to read!

An Everything® Series Book.
Everything® and everything.com® are registered trademarks of Adams Media Corporation.

Published by Adams Media Corporation
57 Littlefield Street, Avon, MA 02322 U.S.A.

ISBN: 0-7394-4159-0
Printed in the United States of America.

This publication is designed to provide accurate and authoritative information with
regard to the subject matter covered. It is sold with the understanding that the pub-
lisher is not engaged in rendering legal, accounting, or other professional advice.
If legal advice or other expert assistance is required, the services of a competent
professional person should be sought.

 —From a *Declaration of Principles* jointly adopted by a Committee of the
American Bar Association and a Committee of Publishers and Associations

Many of the designations used by manufacturers and sellers to distinguish their
products are claimed as trademarks. Where those designations appear in this book
and Adams Media was aware of a trademark claim, the designations have been
printed with initial capital letters.

Contents

Acknowledgments

Thank you to all those who have taught me, and thank you to all those who will teach me. I honor your guidance. I give thanks for the many blessings I continuously receive from God. I thank my family, my son, Taylor, and my daughter, Amber, for their patience and love and support. I thank all my siblings, my peers, and my clients for the love you surround me with. I thank my agent, Barbara Doyen, and my editor, Eric Hall, for keeping me in the running. I thank Elaine Gordon for her unending inspiration. I thank my blessed and beloved friends; your calls kept me company. I thank all the reflexologists everywhere. We are the pioneers in the frontier of complementary and alternative medicine. I thank the readers of this book! Much love, light, and peace.

The Top Ten
Benefits of Reflexology

1. Helps alleviate stress and tension.

2. Improves circulation throughout the body.

3. Aids in the removal of toxins.

4. Helps the body maintain a natural state of homeostasis.

5. Encourages the immune system to work at its optimum level.

6. Helps rejuvenate the system and increase energy levels.

7. Breaks up the blockages affecting the flow of energy throughout the body.

8. Relieves common aches and pains.

9. Contributes to the overall well-being of the body, mind, and soul.

10. Promotes healthy organ function.

Introduction

▶BE PREPARED TO LEARN everything you need to know about reflexology. This healing art is for everyone. Reflexology is not a massage. Reflexology is the gentle application of pressure, using specific thumb and finger techniques. This pressure is applied to points on the feet and hands that reflect areas and parts of the body. Through reflexology you will teach the body to relax, to let go of stress, to recognize a new way of being. Everyone responds to stress differently. The key is, everyone responds. Reflexology teaches the body not to react to stress but to relax, letting the stress flow off rather than in.

This book will help you to better understand the benefits of reflexology. Please note that Appendix A includes reflexology charts you will likely want to refer to often as you learn how to practice on yourself and others by applying the techniques offered here. Reading this book will give you tools to use to help others any time there is a need. Just think, you can help your child's stuffy nose, your spouse's headache, or even your own aches and pains. Everything you need to know about reflexology is here for you to examine. Try it—you will like it.

Whether you want to work on your family and friends or have an interest in pursuing a career, there is a class available to you. It is recommended to try an introductory workshop first; this gives you the taste of what is to come. "Introduction to Reflexology" workshops are everywhere as interest in this trade is growing.

Professional training in reflexology is on the rise as the consumer demands perfection in this trade. Full training in this modality consists of a number of fundamentals. The training courses today meet at least a minimum standard set by a national testing agency. For instance, a reflexology certification course must meet at least a two-hundred-hour training requirement. This standard allows the graduates of such a course to begin the process toward national certification. National certification is voluntary, a postgraduate objective of most professional reflexologists.

State boards of education further support the professionalism of our trade. Most departments of education require licensure of the schools that teach professional training courses. Licensed reflexology schools are now setting this standard throughout the United States. European and Asian countries have long accepted only the highest standards of training in reflexology. Canada also requires professional training in reflexology.

An educational program for professional training in reflexology is extensive, dealing with all aspects of this discipline. Students learn the application of reflexology techniques and when, how, and where to perform these specifics. The history and theory of reflexology is examined as well as the evolution of the modality. The aspiring reflexologist studies anatomy and physiology as it specifically relates to reflexology. Extensive study of the foot and leg is required.

Reflexology schools require an externship or apprenticeship before certification is awarded. Students are required to document a number of practical treatments, following a standard of protocol formulated from their training. Many schools now require a thesis developed from this clinical practicum, as well as the documentations. A formal exam accompanied by a clinical exam is required before certification.

Reflexology is not massage and as such is becoming recognized as a modality in its own right. As awareness grows and the standards of reflexology continue to strengthen, the professionalism of reflexology will be accepted. Consumers are requesting fully trained reflexologists. Reflexology schools are separate entities, establishing standards to satisfy the consumer. An aspiring reflexologist can now feel confident that he or she can receive quality training in this field. This book is designed to help you decide on which path in the journey you wish to travel.

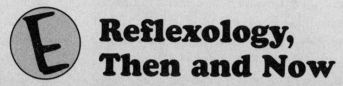

Chapter 1

Reflexology, Then and Now

The history of reflexology is an introduction to understanding complementary, integrative healing modalities. Humans have left records that show an ancient tie to modern reflexology. Be they oral, artistic, or written, these accounts create a connection from the deep past to the clear present.

What Is Reflexology?

Reflexology works points on the feet that are a reflection of the body. The feet are reflected images of the body, with the head at the toes, and the rest of the body following down the foot. If you imagine a body superimposed over the soles of the feet, you can begin to understand the basis of reflexology. A reflexologist works with this concept, visualizing the areas that relate to the body as they are found on the feet. (In this book, we are limiting the discussion of reflexology to the feet; however, keep in mind that the hands are an important medium as well.)

The process is a systematic application of pressure using the thumbs and fingers. The technique is specific—certain thumb and finger movements are used to access the reflex points. The reflex points represent areas of the body, as well as organs and glands. The reflexing of these areas creates an overall feeling of euphoric relaxation.

FACT

Reflexology is found in most eras. In every class of people, in medical practice to home remedy, reflexology has held a place of import. Practitioners of reflexology feel this is a unique form of work that can help anyone and can never cause harm if done correctly. Historically, this belief is constant.

Reflexologists work from the toes to the heels via a slow, gentle progression, reflexing the soles, the sides, and the tops of the feet. They also work points on the lower leg. As these areas are worked, the receiver begins to relax, experiencing the stress-relieving effects immediately. Often the recipient will feel a great sense of well-being flowing through the body. Perhaps the receiver has indicated a certain area of the body that is holding tension. The reflexologist will work both feet, returning to the areas mentioned by the recipient, and reflex yet again.

This modality creates a safe, trouble-free environment in which the receiver can release stress, finding total relaxation. Reflexology begins to teach the recipient the importance of letting go and provides the tool with which to accomplish this level of relaxation. A full session improves circulation, creating a sense of warmth and often restoring some sensation. The process involved with this holistic method allows for an elimination of toxins from the body, as well as restoring peace of mind and a deep sense of wholeness.

Ancient History

The history of reflexology finds its roots in cultures around the world. Many cultures use feet as a way of healing the entire body. Footwork has been around for a long time. Its traces can be found throughout most ancient peoples, with references not only to working on the feet but also to the importance of feet in daily life and spiritual life.

Reflexology in Egypt

In Egypt there is a wall carving in the tomb of Ankhmahor, who was the physician to the king at Saqqara. This pictograph has been used as the definitive reference to reflexology. The section of the picture dealing with reflexology shows two physicians working. One doctor is holding a foot, the other is holding a hand, and both are clearly working on these extremities. Christine Issel, author of *Reflexology: Art, Science and History*, reports that the translation, according to the Papyrus Institute in Cairo, seems to say, "Do not let it be painful." The doctor replies, "I do as you please." Imagine traveling and encountering this historical artifact, especially if the traveler is a reflexologist! Clearly Egypt holds a strong root in the history tree of reflexology.

FACT

During the process of mummification in ancient Egypt, the soles of the feet were removed to free the soul to travel beyond the earthly plane. In fact, many of the ancient cultures believed the feet were a key to the higher being, the sole to soul connection.

Throughout the World

From Egypt we move along now to China where again ancient writings speak of a therapy where pressure is applied by the fingers to the feet, hands, and ears. Eventually, this therapy evolved to the use of needles along energy lines called *meridians*. However, pressure from the thumbs and digits continued to be used as well. Dr. Wang-Wei developed this method in the fourth century B.C.

In India, the feet of Buddha and the feet of Vishnu both have symbols representing life and the flow of energy to live life well. The symbols are not reflex points, but they do seem to be placed in areas on the feet where a reflexologist might work.

Shogo Mochizuki, author and educator, tells us that in Japan you can hear the proverb, "The foot is the gate of ten thousand different illnesses." This proverb illustrates the continued journey of reflexology. Here the ancient art is carried over from China and continued by healers in Japan.

The Bible also mentions feet as a way of healing. To wash the feet of another was a symbol of humility and forgiveness. To remove shoes before entering the temple or holy place is an instruction not only in the Bible but also followed by Buddhists, Muslims, and Hindus. Clearly ancient history demonstrates that footwork has been around!

Native American Influence

You may be wondering where reflexology stands on this side of the world. Some people believe that the Incan people were the first Americans to practice reflexology, but there is no concrete evidence of this. However, it is believed that the Maya show documentation of reflexology. The Mayan civilization is believed to have been an advanced culture, and documentation found on stone carvings preserved many of the Mayan findings. The altar at Copan, South America, has engravings of a Mayan reflexology treatment, according to Jurgen Kaiser. Kaiser is a balneologist, massage therapist, and reflexologist with a special interest in hand reflexology. He discovered a clear connection between reflexology and the Mayan culture.

Native American culture speaks through oral history of the tradition of bathing and treating feet to help bring about balance. The Cherokee nation in particular has a definite custom of footwork for healing, passed down through the Bear Clan. Jenny Wallace, a Cherokee woman who is also a "moon maiden," grew up in the Blue Ridge Mountains of North Carolina. Wallace believes that walking upon Earth connects people to the universe and that our feet keep us connected to the roots of life itself. She practices foot reflexology using her intuitive abilities to guide her.

As you can see, reflexology has crossed all boundaries, circling the world a few times. We have been able to trace the physical and spiritual connection, but what about the scientific aspect?

Another practitioner of reflexology from the Cherokee nation is Jim Rolls. Rolls learned the practice from his great-grandfather, "Coon Dog" Henderson. The practice of reflexology has been passed down in his family since the 1690s. Native American history demonstrates many natural healing techniques, of which most are still used today. These are just a few examples of how footwork has been in the Americas for longer than we can imagine!

Scientific Roots

Reflexology finds its scientific roots in a form of reflexology appearing in a pressure therapy called *zone therapy*, which was practiced in Europe during the 1500s. The working class, as well as royalty and upper classes, received pressure therapy to cure their ills. Science everywhere was exploding with new information as researchers around the world developed theories. Medicine in particular reaped the benefits of this research. From Descartes to Darwin, humans began to stretch their thinking by moving out of the box into infinite realms of possibilities.

Amidst this growth, the term "reflex" first appeared in the field of physiology in 1771. Further research in movement resulted in the concept of "reflex action," which everyone is now familiar with. Thank goodness for reflex action or we *would* step on that tack!

Studies Affecting Reflexology Today

Throughout all arenas in science, European study evolved with major discoveries in psychology, neurology, and physiology, all of which affect reflexology today. From England and France to Germany and Russia, research from the late 1800s through the twentieth century was producing extraordinary theories and hypotheses. Much of that work is reflected in reflexology. For instance, neurological studies connecting the brain and the entire nervous system illustrated how nerve endings in the feet could create a dialogue with the entire body. Conversely, stimulation of an organ can cause movement in the feet.

Major Contributors

As with all work in science, there are different strokes for different people, which is demonstrated by the work of Sir Charles Sherrington from England and Dr. Ivan Pavlov from Russia. Both of these men have made contributions to the work of reflex actions, yet each is significantly unique. Sir Sherrington dealt with the entire nervous system in response, whereas Dr. Pavlov studied conditioned reflexes, the connection between a stimulus and response.

ALERT!

Never apply heavy pressure to a reflex or any part of the foot. It is not recommended to use tools other than the fingers. The use of steady, even pressure is most effective, whereas pushing hard or using inanimate objects such as pencils or so-called "reflexology" tools may cause injury.

Sir Sherrington earned a Nobel Prize for his work with the nervous system, a prize he shared with Edgar Adrian, who is considered to be one of the founding fathers of modern neurophysiology. Further work by Adrian brought about the discovery that the electrical intensity of a nerve depends upon the size of the nerve not the strength of the stimulus. This means you do not need to press hard to be effective in reflexology. What a great discovery!

In Germany, the medical community was also working with pressure therapy and reflexes. Dr. Alfons Cornelius wrote *Pressure Points, The Origin and Significance* in 1902. He developed the theory that applied pressure to different parts of the body assisted in relief of pain. He also recognized that pain had different levels of intensity.

The Twentieth Century

Here is where it really gets interesting. While all this work was going on in Europe, William Fitzgerald was studying at the University of Vermont. Intent upon becoming a doctor, he specialized in the treatment of the ears, nose, and throat while working at Boston City Hospital. From Boston, Dr. Fitzgerald moved on to work in London and then to Vienna, where zone therapy was in use and different publications on this subject were accessible.

Bringing Zone Therapy to the States

When Fitzgerald returned to the United States, he was appointed head of the Nose and Throat Department of St. Francis Hospital in Hartford, Connecticut. Dr. Fitzgerald began to talk about zone therapy, encouraging others in the medical field to learn this drug-free modality. Clearly Fitzgerald was influenced by what he saw and read while in Europe, so much so that he developed his own theories regarding zone therapy and reflexes.

This is where you can see how history has made almost a complete circle, as zones are different from but similar to the meridians mentioned earlier. Meridians come from traditional Chinese medicine and are the twelve energy lines that run through the body either beginning or ending in the feet or hands.

The doctor believed that by exerting pressure on certain areas of the mouth and face a patient would experience a numbing effect mimicking anesthesia without the use of drugs. He took this study further and discovered that pressure applied on the hands, feet, or over joints produced the same results. Fitzgerald soon found that pain relief often reduced or relieved the cause of the pain, further assisting in overall healing.

Dr. Fitzgerald began to record the areas of pain, the conditions that caused the pain, and the resulting relief. He continued to research this therapy he called zone therapy, experimenting with various areas of the body and charting his findings. He divided the body into ten zones. Each zone runs from a toe up to the head and out to a finger and back again, separating the body into ten parts. Any place on a zone can be affected by pressing points on the feet and/or hands. For instance, Fitzgerald found that if you have a headache, you can press your big toe or your thumb to help relieve the pain.

Influencing Others

Dr. Fitzgerald learned through his research and practical application how to relieve painful symptoms often without anesthesia. Fitzgerald published a book, *Zone Therapy*, in 1917 and lectured and demonstrated his findings to his colleagues—some accepted and many did not. Some doctors who did find zone therapy effective felt the practice was too unorthodox and time consuming to adopt. However, there were dentists, chiropractors, naturopaths, and others in the medical field who preferred a drugless treatment and began to use the zone method.

FACT

Fitzgerald advocated using metal clamps, clothespins, rubber bands, and metal combs to apply pressure on the extremities and bony eminences, which would anesthetize an area. Dentists today may speak about pressing the area under the nose with two fingers. Applied pressure to this area will actually produce a sensation very much like Novocain—try it and see!

One doctor who did believe and practice zone therapy was Dr. Joseph Shelby Riley. He was a doctor of medicine—chiropractic and naturopathy—as well as a teacher of these practices. Together with his wife, he operated a school in Washington, D.C., covering many drug-free therapies. Riley did not use any of the tools that Dr. Fitzgerald had employed; rather, he created a technique using his fingers and thumbs. He spent time documenting in charts the regions he felt were affected within the zones.

The Mother of Reflexology

You can see how Dr. Fitzgerald and Dr. Riley introduced this concept in the United States, but there was one person who was responsible for truly introducing reflexology to the modern world. Eunice Ingham, a therapist working for Dr. Riley in the 1930s, accepted zone therapy completely. Ingham is considered the mother of reflexology and is honored by all reflexologists. Through her work with Dr. Riley, Ingham moved zone therapy into a new modality she called reflexology. Ingham saw a correlation between glands and points in the feet and felt that working these points was key to zone pressure therapy.

Ingham connected the actual anatomy of the body with the zones. She introduced the concept of the feet as a mirror image of the body structure. Ingham's belief that the sensitivity of the feet improved the treatment led reflexologists not to consider hands as a medium for many years. We now know both are effective in enhancing the treatment.

In Ingham's book, *Stories the Feet Have Told Thru Reflexology*, published in 1951, she introduces the importance of nerves in the feet. She explains through her method, Ingham Compression Method of Reflexology, that it is possible to help congestion in certain areas of the body, particularly in the glandular system. Ingham indicates that stimulation of reflex points in the feet relieves symptoms throughout the body.

Ingham made other changes in zone therapy. She discovered that alternating the pressure created profound results in encouraging the body to heal itself. Ingham charted where she found reflexes for the body in the feet. She separated reflexology from zone therapy and recognized this as a new modality, further removing the treatment from massage. Equally as important, Ingham continued a dialogue with the medical community, holistic practitioners, and the lay consumer. She traveled around the country writing, lecturing, demonstrating, and teaching.

A Threat to the Medical Profession

The medical profession concurred with Eunice in recognizing the effectiveness of reflexology, particularly in relieving congestion throughout the body and in promoting circulation; some even viewed the importance of this technique as a diagnostic tool. However, many doctors thought reflexology took too long and didn't bring in enough money. The trade of reflexology became a threat, limiting what Ingham and those she taught could do.

Ingham has influenced many people who then began their own training schools. Doreen Bayley, a former student of Ingham's, established the Bayley School of Reflexology in the United Kingdom. Hanne Marquardt met Ingham and developed her own training school of reflexology in Germany. Mildred Carter, another student of Ingham's, developed a teaching program in reflexology and wrote many books on the subject.

Reflexology Today

Reflexologists kept on practicing Ingham's self-help treatment, and the method is still taught in her school, the International Institute of Reflexology in St. Petersburg, Florida. Many renowned authors and reflexologists have studied this method, and it is widely recognized as the root of modern reflexology.

Today, there is a national testing board that administers a voluntary exam that further certifies a professional reflexologist. This board is instrumental in encouraging continuing education and provides a referral service to consumers of nationally certified reflexologists. The serious student of reflexology continues to grow in this field, attending postgraduate courses, joining associations, and attending teaching conferences. The novice is encouraged to join associations and attend conferences. This approach enables the dabbler to be involved on another level.

ALERT!

As you read this book and practice reflexology on yourself, your friends, and your family, do not use reflexology in lieu of a medical consultation. If you or someone you perform reflexology on is under a doctor's care, make sure to work within the guidelines set by the doctor.

Reflexology has come a long way! Integrative health practice is an integral part of healing today. Throughout the world there are many reputable reflexology schools that are graduating professional practitioners in this field. Books abound, as do a variety of charts—even reflexology socks and gloves are available. Magazine articles often mention a condition that may be helped by working a reflex point. There are professional associations worldwide; we even celebrate World Reflexology Week. Teaching conferences are held annually, hosted by various countries and states.

Current Applications

CAM, the U.S. government Complementary and Alternative Medicine Board, is exploring reflexology as an acceptable modality. The field of cancer research is using reflexology, as is holistic nursing. Hospitals employ reflexologists in many capacities. Doctors are sending their staff to become trained reflexologists. Hospice is beginning to see reflexology as compassionate touch. Science has proved that stress is the number-one cause of disease. This allows the practice of reflexology to at last come to the forefront, as reflexology reduces stress and promotes whole health. The recognition of reflexology as a true integrative health treatment has begun.

Major research is now interested and involved in reflexology and its results. As reflexology is recognized for the viable healing modality that it is, the research will expand. Today you can buy a book like this and be introduced to reflexology in an informative, understandable way. You can learn how reflexology works and how to do a session on your family and friends. You can help people become less stressed and feel great yourself!

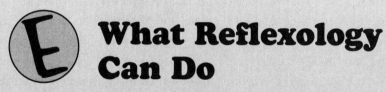

Chapter 2

What Reflexology Can Do

It is amazing what reflexology can actually do! Consistent, uniform sessions of reflexology create a receptive environment for whole health. The message to relax and to let the body function properly is relayed with every session received. The body, mind, and spirit respond to this technique, allowing for overall self-improvement.

Reduce Stress

Stress is part of life. Without stressors we would have no challenge, no stimulation—what would excite us? To be alive is to experience stress. Some people function best under crisis, while others cannot move. How people adapt to stress dictates the effect the stressor will have on them.

Pick up a book or article on stress today; within the first few lines you are likely to discover that disease and stress are closely connected. Even everyday activities such as going to the store, finishing a project, relaxing, talking with someone, or picking out what clothes to wear can be affected by stress. Each time a person overreacts to the experience of a negative stress factor, the proper flow of energy throughout the body is disrupted, allowing weakness to begin. Ultimately the body system may become too congested and begin to shut down, causing a break somewhere in the proper function of the miraculous body.

Response Is Key

Carrying an overabundance of stress may invite such developments as chronic fatigue, headaches, teeth grinding, and excessive anger. Chronic muscle fatigue is another side effect of stress overload. Excessive stress may cause anxiety and depression as well as a weakened immune system. Heart disease and cancer have also been linked to constant stress. However, it is how you respond to stress that is the key factor.

Some people are able to go through the day without overreacting to everyday stressors. They can sit patiently in traffic, listening to the radio or making out a grocery list. They are better able to deal with the whispers and looks in the work environment, not personalizing these behaviors. Some are able to flow with the responsibilities from work and home, while others cannot cope as well. Any negative responses generated from stress may weaken the body's systems, leaving you open to future complications.

Producing Results

Dr. Koop, the former United States Surgeon General, advocated the use of relaxation techniques to reduce stress, keeping the immune system healthy. Reflexology can help to reduce stress. This is a relaxation technique that produces profound results. Imagine sitting back in a comfortable lounge chair with your feet up as someone applies alternating pressure on your feet. Aaaah! Before long you are snoring or at least so relaxed that you cannot keep your eyes open. Now that is stress reduced!

FACT

Stress is a very real physiological reaction. Undue stress causes a rapid release of hormones into the bloodstream as the body prepares to use more energy. To be constantly "on" is what produces chronic stress. Many people do not know how to slow down.

Balance the Energy Flow in the Body

When your body is functioning at its optimum, you are in a state of homeostasis, which means balance. With homeostasis, every system of your body is working properly; you are a fine-tuned machine, running at full production. The central nervous system, which consists of the brain and spinal cord, sends messages through the nerves directing every part of your being to act properly. This basic operating function happens without any outside stimulus.

Energy flows through the body by way of electrical impulses, which may be nerves or chemical messengers such as hormones or endorphins. How does that work? Some pathways of energy do move with the nervous system, and others use meridians, zones, chakras, dermatomes, or, simply put, the universal life force. We aren't going to discuss the different pathways here—that's a whole other book! What we are concerned with is the fact that energy does exist and that reflexology assists in removing any resistance to the flow of energy.

Congestion and Blockages

Congestion or blockages can occur throughout the body, and stimulation through reflexology may break up this interference, allowing the energy to flow freely. An area becomes blocked or congested when the body overloads with toxins. Toxins are any substances that interfere with homeostasis, interrupting the smooth flow of body function.

Some of these congested areas may be actual stressed regions found in the feet. Scar tissue from a past injury, calluses, or pinched nerves, as well as a buildup of uric acid can all be the cause of blockages. Other causes may be emotional upsets, which can produce an overall feeling of listlessness and exhaustion. Emotional stress can bring about muscle tension, headaches, and even upset stomachs. The extended blockage of energy channels can result in long-term illness or pain.

Chronic pains, which may manifest as fibromyalgia, myofascial syndrome, arthritis, or irritable bowel syndrome, are clear examples of energy disruption. Meridian therapy is based on the concept that the flow of energy is blocked, not allowing smooth passage of blood, lymph, and nerve supply to the organs. When an area on a meridian indicates stress, or a reflex feels tight, this reflects congestion of an energy pathway.

There are ten zones, twelve main meridians, and seven main chakras, all of which divide the body into sections. Each of these sections is connected to the structure, function, and well-being of the body and is accessed through reflexology.

What Is This Energy?

The energy we are talking about here is the same shared energy that makes up everything on this planet. Humans connect into this universal energy through their own energy fields. The body's energy fields are composed of many electrical functions dispersed throughout the organic systems. You have electrochemical, electromagnetic, and many other electrical impulses working to maintain balance in your body. The molecules of the body run through many pathways of energy, continuously balancing your systems in a circuitous cycle.

Energy is measurable though not always seen. The machines used in conventional medicine such as EKG, EEG, EMG, MRI, and EKY are used to diagnose disruptions in body systems. These diagnostic implements seem to be based on the concept of energy and energy fields. The idea of seeking out imbalance and correcting the energy field is now being developed in today's medical practice. A meeting of conventional and ancient wisdom is taking place.

The Practice of Holistic Energy Medicine

Holistic means *whole*. Energy means *life*. Medicine means *to heal*. Whole-life healing is the practice of holistic energy medicine. This does not mean that reflexologists practice medicine. Far from it! Reflexologists and other energy workers assist the receiver in helping themselves by using the whole-body concept. The only true healer is the body, mind, and spirit of the person being administered to. The integration of many modalities contributes to whole wellness.

The balance of all three elements—body, mind, and soul—is essential for true wellness. Being healthy is a many-faceted component. Physical health exists when all systems are functioning at the best for the individual, who is then full of zest and exuberance. A healthful environment is essential and includes the food you eat, the water you drink, and the air you breathe. Honoring your living space and those you live and work with is also part of whole health.

FACT

Universal life force energy has many names throughout the world's cultures, such as Chi, Qi, Ki, Prana, Shakti, Reiki, Spirit, Yesod, Waken, Baraka, and Orenda. You have probably heard one or two of these mentioned before. The energy systems are accessed through zones, meridians, or chakras. The practice of yoga, with its postures and breath work, is another way to connect with these systems. Prayer and meditation are also powerful tools.

Mental health is another part of the holistic picture. Living a satisfying life and feeling fulfilled by your experiences are necessary aspects of a healthy mindful state of being. Emotional well-being is intrinsic to the quality of mental health desired. Many also believe that spiritual health connects you completely to the universal energy. A healthy spiritual self allows for unconditional connection and recognition of a Greater Source.

The social aspect of whole health is an important connection. An energetic, vital being lives a longer, happier, and healthier life than one who has minimal social contact.

Improve Circulation

Have you ever noticed your feet when you have been sitting for a very long time, perhaps on a transatlantic air flight or a cross-country drive? They may look puffy, swollen, or discolored because the circulation of blood in your body hasn't been energized for a while. In other words, you didn't move around a lot. Poor circulation may exist for many reasons. Reflexology is a powerful adjunct for improving circulation, along with whatever has been prescribed medically.

Blood circulates to every cell in the body through an intricate system containing over 60,000 miles of blood vessels. Reflexology encourages oxygen, blood, and lymph to move through the body, assisting in proper circulation. Normal blood pressure is restored through the process of reflexology. Fresh oxygen and food move through the body as it reacts to the reflex action provided by the thumb and finger techniques.

Regular sessions of reflexology help chronic circulatory issues. A receiver may indicate during the initial intake that she or he has diabetes or Raynaud's phenomenon. Perhaps the recipient smokes or is on a medication that may affect circulation. In any of these cases, a series of eight weekly sessions will bring about noticeable improvement. Following that, continued monthly sessions help to maintain enhanced circulation.

Another added bonus is that improved circulation allows proper blood flow to the muscles and the liver, which contributes to a warming of the body. During a reflexology session many people actually feel the warmth spread through their body—a calming glow of subtle heat.

Release Toxins

Our bodies are exceptional creations; the way we function is amazing. The heart has chambers to store and pump blood, while working with the lungs to give the blood oxygen-rich food. The oxygenated blood moves through the body via a system of arteries, and then veins bring the deoxygenated blood back up to the lungs and heart to begin the process again.

Picture the food-laden blood traveling through the arteries down your body, the rich blood nourishing you, eventually reaching the feet. Here the law of gravity kicks in and many of the toxins that the blood may have picked up are dropped off in the feet, as the veins begin the process of carrying the oxygen-stripped blood back up to be recharged. Reflexology helps with the removal of these toxic wastes by revving up the body to work smoothly and efficiently, flushing out waste material. As all the systems join together in harmony, the toxins are removed from the body. The removal comes through some form of excretion, as the body works to rid itself of any unfriendly substances.

FACT

The lymphatic system is another waste-removing component within our bodies. The lymph vessels and organs deal with the absorption of fats, the distribution of excess fluids, and the elimination of other harmful substances. Reflexology helps to support the work of the lymph and spleen, thus encouraging the lymphatic movement throughout the body.

Stimulate the Body's Own Healing Potential

By now you can see that our bodies are very smart! Sometimes they may need a little push (on the feet) to get them working correctly, but they can pretty much take care of themselves. Reflexology is the gentle guide to remind the body to wake up and act right! Every system of the body needs to work in union with the others. Bones without muscles would fall on the floor and blood without oxygen couldn't feed the body, just as food couldn't turn into energy without digestion and elimination.

Whole Health

Reflexology affects every system, creating an environment for whole healing. The immune system is the integration and interaction of all systems to protect the body from organisms that are not part of the overall system. The body works to recognize, eliminate, and resist all outside influences that detract from homeostasis. This modality encourages the immune system to continue to defend the body from all toxic invasions.

Guided visualization is a tool you can use with reflexology or at any time to help you be healthy in body, mind, and soul. By using your imagination, along with specific thoughts, affirmations, pictures, sounds, and colors, you can create the space in which to reside during this journey through life.

Whole health is what you are capable of producing for yourself by being proactively involved with your body. Prevention through lifestyle is a natural way to reach your highest potential. Reflexology can help you stay healthy, along with good eating habits, exercise, and positive thinking. What you believe you are—you are! Picture yourself as happy and healthy and go for it.

Create Your Own Reality

As you take charge of your wellness, begin to look at the concept of body, mind, and soul as an actual tool toward health. Try to understand how important it is to set a positive intention, allowing you to manifest a positive reality. You are what you eat, what you think, what you act, what you feel, and what you believe. Your well-being depends on the existence of internal harmony.

We all have heard of the idea "create your own reality." As you become more involved with the homeostasis of self, you will recognize integration of the soul with the mind and the heart. If you decide you are going to have a good attitude, no matter what anyone else implies, you will have a good attitude. Creating a new reality that is happier, more content, and less frustrated will allow you to live in a better space, a space you have taken control of.

FACT

Some people believe that the next step in total wellness is to trust in a power higher and greater than us. This means to believe that whatever is for your best will be. Of course, you do have to work toward the best and highest—your involvement is key to success.

Assist in Maintaining a State of Health

If you are healthy, reflexology will support your continued good health. Reflexology gives a jump-start to a healthier lifestyle when needed. If you know someone who can use some positive reinforcement and support, this is a great tool. Invite them to come for a session and watch how they are able to relax and let go of what ails them, at least for the hour they are in the chair. Recognizing the ability to relax and to let go allows people to believe they can be in charge and move forward.

A reflexology session is a loving gift to give. Everyone benefits from compassionate touch. Whatever age or condition, a gentle caring session of reflexology will enhance the life of the receiver and the giver.

The more reflexology treatments a person receives, the better that person will feel. Subtle changes will begin to take place within the internal balance. Reflexology joins with orthodox medicine, working to complement and support any existing treatment. As a healing art, reflexology encourages healing from within. The body works with the innate intelligence of your mind and the spiritual wisdom of your soul in developing whole health.

Body, mind, and soul work together to create a state of well-being. Dr. Herbert Benson, the founder of the Mind/Body Medical Institute in Boston, Massachusetts, suggests that wellness is a three-legged stool. One leg is the miraculous practice of medicine, without which many people would not be healthy. Another leg is the continued research and use of pharmaceuticals, which can be lifesavers. The third and equally important leg is holistic practice, the integrative work that supports and connects. A stool without all three legs *will* fall down. Reflexology is that third leg.

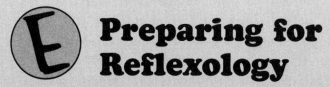

Chapter 3

Preparing for Reflexology

Whether you want to work on family and friends or want to practice re-flexology professionally, you will need to create a space and gather the proper items needed to make the most of a session. This chapter will show you what you need to create the ultimate relaxation setting for reflexology.

Create a Healing Space

So far you have learned how reflexology can relax a person. But where do you perform the reflexology techniques? In the middle of the den with all the children running around? In the garage among all the tools and bicycles? Setting aside a place to practice is important.

Take a walk through your living area and feel where you begin to relax. Sit in this place and see if it is comfortable to you. Make sure there is enough light—natural, if possible. Check to see if the air is clear; see if there is enough space without clutter. Even if you live in one room, you can be creative with the section where you will be working.

FACT

The rule for space clearing is keeping it simple. Getting rid of clutter is essential. Whether physical, mental, or emotional, releasing old junk allows you to function in balance and harmony. The areas of living and working need to be not only physically clean but also spiritually clean as well.

Once you have decided where you want to work, use lots of elbow grease and clear out all dust, dirt, and dinginess. Let yourself look through the eyes of the person who will be receiving reflexology in that setting. The size of the area is not important. Rather, it is the energy of the space that is key. The region you are working in should say, "Welcome! Come and relax, put your feet up and enjoy." Remember, for the next bit of time the person you are working on will have nothing to do but relax, so the arena you have developed is important.

The Right Chair

You've created an excellent healing space. Now, what are the people going to sit in? Reflexology can be done anywhere and basically on anything, but a good chair makes all the difference. Finding the right chair needn't be difficult. In fact, it can be fun!

RV Recliners

Reflexologists use a multipositional recliner, the kind that can be bought in a recreational vehicle (RV) store. Go on a field trip to your local RV facility and ask to see all of their recliners. These chairs are great because they have been created with the thought of saving space as well as providing comfort.

Generally the RV store will carry two or three brands of these chairs in different colors and styles. The chairs may cost as little as $130 up to $200. A higher price does not necessarily equate to a better chair. Sitting in the chair to make your decision is a must. Let the chair fully recline while checking to see that the back is down, your feet are up, and your arms are supported. Make sure the frame of the chair is sturdy and ask for the maximum weight the chair will hold. These chairs are great for house calls.

The Best Position

Not everyone will be rushing out to buy a chair; sometimes what is in the house works just as well. A lazy recliner or any chair that goes back will put your receiver in the proper position. The best position is with the head back and legs a bit above chest level. This position supports the back and assists with blood flow. Some people cannot have their head all the way back, so adjust the chair for their comfort.

FACT

If someone is restricted to bed rest, pull a chair up to the bottom of the bed and go to work. If someone is wheelchair-bound, place a stool or hassock in front of the chair and commence with the session. Always check with the person to see if they are comfortable, or if they need a bolster or other implement for support.

If you already have a massage or reiki table, this will work using pillows or bolsters. Again the proper position is with the feet raised basically in line with the chest. The head is back and resting comfortably with the legs slightly raised by a pillow placed under the knees and under the calves. The knees must always be supported; never let the knees sag.

If you do not have a chair or a table and are going to work on someone's feet, there is an easy solution. Place two chairs facing each other and have the receiver place one foot on your lap at a time. You can use a pillow on your lap for comfort. This is a quick fix and not recommended for every session, but it will do in a pinch.

Proper Props

You have begun to realize by now that pillows and bolsters are necessary utensils in reflexology. One of the best pillows or bolsters to acquire is a foam wedge, one that is large enough to slip under the receiver's knees. The wedge will have a narrow edge that fits under the knees and a wide edge that will support the feet. The wedge places the feet perfectly in front of the giver's chest, so you can see the feet and work on them easily. Wedges can be found in catalogs and better bed-and-bath stores.

Pillows of all shapes, sizes, and thickness are important, as they offer support and assistance in positioning. Some people need pillows behind their head; some need more height or support under their feet and legs. Have a variety of pillows on hand to assist in making people comfortable.

All of the linens used must be properly cleaned. Universal precautions for laundry are simple: use hot water and bleach. Any towels or pillowcases used should be changed after each session. This simple precaution will keep everything germ free.

Covers

Blankets are necessary to cover the receiver, especially during the cold months. Think about what happens when you really relax: Your temperature drops and you feel chilly. This is exactly what happens during a session. A cuddly fleece or other lightweight throw is often all that is needed. The act of tucking in the receiver as she lies back in your chair is very nurturing, setting the scene for continued trust and acceptance of the work.

Towels are an additional cover. After the covered pillows are positioned, a towel is placed on top of the pillow. You should arrange the pillow before you lay out the towel, so the entire surface area will be smooth and comfortable. Towels are also used to wrap up around the feet, and may be used under the head.

The Reflexologist's Chair

What the reflexologist sits on has been a challenge in the past. Nowadays there are a variety of chairs that work for the giver. The exercise ball is a favorite, as they come in all sizes and allow complete freedom of movement during the session. Rolling office chairs are great, especially those with seats that move up and down. Drummer stools work, too. Some reflexologists like chairs with a back, while others like the freedom of backless chairs. Folding camping stools are great. Not only are they the right height, these stools can travel. Hassocks are also often the right height, allowing you to rest your legs under the chair, and are soft to sit on.

FACT

Proper hand washing is essential. Before and after a session, the giver must wash her hands in hot water and soap, rinsing with cold water to close the pores. Do not use the waterless antibacterial cleaners, as they cause the skin to crack and split around the fingers. Feet to be worked are always cleaned as well; nonalcohol baby wipes are great.

You will know you are at the right height to work if your legs are comfortable and the receiver's feet are at your chest level. You need to be able to move your arms easily without raising your elbows. Check when you are beginning to make sure you are able to see the feet and move your arms freely, and that your leg position feels comfortable.

Music

Music plays a part in working to reduce stress. Today there is a variety of relaxation music to choose from. The key to appropriate sound for reflexology is to find music with soft, even beats and tones. Music for meditation, massage, yoga, or any healing art is fine, as the use of repetitive melodious combinations with instruments and beat is the preferred style.

Flute, drum, sitar, piano, and guitar are often the roots for the harmonious blend of music in the healing genre. Musicians pull from indigenous world cultures, incorporating ancient rhythm with newer harmony. The calming cadence used in the music of today is compassionate and joyful.

Peaceful, soothing music used repetitively is best to promote relaxation. If you use the same music during the reflexology sessions, the receiver will be given a subtle message to begin relaxing every time the music is played. Perhaps it is the beat or the melody, or maybe it is the repetition—whatever the cause, play music!

The use of music is good for the giver, too. Recorded rhythm is a subtle reminder to move your body while applying the treatment. Remember, if you move while you are giving, you will protect your body and give a better session.

Foot Soak

To soak or not to soak, that is the question. Foot soaking is a way to further the caring and guarantee cleanliness. A simple soak with warm water and Epsom salts is a fantastic way to begin a session. The warmth of the water coupled with the soothing relief from the Epsom salts introduces relaxation immediately. A clean dishpan (used only for foot soaking) is a fine implement for the soak. White is a great color and easy to keep clean. Just use bleach after each soak to sterilize the container.

What if you want something a bit more fancy? Currently there are many foot-soaking products on the market. You can buy a machine designed specifically for cleaning and relaxing feet, with all the bells and whistles. If you are drawn to this type of product, pick a machine with minimal vibration or at least multiple speeds. Generally this equipment does not keep the water warm, so remember you will be putting in the hot water. The object here is relaxation, so you don't want a noisy machine that jumps all over the place with cold water. The point is to reduce stress not shake people up.

ALERT!

Sterilizing the equipment used is essential. The simple step to ensure the absolute cleanliness of our paraphernalia promotes the safety of the receivers. Sheets, towels, pans, and hands all need to be properly cleaned and cared for. Strict adherence to these precautions protects the receiver as well as the giver.

Starting a session with soaking the feet allows the receiver a few moments to kick back and disengage before the hands-on work begins. Imagine the luxury of putting your head back and listening to peaceful music while your feet are soaking, with no directive to talk or otherwise entertain. Reflexologists believe this is an essential piece of the work; whether you soak the feet or wipe them clean, give the receiver permission to unwind.

Essential Oils, Lotions, and Powders

Reflexology doesn't use much gliding, sliding, or rubbing; therefore, a lubricant is not necessary. It is simply supplementary. A pinch of product before the session may help with movement if the feet are excessively dry or sweaty. If you choose to do this, it is recommended that you apply this to your hands rather than the feet to be worked. You have a wide variety of products to choose from including essential oils, lotions, and powders.

Whatever you choose to use on the feet, always apply it liberally *after* the session. In Europe, where it is very clear that reflexology is not a massage, reflexologists do use products before, during, and after sessions. However, here in the States, using lotion, oil, or powder indicates massage only. Recognizing the practice of reflexology and massage as separate modalities is ongoing at this time.

Essential Oils

The use of essential oil in reflexology has grown in importance over the past few years as practitioners recognize the healing properties of aromatherapy. The practice of aromatherapy can trace its roots to ancient cultures worldwide. Just as reflexology has evolved, so has the use of aromatic oils.

Research has shown the medicinal value of these oils. The scientific research dealing with essential plant oils began in France during the late 1800s. Like many famous stories in history, an accident proved the value of aromatherapy—an accident and a reflex! René-Maurice Gattefossé, a chemist, burned his hand during research. He reflexively plunged his hand into a vat of lavender oil. Not only did his pain lessen, the healing process was quicker.

ALERT!

A guideline for aromatherapy is to understand that less is more. Do not overuse; a drop of pure oil goes a long way. Remember to check with your receiver for any known allergies. If you have any questions about essential oil use, consult a professional aromatherapist.

The myriad of oils available may be confusing. A rule of thumb is to look for organic oils, those that have been prepared and infused without alcohol. Generally, essential oils are packaged neat, then mixed with carrier oil for safe dispersing. The label should read "100 percent pure," which means it is not blended, or "100 percent natural," which indicates there are no synthetic additives. However, commercially produced oils may use alcohol. Read all labels before buying any individual or combination oils and stay away from additives.

Lotions

Everywhere one looks, lotions for feet can be found. Magazines teach you how to make your own, retail stores stock several different kinds, specialty stores carry their own blend, and catalogs allow the consumer to buy herbal lotions, essential oil lotions, even lotions for aches and pains. Specific aromatic oils used for relaxation may be included in the lotions you purchase, either in a blend or singly. Lotions come in all colors and scents and have a thicker texture than essential oils.

Peppermint and lavender are often the scents used in lotions since they contribute to relaxation. Lotions that contain tea tree oil are good for antifungal and antibacterial use. Generally the use of lotions is preferable, as the incident of reaction is far less with lotions than with pure oils.

Powders

Powders assist in absorption. If your hands or the receivers' feet are sweaty, sprinkle some powder on your hands and go to work! Cornstarch, talc, and alum are all used as a base for powders. The roots from certain underground plants are ground into powder, and the use of these products will not clog pores. The more natural the powder the better, but good old baby powder works just as well.

The purpose of the powder is to allow the treatment to move along without interruption—a free transition from one reflex to another. Often powders are scented, which lends an aromatic flavor to the session. Powder applied at the end of a session may be used more liberally than at the beginning of the treatment.

Most practitioners find a cream they resonate with and use it exclusively. Some reflexologists make their own lotions or combine essential oils in their homemade creams. Generally, oils, creams, lotions, and powders are not combined in a session. Most work with just one consistently since it is used at the end of the treatment.

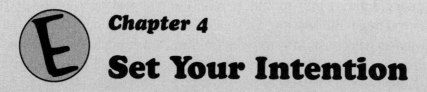

Chapter 4

Set Your Intention

The right intention allows you to remove all worry from a session. By intending to do the very best and most appropriate work, the encounter will only be positive. Reflexology cannot hurt anyone, and this allows the giver to practice without fear. When you perform without fear, you instill peace and harmony, further empowering the receiver.

The Importance of a Calm, Even Touch

Touch of any kind should always be even and steady with good pressure, and given in a calm, caring manner. Think about what you are doing as you prepare to work on the receiver. A gentle approach allows the receiver to become accustomed to your touch. Remember, you are entering into another person's energy space, so be respectful. As you begin the session, let yourself be calm and honoring of the receiver, who trusts you to work on him. Never push too hard, use tools, or dig in with your thumbs and fingers, even if the receiver asks you to.

The touch depends on the movement of your body and the reflexes you are working on, not brute force. It is incorrect to believe that reflexologists work so hard that they hurt people. They do not hurt anyone! Remember, they base their technique on the scientific fact that it is the size of the nerve not the amount of pressure that is important.

FACT

With the acceptance of complementary care, research agencies are currently funding studies in many areas of holistic treatment. Reflexology has been identified as a viable modality, creating an exciting interest in the field of investigative analysis. The productive feedback will promote the further use of reflexology as an integrative model, supporting conventional treatments.

Clearing Your Energy

Now that you have set your intention, make sure that your energy is clear; do not bring any of your stress to the session. It is important for givers to practice staying focused in the moment of the giving, without any outside interference. While you are in the role of practitioner, remember that you are the good listener; you are the one who is providing the quiet space and giving permission for the receiver to let go. Practice manifesting a calm and stress-free environment, creating the reality you will demonstrate to your receiver. A significant relationship is developing between the giver and the receiver.

You Are a Leader

Always enter into a session baggage free; check that backpack at the door! The more you let go of your old stuff, the freer you are and the taller you stand. Give thanks instead of complaining—you will find you are happier. As you become stronger and clearer, so shall your receivers; they often follow your lead.

In our humanness we have all learned to whine when life doesn't go our way. We may judge or cast blame. Sometimes we are unkind. Maybe we try to make bargains: If we act a certain way, we will get what we want. Negative behaviors begin to chip away at our energetic being, creating aches and pains, perhaps manifesting depression or other illnesses.

Begin from today to create a beautiful existence for yourself. Believe you are worthy of abundance in every aspect: spiritually, emotionally, intellectually, and materially. What you believe, you will be. Present a strong, positive, and caring reality to all around you and you shall maintain this truth for yourself, as well as encouraging others to follow a positive path.

Take Time for Yourself

The profound beauty of life is lovely to behold, if you take the time to do so. The fast pace today not only creates stress, it also does not allow people to take the time to appreciate being alive. Take the time to breathe and feel the joy of the day and the peace of the night.

Meditation and guided visualization are tools to help you clear out the old junk and create a positive reality. Plan to spend five to ten minutes a day, either early in the morning or last thing at night, becoming still, releasing anxiety and stress. Use meditation and breathing to clear out negativity. Guided visualization is useful in generating the beginnings of a new lifestyle.

Classes in yoga, meditation, or tai chi are all helpful in teaching you how to create a serene space for yourself. A holistic practitioner is as good as the practice he follows. Remember the adage to "practice what you preach"? A newer version is to "walk your talk." This basically means that the more open you are to change, the better you are at helping others. Reflexology is about excelling at the craft of helping others. The best way to achieve this is through helping yourself as well. Always enter into the relationship of giving with clarity and good intention.

Focusing on the Task

Once you have set up a space within which to work, you'll then need to prepare an interview format. Reflexology is about touching, and it is imperative to be familiar with the health history of the person you will be working on. You must also receive permission from the receiver before you begin the session. It is good practice to discuss briefly what is to be expected during and after the treatment. Before you begin working on a new receiver, carefully go over the details of the following list.

1. Create the receiver's history sheet.
2. Create a release form.
3. Explain what reflexology is.
4. Explain what will transpire.
5. Discuss the outcome.
6. Give suitable homework.
7. Reschedule if appropriate.

The receiver's history should include questions regarding current health, any allergies, old injuries, and any medications. Find out what the medications are treating, as this will help you to understand what conditions are present. Ask about current stressors and how the person is feeling at the moment.

The Release Form

A release form should plainly state that you do not practice medicine, you do not prescribe or change medications, and you do not diagnose. This simple form indicates permission given to perform reflexology. Take a look at the sample release form. This includes the basic information you will need to include on your own release form.

While the release file explains what reflexology is not, make sure you give a brief definition of what reflexology is. Explain how reflexology reduces stress, releases toxins, and helps with circulation. A discussion of stress and disease is helpful and educational.

Letterhead of Your Practice

To the Clients of Such-and-Such Institute of Reflexology

For your information:

- I am not a doctor or medical practitioner.
- I do not diagnose, treat, or prescribe.
- I am qualified to provide a professional reflexology session for the purpose of stress reduction and the promotion of relaxation. Further, reflexology works with the body to encourage a sustained balance and harmony. Reflexology helps to improve circulation throughout the body.
- I will provide the reflexology session using specific thumb and finger pressure applied to reflex points and areas on the feet, hands, and ears.

You need to know that:

- Reflexology is not a substitute for a medical examination, diagnosis, or any other medical care.
- It is your responsibility to stay current in your medical care and report any changes in your health to your medical practitioner.

I, *(insert client's name),* understand the above benefits of reflexology. I give my consent to receive reflexology for the purpose of stress reduction and the increase of circulation, as well as the promotion of homeostasis. I understand that this is not a medical treatment, nor a substitute for services as would be provided by my primary health care provider. I understand it is my responsibility to provide correct information to the reflexologist with regard to my health. By signing this consent, I give permission to *(insert the reflexologist's name)* to provide professional reflexology sessions until such time as I wish to discontinue the service.

_____   _____
SIGNATURE OF CLIENT/DATE   SIGNATURE OF PRACTITIONER/DATE

Stress and Disease

It is important for a receiver to understand what stress is and what it does. Give the recipient a brief description of stress. Stress is the way people respond to change. The response is registered physically, mentally, emotionally, and spiritually. If a person can adapt to change, he is able to flow with the stress. If a person finds change unbearable, he creates resistance. It is this resistance that encourages the growth of congestion and blockage in the body systems.

Point out that stress is essential to life. Explain that stress itself is not what causes the upset to our balance and harmony. Rather, it is the reactions to stress that will produce physical upsets. If you react in a negative, combative, hostile, or withdrawn manner, you are allowing the stressors to dig in. This digging-in forms an environment conducive to the growth of disease, whether that disharmony is physical or emotional.

Reflexology is an effective tool in dealing with the way people deal with stress. Introducing a positive reaction to stress empowers the recipient. Talk about what to expect during a session, letting the person know he will actually relax and begin to release stress almost immediately.

At the Finish

Once the treatment is finished, it is important to reassess and evaluate what transpired, letting the receiver know what to expect. Ask how the person feels at the end of the session, and give a reminder to drink water, which will allow the release of toxins to continue. Explain how he or she will remain relaxed and will have a peaceful and uneventful sleep later that evening. Point out that the calming effects will last for a few days.

At the close of the session, it is helpful to remind the receiver to practice proper breathing. Explain the difference between chest and abdominal breathing. Demonstrate with diaphragmatic breathing, letting the belly out with the inhalation and contracting the abdominal muscles when exhaling. Another piece of homework is to suggest listening to meditative music for ten minutes a day. Keep a handful of tapes available for lending or giving.

Often rescheduling is essential to continue what has begun. One session is an introduction. However, the benefits unfold with future sessions. Encourage the receiver to come back on a regular basis over a period of time; this will provide the most benefit. Of course, whenever a person can come is always appropriate.

Most reflexologists recommend a series of treatments, usually performed weekly over a period of six to eight weeks. At the end of that time, the receiver and the practitioner re-evaluate the receiver's needs. Generally the recipient contracts to a regular schedule of once a month for maintenance.

Being the Giver

Have you ever been on the receiving end of a service and felt the giver was not really present? Maybe she or he had problems at home, was bored, or was already thinking about what was happening after you leave. Didn't make you feel like returning, right? The point here is that you should be involved only in the person and the exercise of the moment. The element of trust displayed by the receiver requires you to be totally engaged. You are committed to stay focused on the needs of the receiver during the time of the session.

Don't Make a Laundry List

Working on feet is so rhythmic that you can think about what you are preparing for dinner and who will pick up the kids as your hands do the work, right? Not likely! Even though your hands perform the task, your brain needs to be actively present. Your body, mind, and spirit have entered into a contract to provide the best care to the person who has entrusted you with his or her feet.

Information about the receiver is constantly transmitted through the feet. If you are in the room with her, you will get the message. Your hands pick up the information first; then recognition kicks in and your mind carries forth. As the session progresses, the texture, temperature, and color of the feet change, alerting you to the physical response. You can see by the facial expression how the person is feeling during the session.

Give the Gift of Relaxation

Often people begin to unwind by nervously talking, sometimes throughout the entire treatment. You aren't expected to respond, only to listen. Eventually the relaxation will take over, allowing the stress to be released. A gentle suggestion to lie back and relax at the beginning could be all that is needed to prevent excessive talking.

The giver listens and works steadily with firm yet gentle pressure as the receiver accepts. Your job is to ensure a proper treatment delivered efficiently with compassion. To be effective, you need to be available throughout the entire session and constantly aware of the receiver's needs. It is an honor to be the one providing the treatment.

ALERT!

If you are not present when working on a person, you may miss important cues that the feet offer. You may not recognize tension still held in the body or the area that may need more work. The sense that you are not fully invested in the well-being of the person you are serving will be transmitted.

Short Nails and Clean Hands

Universal precautions cannot be overly discussed; learning how to care for your hands will keep you healthy and happy. First, let's talk about nails. It seems that everywhere one looks these days people have fancy, long nails. Red nails, pink nails, nails with squiggles on them, nails with little charms hanging off them, nails that are way too long! Imagine trying to hook into a reflex with nails the length of your little toe.

Reflexologists need to have well-manicured nails and hands. The nails must be short so you can perform your tasks without worry. Nails that are too long may scratch, pinch, or prick the receiver, which is not an effective technique. A reflexologist's hands are the tools of her trade, so she wants them to look good, neat, and clean. So say good-bye to long nails and concentrate on learning the moves to make you a great reflexologist.

FACT

Hand washing is an age-old concept. The old adage "cleanliness is next to godliness" could be used here since everything begins and ends with clean hands. Surely you can remember your mom always telling you to wash your hands—before dinner, after dinner, when you came in from play, work, or any activity, or any old time? There is a lot to be said for simple hand washing.

The best way to prevent transmission of germs is to have clean hands. After trimming the nails, wash your hands with warm water and soap and rinse with cool water. There are a variety of soaps to choose from: sweet-smelling soap made with essential oils; antibacterial soap; liquid, bar, or powder soap. The important point is to use the soap, along with warm water, in the hand-cleansing process.

Establish a pattern that becomes second nature during your treatment process. After asking the health questions, relax the chair into the reclining position; then excuse yourself to wash your hands. If you move from feet to hands during a session, wash your hands before the move. Upon completion of the session, wash your hands again.

Using Wax

With all this hand washing, there is a loss of natural oil from the skin. Make sure to rehydrate by drinking plenty of water and using a good hand cream. Paraffin wax machines used on a monthly basis help restore moisture and heal cracks in the skin.

Using Wax on the Hands

These machines are designed to fit a hand or a foot, singly, into the basin. Clear bars of paraffin wax are melted in the well of this machine, creating a hot bath. Once the wax has changed from boiling to warm, you can dip your hand in completely and then lift it out. The warm wax will form a coating around the entire hand.

This process is repeated three to five times, until a firm wax glove is formed. Dip the other hand as well. The wax forms a protective coating that encourages the oils of the skin to the surface, helping to mend dry skin and cracks. Keep the wax gloves on for close to ten minutes. Once you peel the wax off, a moisturizing cream will reinforce the work of the paraffin. Hands treated in this way feel soft and renewed.

Overuse of the wax can leach all the moisture from the hands, which can lead to breakdown of the protective outer layer of skin. The recommended time between treatments is approximately three weeks to a month. If you decide to use paraffin, make sure you adhere to the guidelines provided on the package.

Using Wax on the Feet

A great use of the paraffin treatment is to apply it to the feet you are working on. Do not soak the receiver's feet in the machine, but rather dip a disposable towel in the hot wax and drape it around the foot that is not being worked on. When you finish with the first foot and are ready to begin on the other, use another disposable sheet dipped in the hot wax to cover the foot you have completed.

Tissue works well, too. After it is dipped in the wax, place it directly on the foot. Your receiver will love the feeling the hot wax generates as it actually permeates throughout the foot. The heat felt in the foot will spread up into the body giving an added feeling of comfort and contentment. It's fun to pamper people, especially since people these days are so busy they forget to take time for themselves.

Giving is easier than getting. To sit and receive requires an element of trust. For many people it is very hard to let go of the control, to relax enough to feel safe. Reflexology provides an environment that nurtures, developing a new memory of harmony and balance.

Chapter 5

Understanding the Body as It Relates to Reflexology

Reflexology is based on the premise that the feet and hands are a microcosm of the body. Imagine a tiny body superimposed over the feet. Everything of the body is designated on the feet—every bone, muscle, nerve, blood vessel, and organ. This chapter will show you how reflexology connects with the different parts of the body.

The Structure of the Body

The anatomical structure of the body is the organization of the body and the relationship between the levels of this organization. The very essence begins with the chemical roots of life. Chemicals combine to form the cellular level—the cells that form the structure of all living organisms. Although cells share a common structural bond, they perform different specialized tasks as well. Each cell is styled to perform life processes. Cells are minireplications of the body and operate as such. Each cell metabolizes, breathes, reproduces, and excretes.

Metabolism is the interaction of all the chemicals that pass through a cell. One aspect of this process is catabolism, which is the action of releasing energy, the food needed to sustain life. Another aspect of metabolism is anabolism, which converts the food into structural and functional compounds. Metabolism is continuous. Food is taken in and then used in whatever part of the cell structure it is needed. After the food is processed, the waste is eliminated and the process begins again.

The Tissue

Cell groups that have the same structure and function become tissue. The human body has four major types of tissue. The categories are epithelial, connective, muscle, and nervous tissue. Each of these groups performs a particular function. Epithelial tissue covers the body and lines the organs. Connective tissue basically provides support and protection to the body. Muscle tissue allows movement. Nervous tissue is the major component of the nervous system, which has the ability to receive and send signals as well as organize the body's activities.

The Organs

The next level of structural organization is formed when tissues group together to become organs. Organs are structures with specific functions. As the organs group together in related function, they form systems. Finally, body systems work in concert to produce a complete living entity, an organism. The cycle from cell to organism is a total experience.

The anatomical regions that contain the internal organs are known as *body cavities.* Knowledge of these areas is helpful in explaining the position of many of the reflexes. There are two main cavities. One is the cavity found in the back of the body and the other is found in the front. The back region is divided into two parts—one holds the brain and the other the spinal cord. The front cavity is also two parts—the chest region and the abdominopelvic region. The two divisions of the frontal cavity contain all the major organs of the body. These divisions help us to picture the body superimposed over the foot as we locate the reflexes associated with these areas.

Homeostasis

Homeostasis is the state of equilibrium that attains and maintains balance among all the systems, allowing the body to function at its best. Many factors can interfere with the exact state of balance essential for good health. For instance, stress upsets the delicate balance maintained within the internal environment. The stimulus of stress may come from external pressures such as heat, cold, lack of oxygen, or noise. Internal stimuli like high blood pressure, chronic pain, unpleasant thoughts, or an imbalance of chemicals can interrupt the harmony of homeostasis. Reflexology works to restore this balance.

As you walk, you are affecting your entire body. Every feeling—good, bad, or indifferent—emanates from the feet. The way you walk dictates how the entire body functions. Proper gait allows for good posture and pain-free existence. Many aches and pains in the body can be directly related to the feet.

The Function of the Body

There are eleven principal physical systems within the human body. Each of these structures has related functions indigenous to that system. However, organ systems need to work together to survive. For instance, bones without muscles would fall down as would muscle without bone. Imagine a pile of bones trying to move with nothing to attach to. Picture skin without bones and muscles to cover. Think about food sitting in the body with no way out. The cooperative relationship between the systems presents the highest level of organization within the body.

The eleven major organ systems of the body are:

1. **Integumentary**—the skin and related structures
2. **Skeletal**—bones, cartilages, and joints
3. **Muscular**—muscle tissue
4. **Nervous**—brain, spinal cord, nerves, and sense organs
5. **Endocrine**—all the glands that produce hormones
6. **Respiratory**—lungs and all air passageways
7. **Cardiovascular**—blood, heart, and blood vessels
8. **Immune**—lymph, lymph vessels, and lymph structures
9. **Digestive**—teeth, esophagus, stomach, and associated glands
10. **Urinary**—kidney, bladder, and related ducts
11. **Reproductive**—ovaries, testes, and all reproductive structures

The Integumentary System

The integumentary system is primarily the skin, and it provides a protective covering over the entire body. Skin regulates the temperature of the body, metabolizes food from the sun, and excretes waste through sweat. Skin is a receptor for stimulus from the environment and communicates this information to the nervous system. Reflexology is a powerful stimulus that works to support the efforts of the integumentary system.

The Skeletal System

The skeletal system is all the bones, joints, and cartilages of the body. The skeleton contains 206 bones that are attached by ligaments, tendons, and muscles. Bones provide support for motion and leverage, as well as protection for the body and its organs. Bones also store minerals and produce blood cells.

FACT

Bones are classified by shape. The four main shapes are flat, long, short, and irregular. Flat bones are compact in shape and are found in the skull, shoulders, ribs, sternum, and pelvis. Long bones are very long, weight-bearing bones such as those in the legs and arms. Short bones have small block shapes, such as the wrist bones. Irregular bones have many shapes, such as the vertebrae or the kneecaps.

The Muscular System

While bones provide leverage and make up the frame of the body, they cannot move by themselves. The muscular system provides the movement necessary for the body through the contraction and relaxation of muscles. When muscles contract, their function is to perform motion, maintain posture, and produce heat.

Muscle tissue can be classified as cardiac, smooth, or skeletal. The functions of these muscles are distinct. Cardiac muscle is found only in the heart and it is involuntary. Smooth muscle lines the walls of organs and is also involuntary in movement. Skeletal muscles are the most abundant muscles, and these are voluntary.

Muscles that move voluntarily can contract by the use of your conscious mind. Walking, running, talking, or any conscious intent of motion is the voluntary use of skeletal muscles. You can decide not to move out of your seat to greet a friend or to shake hands upon an introduction.

Cardiac muscles and smooth muscles take direction only from certain systems and are not controlled by you. You can hold your breath until you pass out, but the lungs will continue to pump against your will, as the smooth muscle takes over responding to the lack of oxygen.

The Nervous System

The nervous system is responsible for the proper function of the body. The activities of the body are regulated through this system. This structure detects and responds to changes in the internal and external environments. The nervous system promotes reasoning and memory.

The nervous system has two major divisions. There is the central nervous system (CNS), which is the brain and spinal cord; and the peripheral nervous system (PNS), which is composed of the spinal and cranial nerves. There are further divisions within the PNS creating voluntary and involuntary responses through specific nerves.

The essence of the nervous system is its ability to keep communication active among all systems in the body. A breakdown in contact would lead to anarchy within the body. This system takes into consideration all of the body's needs, continuously supplying what is necessary for proper function. Reflexology works with the 7,200 nerve endings in the feet, affecting the nervous system and all related areas.

The nervous system is like a computer. The brain is the mainframe. The nerves are the connecting wires that reach out through the body to all the systems that are connected to the brain. Sensory nerves send messages from the body systems to the brain and motor nerves send the brain's response back to the body.

The Endocrine System

The endocrine system controls and integrates body functions through hormones that are secreted into the bloodstream. The endocrine system—together with the central nervous system—holds the primary responsibility for controlling the complex activities of the body. Both are communication networks. The CNS transmits its messages through electrochemical impulses while the endocrine system employs chemical messengers in the form of hormones released into the bloodstream.

There are many hormones, and they affect the body in various ways. This system can be characterized by four basic actions:

1. Hormones control the internal environment of the body.
2. They help the body cope with emergencies.
3. Hormones assist in growth and development.
4. They are essential in the process of reproduction.

All hormones are essential in the maintenance of homeostasis, as they alter cell activity to promote balance. Endocrine glands are ductless, meaning the chemicals move directly into the bloodstream. The body controls the production of these chemicals, only producing what is necessary. Reflex points relate to the hormone-producing glands; reflexology helps to maintain the desired balance.

The Respiratory System

This system supplies oxygen to the blood and eliminates carbon dioxide. The organs of the respiratory system carry air in and out of the lungs. The process of respiration involves three procedures. The first step is breathing, the act of exchanging air between the lungs and the atmosphere. The other two steps, known as external and internal respiration, involve the exchange of gases between the lungs and the blood, and then the exchange of gases between the blood and the cells. Reflexology helps to create a healthy environment for breathing, with constant reminders by the giver to relax and breathe.

ALERT!

The respiratory and the cardiovascular systems have equal input in the process of respiration. Homeostasis depends upon the participation of both units. Failure of either system will disrupt the harmonious operation of the body.

The Cardiovascular System

The cardiovascular system transports respiratory gases, nutrients, wastes, and hormones. This system protects against disease and fluid loss while regulating body temperature and acid-base balance. While the cardiovascular system provides nourishment and life to all parts of the body, it also transports energy for thought and action.

Cardio means "heart" and *vascular* denotes the blood vessels—these are the principals of the cardiovascular system. The heart is built to pump large quantities of blood that is carried by the vessels throughout the body for the exchange of oxygen and carbon dioxide to occur. Arteries carry blood out into the body and veins bring the blood back to the heart.

Working together, the lungs and heart cleanse the blood and the circle continues infinitely. Reflexology promotes circulation, augmenting the work of the cardiovascular system and supporting the heart and the vessels.

The Immune System

Lymph vessels and organs work with the cardiovascular system as they transport food and oxygen to the tissues of the body. Both systems remove waste as well. However, the lymph system moves in only one direction, toward the heart. The fluid recovered from the tissues, known as *lymph,* is returned to the circulatory structure to be used again. The lymph nodes filter out bacteria before the fluid reaches the blood for reuse. Reflexology works to keep the pathways clear, allowing for smooth transition of lymph.

FACT

Lymphocytes, working with substances from the blood and other organs, seek out and destroy invaders. T cells are produced in the lymph system and, with other fighter cells, work to eliminate foreign matter that weakens the body.

The Digestive System

The digestive system begins with the mouth and travels throughout the body ending with elimination. Many organs are involved with the function of digesting and eliminating. This system works by breaking down food to be digested and then absorbing that food into the body. The nutritional substances are converted to replenish and refuel our cells giving vitality, strength, and continued growth.

Digestion is a process involving certain activities such as the following:

- **Ingestion**—eating.
- **Movement**—muscle contraction.
- **Digestion**—chewing, swallowing, and gastric chemicals.
- **Absorption**—digested food moves into blood and lymph.
- **Elimination**—waste products leave the body.

The alimentary canal and the accessory structures are composed of the organs used in digestion. The canal consists of the mouth, pharynx, esophagus, stomach, small intestine, and large intestine. The accessory organs are the teeth, tongue, salivary glands, liver, gallbladder, and the pancreas. Each of these formations performs an essential job within the digestive system. Reflexology works with the digestive system to bring about homeostasis within each organ, assisting in the overall proper function of these structures.

The Urinary System

The urinary system removes toxins from the blood and maintains the acid-base balance of the body. This system regulates the chemical composition, volume, and electrolyte balance of the blood. The urinary system works in conjunction with the respiratory, integumentary, and digestive organs to eliminate waste. The excretory organs of these systems offer other avenues for the waste products of metabolism to be released. A primary function of reflexology is to remove toxins and help to re-establish harmony. Reflexology supports and enhances the urinary system.

The Reproductive System

This system can be divided into two branches: the male and female reproductive systems. The organs are different yet the functions are basically the same. Reproduction is procreation, the continuation of our species, the sustaining of human life. This miraculous process not only reproduces cells, but also allows genetic material to be sustained through generations.

FACT

All of the body systems work together to produce homeostasis. All systems interact; none can exist without the whole. Reflexology treats the whole person and supports the work of the body in its entirety.

The functions of the organs in this system are to produce sperm and ova, to secrete hormones, and to produce materials that support these functions through storage and transportation of the reproductive cells. The reproductive system interacts closely with the urinary, nervous, and endocrine systems. The many hormones necessary for reproduction and development play an integral part in the operation of this system. The nervous system is involved in the regulation of these activities through the impulses of the nerves. Some of the organs of the urinary system are involved with the reproductive system as well.

The Body Is Mirrored in the Feet

The feet are tiny mirrors of the body. Each and every part of the body is replicated on the feet. The right foot contains all of the right side of the body, back and front. The left foot holds the left side of the body, back and front. The tops of the feet are representative of the back of the body and the soles of the feet symbolize the front of the body. The inside arch area of the feet represents the spine. The outer edge and side denote the outer edge of the body from the head to the feet.

The temptation to diagnose a condition may arise when performing reflexology. Do not give in! Reflexology fights stress and makes people feel better. Reflexology does not cure. Reflexologists do not prescribe either. Always refer people back to their doctors for treatment of a condition.

The feet tell many stories about the people they are connected to. The color and temperature are important indicators of a person's state of well-being. How the feet are cared for is a sign of how the person cares for herself or himself. Every area of the foot represents an area of the body, and every reflex is connected to an operation of body function. If there is congestion, pain, swelling, discomfort, or discoloration on the feet, these are representative of some stressful element in the body.

The correlation between sensitive reflex points and specific body areas is fairly straightforward when you remember the foot is a microcosm of the body. An area of congestion may indicate a blockage of energy or it may simply mean that part of the foot is sore. Whatever the cause, the reflexologist will gently work the area to relieve the discomfort if possible. The giver works with the intention to release stress and promote relaxation.

Understanding where the body is represented on the feet gives us a deeper understanding of what may be affecting the person we are working on. Feet have a story to tell. All feet speak through their sole, which is considered a connection to the soul. The temperature, lines, spots, freckles, beauty marks, textures, and colors found on the feet create a tapestry.

Zones

Do you remember Dr. Fitzgerald? He was the doctor who introduced zone therapy to the States. Fitzgerald worked and researched in Europe where the concept of zone therapy was evolving. He worked with the theory of longitudinal zones dividing the body. The body has ten zones that run from the head to the feet, as shown in **FIGURE 5-1**. Every organ and body part in a zone can be affected by applying pressure to the feet and hands. There is an imaginary separation at the centerline of the body, with five zones on the right side and five zones on the left.

The vertical zones allow us to work with each toe or finger and touch the entire zone within that energy field. If there is a blockage or congestion anywhere along that line, pressure applied to the corresponding reflex will help. Often pain or discomfort manifesting in one area of a zone may actually be a referral from somewhere else along that zone.

Within the concept of zones, there is another aspect known as the *transverse zones*. These imaginary horizontal lines divide the feet into four sections. These areas are called the shoulder line, the diaphragm line, the waistline, and the sciatic line. As the names indicate, the lines divide the feet into reflex areas related to parts of the body located between these lines. The shoulder line is located under the necks of the toes while the diaphragm line is tucked under the ball of the foot. The waistline is in the middle of the arch, and the sciatic line is found across the center of the heel.

FIGURE 5-1
The body is divided into ten longitudinal zones.

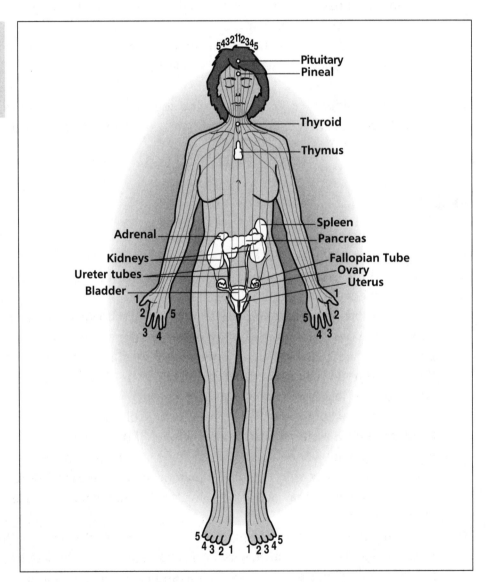

Meridians

Traditional Asian medicine looks to balance chi (the life force energy flowing through the energy channels) by keeping the opposing forces, yin and yang, functioning in harmony. The concepts of environment, seasonal changes, the elements, and the meridians are all considered in the pursuit of good health. The relationship between these elements must remain stable for continuous vitality. The constant force that is shared is the electrical energy of life, the ebb and flow of our essence, as we exist in rhythmic partnership with our environment. Reflexology works toward the goal of homeostasis, and the meridians that run through the body are a connection with the electromagnetic field.

Reflexology and the Meridians

Reflexology and acupuncture are two modalities that base a central focus of their work around the concept of energy channels. Both believe there are specific pathways through which energy travels and that by manipulating these paths, blockages that could cause disease can be prevented. While acupuncture points are found all over the body, reflexology points are on the feet and reflected on the hands. By using pressure that disperses congestion along the energy pathways, the molecules can flow freely, encouraging wellness.

The meridians run vertically through the body, beginning or ending in either the hands or feet. Reflexology affects the meridians, as many of the reflexes are actually on meridian lines. These energetic pathways connect with the systems of the body. An obstruction along a meridian may disrupt the function of organs found on that channel. Six meridians run on the legs—three yin and three yang. Six more run on the arms with the same divisions.

Foot reflexology works with six of the main meridians. These are each connected to a specific organ. The energy of these, and all, meridians moves continuously. Yang energy comes from the sun and yin energy flows from the earth. The movement of this energy along the channels is from one meridian to another in a steady flow. Some studies have connected meridians with nerve pathways; others point out that the transparent liquid that moves along the pathways functions as a nerve.

There are many thoughts and theories surrounding meridian work, which dates back over 3,000 years. The concept of energy flow is consistent throughout all analysis of this healing work. Meridians run through the body with connections to organs and the overall structure. The flow is constant, with chi moving through in a never-ending cycle of two-hour periods, and each two-hour unit is linked with a meridian and its organ.

FACT

Meridians are part of an overall system of healing known as *acupuncture*. These energy lines are also found in other healing systems such as shiatsu, acupressure, and reflexology. The meridian system has 100 meridians and connections. There are twelve standard meridians that are connected to one another by organs and are bilaterally symmetrical. Two vessel meridians are also involved.

The Twelve Standard Meridians and the Two Vessels

The twelve meridians are affiliated in a twenty-four-hour cycle. The energy follows a pathway through both sides of the body. The two vessels that are most often used with these twelve meridians run along the middle line of the body, in the front and the back. These two vessels divide the body and balance the meridians. The twelve standard meridians and the two vessels are as follows:

1. Lung meridian
2. Large intestine meridian
3. Stomach meridian
4. Spleen/pancreas meridian
5. Heart meridian
6. Small intestine meridian

7. Bladder meridian
8. Kidney meridian
9. Circulatory/pericardium meridian
10. Triple Burner/endocrine meridian
11. Gallbladder meridian
12. Liver meridian
13 Conception vessel
14. Governing vessel

The Six Meridians of the Feet

There are six meridians represented in the feet, specifically the toes. Using a basic knowledge of the meridians during reflexology, a giver can have a better understanding of a receiver's condition. The meridians of feet are the spleen/pancreas, the liver, the stomach, the gallbladder, the kidney, and the bladder.

The stomach meridian starts under the eye, curves along the face and up to the temple, then continues down the body and ends on top of the second toe. This is a yang meridian with earth energy. Meridians are related to elements that are the varied qualities of chi energy. The elements are known as fire, earth, water, metal, and wood. A yin and yang meridian is paired to each element, except for the element of fire, which has two pairs of meridians.

Although a pain or disorder may appear on the feet, often the cause is elsewhere in the body. The relationship along these energy channels presents a deeper, yet simple, explanation. The basic premise is that everything influences everything.

The spleen/pancreas meridian, which works in partnership with the stomach meridian, starts at the tip of the big toe, runs up the leg, turns in at the pelvis, goes up the side of the abdomen, and ends in the shoulder. This is a yin meridian with earth energy.

The functions of the spleen and stomach pathways work in relationship.

The stomach deals with digestion, then passes the energy of the food to the pancreas and spleen. The spleen takes the energy and works it into the blood and the chi. Many believe the stomach to be one of the root causes of upsets throughout the body. The stomach meridian is the channel that actually touches all the major organs. Stomach problems are often reflected elsewhere in the body.

The kidney meridian begins on the sole directly in the solar plexus reflex under the center of the ball of the foot. The path runs along the inside of the leg and thigh up to the bladder area, past the navel and breastbone, and ends on the sternum side of the clavicle. Changes in this meridian can indicate kidney and/or circulation irregularities. This is a yin meridian with water energy. The kidney pathway works in partnership with the bladder meridian.

The bladder meridian starts at the inner corner of the eye and runs up and over the skull, dividing into two strands at the back of the neck. The strands run down as parallel lines along the entire back to the coccyx area. From the coccyx, one strand of the pathway continues through to the heel and ends on the little toe. The other strand ends in the hollow of the knee. Changes in this meridian may denote painful conditions such as headaches, rheumatic pains, sciatica, and eczema. This is a yang meridian with water energy.

FACT

Meridians and reflexes often cross paths. Reflexology includes the stimulation of points along meridian lines. Zones connect with meridians throughout a reflexology session, giving further explanation to problem areas that have manifested on the feet.

The liver meridian begins in the leg and works in conjunction with the gallbladder and lung meridians. The liver meridian receives energy from the gallbladder line and transmits it to the lung pathway. This line starts between the first and second toe, runs along the inside of the leg, past the groin and bladder, touches the ribs, and ends in the chest. Changes in this meridian may be indicated by jaundice, fatigue, swelling of the liver, intestinal disorders, allergies, and headaches. This is a yin pathway associated with the element wood.

The gallbladder meridian is the last of the meridians in the feet. This meridian begins at the outer eye and runs through the temple to the back to the top of the pelvis and along the outside of the leg to the fourth toe. Congestion along this meridian may be associated with acute and chronic pain. The disorders affiliated with the gallbladder pathway are migraines, teeth and ear pain, jaw pain, pain in the lower limbs, and neuralgia. This is a yang meridian connected with the wood element.

Chakras

Chakra is a Sanskrit word meaning "wheel." This concept of energy focuses on wheels that spin at key positions within the body. This system of healing connects with the electromagnetic impulses found throughout the body. Chakras deal with the expression of energy in our physical, emotional, mental, and spiritual essence. The main physical structures are the endocrine and nervous systems.

The human energy system flows freely with the help of the chakras. There are many chakras found, not only aligned with the spine and hormone-producing glands, but also in the hands, knees, feet, and scattered throughout the body. The feet also reflect the spine and the endocrine system, so they have direct and mirrored representation.

Chakra balance distributes life force energy to create homeostasis among all systems and functions within the body. Congestion of the body can cause these wheels to become blocked, operating at less than optimum potential. Chakras and meridians share many connections. These vital energy centers influence our whole being.

Location of the Major Chakras

The major chakras connect to the major nerve plexuses located near the spine. Perhaps it is through this contact that the chakras affect the flow of energy through all the systems, determining health or disease. Clear, unblocked flow creates a healthy environment, whereas congestion can lead to disruption and disease.

The *root* or *base chakra* is the first wheel and is located at the coccyx, the tailbone of the spine. The gonads, which are the ovaries and testes, are the glands connecting this chakra with the endocrine system. The areas of the body affected are the lower extremities, legs and feet, and also the skeletal system, large intestine, and spine. The nervous system is also connected with the root chakra.

The second wheel, known as the *sacral chakra,* is found at the sacrum. The organs affiliated with this chakra are the reproductive organs, the kidneys, and the bladder. The circulatory system and the lymphatic system are linked as well. The adrenal glands are the connection to the endocrine system.

The third chakra is the *solar plexus center,* located in the center of the body. The respiratory system, stomach, gallbladder, and liver are the functions of the body connected to this chakra. The pancreas represents the link to the endocrine system.

The fourth wheel is the *heart chakra* and is directly related to the physical heart. The respiratory, circulatory, and immune systems are connected with this center, as well as the arms and hands.

The fifth chakra, which is in the throat, is known as the *throat chakra* and is associated with the thyroid and parathyroid glands. This center also governs the nervous system, ears, and voice.

The sixth wheel is known as the *third eye* or *brow chakra.* This center, located between the eyebrows, is connected with the pituitary gland. The sixth chakra also deals with the eyes, nose, ears, and the hypothalamus, which is part of the brain.

The *crown chakra* is the seventh energy wheel and is found at the top of the head. This center allows direct access to the flow of energy from the universe. The pineal gland is the crown chakra's affiliation with the endocrine system.

FACT

Reflexology does affect these energy centers in a profound and dynamic sense. Reflexologists directly work with the nervous system as they perform reflexology. They are also dealing with energy and are therefore connecting with the chakras on both levels.

Three Other Chakras

Three others carry a tremendous amount of importance. The *splenic chakra* is located near the spleen area on the left side of the body just above the waistline. This wheel stores the life force just as the spleen stores blood. Of equal importance is the *etheric chakra* connected to the thymus. This chakra is found on the centerline between the heart and the throat. Another major chakra is the *opal essence wheel,* an energy center above the body that opens to allow energetic light to flow around and through the entire body.

Colors Are Important

Colors are an important piece in chakra work. All colors exist in all chakras; however, each wheel has a signature color that is the essence of the energy found in that area.

- Root is red.
- Sacral is orange.
- Solar plexus is yellow.
- Heart is green.
- Throat is sky blue.

- Brow is midnight blue.
- Crown is white.
- Splenic is the rainbow.
- Thymus is pink.
- Opal essence is opal.

Chakras are energy wheels that connect not only with the physical but with the emotional and spiritual aspects of our lives as well. The root chakra deals with the issues of survival and security, connecting us with our family and our profession. The sacral chakra connects with our awareness of abundance, sensuality, and sexuality. The solar plexus center deals with our sense of self, connecting with our sense of empowerment. The heart chakra is our emotional center, responding to our feelings of love and joy. The throat chakra is associated with the ability to speak our truth. The third eye is our sense of awareness, our intuitive self. The crown chakra helps to bring together the connection of body, mind, and soul. Ⓔ

Chapter 6

Basic Reflexology Techniques

Reflexology tools are very simple; the thumbs and fingers are used with specific techniques to apply pressure in a particular way. Before you begin a routine, it is important to master the techniques you will be using. Do everything slowly and with exaggeration until you feel comfortable enough to advance. Get ready to start walking!

Thumb Walking

Thumb walking is the main movement made during a reflexology treatment. Apply steady, even pressure, moving along slowly over each area. The thumb is a tiny lever, touching the fine-point reflex areas in the most effective way. The nail must be short and neat with smooth edges so there is no dragging or digging on the foot.

Don't concern yourself yet with identifying reflex areas and points. That will come later in the book. You must learn how to walk before you can journey into performance.

Learning the Technique

Place one hand, palm down, flat on a table and let your other hand gently rest on it, palm down. Let your thumb rest at the top of the hand by the first knuckle joint and your fingers loosely rest above this. (You may use either thumb to practice this move, as you will interchange thumbs and fingers during a session.) See how the top thumb touches with the tip and outside while resting on the top surface of the bottom hand. Bend this thumb up now so it is flexed at the first joint. This will allow the tip of the thumb to be on the skin with the remainder of the thumb bent up.

Push off with this thumb on the surface below so that the pad comes in contact with the skin. When doing this, your thumb will once again lie flat while the rest of the hand lies slightly across the surface with the fingers relaxed and wrapped easily around the outer edge of the hand. Pull the thumb back up into a bent position, hold down on this spot, and then move forward again. (See **FIGURE 6-1**.) The thumb continues to perform this creeping motion, just like the little green inchworm that announces the beginning of spring. You will notice how more of the thumb surface comes into play as you walk along. This movement continues with tiny little bites across the top of the hand. When you work across the top surface of the hand, the fingers will be resting along the top of the hand above the knuckles.

Each movement is slow and controlled. Pull up at the joint and count 1, 2, 3. Push down and creep forward on the pad of the thumb and

FIGURE 6-1
Thumb
walking is the
most impor-
tant technique
you will learn.

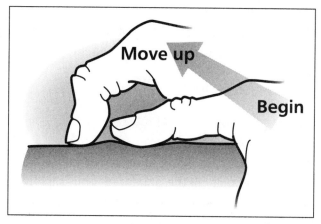

Move up

Begin

count 1, 2, 3. Bend up again at the joint, pull back a bit with the thumb, and count 1, 2, 3. Switch hands and work the same movement across the other hand with the opposite thumb. You do not need to apply extra pressure, just concentrate on the thumb walking right now.

Lift your hands off the table and continue to practice this movement, with your hands resting on your lap or on each other. Then turn your hands over and thumb walk along the palm surface, switching back and forth. Allow the fingers of the hand working to gently cup the back of the hand being worked, while working across the palm with your thumb.

ESSENTIAL

Remember the ad that told us to let our "fingers do the walking"? This is exactly what you are doing with your thumb. Let your thumb do the walking across the surfaces—the top and palm— of your hand.

Practice, Practice, Practice!

Rest a hand on the counter and see how the thumb again assumes the position. Your thumb will automatically rest almost in the thumb-walking position. Once you bend and begin the process, the thumb comes up a bit more on the surface you are walking on. Reflexology is so natural; the hand seems to be made specifically to perform this task. Don't worry if you feel you are not doing it exactly right. If you follow these simple directions, you will be fine.

The best way to master this is to practice, practice, and practice some more. Practice on the back of your hand, on the countertop, on the steering wheel (not while you are driving, of course), practice while you are waiting in line, or while you are sitting at a meeting. Practice on your friends, mate, mom, dad, children, and pets—practice on anyone and any surface available.

Finger Walking

Finger walking is similar to thumb walking; it uses the same motion and form. The index finger—sometimes all the fingers—is bent slightly at the first joint then pushed along in a walking or creeping movement. Practice again on your own hands.

Learning the Technique

Close a hand into a loose fist, the top surface facing up; this is the hand you will work on. Grasp this hand with the other hand, letting your thumb slide between the thumb and index finger of the fisted hand and rest in your palm. The fingers are on top of the hand. While you are using the index finger, the other fingers will rest on top, slightly closed in. These fingers move along without working as the index finger walks down the top of the hand.

Begin at the first knuckle under the index finger of the hand with the closed fist. Begin by placing the finger, tip surface touching, just below the knuckle. You will be moving away from the fingers down toward the wrist. From the tip touching the hand, the finger is bent with the first joint pushing out. Bend the working finger down at the first joint, pushing forward slightly. This straightens the finger a bit, so that the pad of the finger is touching the surface of your hand. Pull back up into the hammerlike position. Again the movement is a push/pull motion, creeping along just like the inchworm. This is one finger-walk move.

Walk down the top of the hand, in between the thumb and index finger, in the fleshy section. The thumb will rest under this area; the other fingers are slightly tucked under, just along for the ride. Begin with the finger bent up in the hammer shape, and count 1, 2, 3. Move the finger down into a straight line, with the pad touching the skin pushing forward, and count 1, 2, 3. Pull up into the hammer shape, and pull slightly back again. Imagine you are pinching the skin. You aren't, but it does seem as though you are. Continue this exercise with the finger walking down the fleshy pad, and the thumb moving underneath. The thumb holds the underside, providing leverage, keeping the hand steady, and pushing back a bit.

Bring the index finger back to the first knuckle, unfurl your other fingers, and place these fingers at the other knuckles. Bend all the fingers up onto the tips. Move forward ever so slightly, straightening out the fingers as the pads touch the skin. Bring the fingers back up onto the tips; this will pull the skin back toward the knuckles a bit. Move forward again and continue the push-pull movement down to the wrist.

ALERT!

Never use tools. Pushing a pencil or an implement that says it is a "reflexology" tool can hurt the foot! Tools have no feeling; you cannot gauge how deeply they are going into the foot. Remember, fingers and thumbs are all that is needed to do an excellent job. It's not how hard you push; it's where you are working that is important.

Why the Fingers Are Used

The index finger is used to reach certain reflexes, on the top or side of the foot. When the fingers are used, the thumb generally is held in place on the opposite side of the foot to provide leverage. Finger pressure is steady and even, not abrupt or heavy. Using the fingers also gives the thumb a break so the hands don't become tired.

Finger walking allows the area of pressure to broaden. Always move forward with tiny bites. Watch that you are not bending your finger too much; this will cause your fingers to ache later. Slow movement ensures all the reflexes will be stimulated.

When you use all four fingers at once, you are covering a greater region at one time, which is useful in some areas. The back reflexes are a part of the foot where using the fingers is very effective. This technique is also excellent for working on the lymph reflexes, but you will learn more about that later. The more you practice, you will begin to find places on the foot where the index finger or all the fingers are more efficient than the thumb.

Rotation

In rotation, the tip of the thumb is placed directly on the point to be rotated. Using your hands to practice on, turn a palm up and find the space just below the little finger. Whatever palm you choose to work on, let it rest cupped in the other palm. The fingers of the holding hand, which is also the working hand, rest under the knuckles. The thumb is going to work on the palm surface from the little finger side.

Learning the Technique

Feel under the little finger, on the palm surface. Find the undersurface of the knuckle bone and place your thumb on it. Back up to the edge of the hand and gently thumb walk over the bone, thumb walking in along the ball of the hand. You are walking horizontally across the palm. This thumb-walking movement will take about three tiny inchworm bites to reach past this bone. Notice how the tip of the thumb drops into a space after the joint bone is passed over. If you have gone too far, you will find another bony bump, not quite as big as the first.

FACT

The five long bones in the hand are called *metacarpal bones.* The beginning of each bone has a head. These heads join with the ends of the fingers—the bones known as *phalanges*—to form the knuckles.

First, hold the hand steady. Then gently circle in a small rotating motion on this area. Staying right here, continue this move for about the count of three. Now press in and actually rotate the hand a bit, moving it around as the thumb holds the spot. The moving of the hand is minimal;

you aren't actually turning the hand for the sake of turning. The movement of the hand is to allow the thumb to move in deeply without much force. To transition from this, move forward in a thumb walk along the rest of the area being worked.

When to Use Rotation

A reflexologist does not always rotate the foot. It depends upon what reflexes or areas are being working on. Rule of thumb, if anatomically—meaning physically—the foot cannot rotate, such as when working on the toes, do not turn. If the foot can move easily, such as when working on the solar plexus reflex, then go ahead. Again all of this will come with practice.

Rotation is a technique that allows the thumb to work steadily and directly on a reflex point. The thumb is walking along, when a reflex point is reached that needs more attention. Perhaps the skin is tougher, there is a crunchy feeling under the thumb, or the technique for this particular reflex calls for rotating in on the point. Whatever the reason, rotation feels great to the receiver.

Pressing

This technique uses the entire thumb surface, holding flat along the bottom of the foot on a particular reflex. The thumb is in a holding position, without undue pressure. When pressing is indicated, generally after rotating, press down and hold firmly without moving. Pressing allows you to reach an entire reflex surface in a gentle, connected way. This is another technique that when used properly will give your thumbs a break.

Pressing on a reflex allows you to feel the subtle shift that will happen as the reflex connects with the energy, releasing any tension in that area. The amount of pressure used with this technique is slight; there is no need to push hard or dig. As the reflex relaxes, the thumb will actually lift up a bit from the skin, an indication to move on.

At times you can rotate the hand as you press, which will broaden the area you are working on. Place your thumb in the center of your other hand. Let the thumb press from the center outward toward the side of the hand. Your thumb is pressing on an imaginary line from the center to the outside edge (lateral side) of the hand. Lift your fingers and turn your hand toward the thumb side of the hand you are pressing on; feel how you stay connected to the reflex, yet allow the area to grow. Try this technique whenever you have a flat area to work, and see when it is effective and when it is not.

Imagine your fingers are your eyes. Once you have learned a basic technique and routine, your thumbs and fingers will be your guide. Through informed touch you will know how much time to spend on a reflex and where to return, if needed. Reflexology never ever hurts.

Hooking and Pulling Back

This is an advanced move, which allows you to reach way into a reflex, stimulating deeply, without hurting. The hook technique is actually approached in three parts. First, thumb walking is used to move to the reflex, pinpointing the spot. Then, rotation is used to zero in on the exact point. Finally, the thumb hooks in on the reflex. Reflexologists pay close attention to the skin under their thumbs to see if the surface is tense or pliable.

Only the thumb—on the particular reflexes that you will learn—performs the hooking technique. These reflexes will be discussed later in this book. For right now, just concentrate on practicing the technique.

Learning the Technique

Hold your left thumb up, curling the other fingers in, giving the thumb plenty of room. The thumb's fleshy pad is facing you. Look at the first section, and imagine a line running from the top of the thumb, down the center to the first joint. Find the center of that line and draw an imaginary line across it.

Use your other hand to thumb walk up from the neck of the thumb to the place where the two lines cross. Let the tip of your thumb rest on the crossing point. Now rotation comes into play as you circle in on the exact point. You may feel the point pushing back to you. This is exactly what you want to feel.

FACT

Reflexology is a technical modality that also depends upon the senses of the practitioner. As you become better with the actual technology of application, you will begin to trust what you feel as well. For instance, pushing back is a feeling; you will sense it with time.

Gently continue to circle on the point, using your thumb to apply gentle, steady pressure as the circles move in, targeting the exact spot. Once the rotation has allowed the thumb to touch in deeply, the thumb is then turned halfway around (180 degrees) on the reflex, pushed in, and hooked up.

The hooking movement is done with the tip of the thumb. As the thumb pushes in, it actually hooks on some of the skin. With the hook movement in place, pull the thumb back, as though you have just secured bait on a hook. Don't worry, you cannot hook in too far; the body will stop you.

Hold in this hooklike position, gently pushing in even farther. Please make sure your nails are short, as this technique goes in quite deep. Hold in this position for a count of three to five, then slowly release as you move on.

The Possibility of Pain

Sometimes there is a slight flash of pain, but this will subside as the point is held. The pain, which feels like a pinprick or a long fingernail, is an indication that there may be congestion at this particular reflex. If the pain does not abate, move on to the solar plexus reflex where you should press in with your thumb and hold, asking the receiver to breathe slowly and deeply. Releasing this reflex, return to the painful spot and hook in again. The pain should be gone or minimal. If there is still pain, just move away from the reflex at this point and continue on with the session.

Holding

There are two types of holding. One holding is what the nonmoving hand does. It is very important to support the foot that is being worked on. The hand holding the foot keeps the foot stable and provides leverage for the working hand. As you switch back and forth during a session, each hand has a turn holding or working.

Hold the foot you are working on by placing the fingers behind the foot with the thumb resting on the sole. If you are working near the top of the foot, hold near the top. If you are working at the bottom of the foot, you will generally hold near the ankle. When you are working on hands, one hand supports and the other works.

Holding the feet in this way provides leverage and support. Leverage allows the thumb or finger doing the work to have a strong hold on the surface being reflexed. The fingers support the foot as the thumb walks on the other side, creating a circle of healing. As the thumb moves, so do the fingers—the leverage and support is always there.

QUESTION?

What happens if we have to use both hands during a technique?
There are times when we will not be using one hand to hold and one to work. The support comes from the pillow under the feet as well as the hands working on the feet.

The other type of holding is that of holding on a reflex point during certain techniques. For instance, you may rotate and hold, hook and hold, or press and hold. Remember, reflexology is a steady, smooth system, so holding on a point is integral to this style of work.

When you rotate or press and hold on a point, often the receiver will feel a warm sensation begin to radiate through her body as the thumb stops moving and holds. Holding at the reflex point is amplifying the healing effect. With the hook and hold, you are pinpointing a very specific region of the reflex, again creating a direct pathway.

Butterfly

Butterfly is a wonderful two-handed technique used to smooth out an area and to work a bit deeper. It is named the butterfly because the imaginary shape the thumbs make are like the wings of a butterfly. This technique is done with both hands holding on to the foot, with the palms resting on the top surface of the foot and the thumbs on the sole. The movement is with the thumbs; the rest of the hand comes along for the ride. Let the thumbs move in toward the center of the foot and back. Imagine your thumbs look like butterfly wings as you move in and out.

Learning the Technique

The thumbs move in a less exaggerated thumb walk toward the center, and then quickly slide back to the edge. Move your thumbs up each time you are along the edge, basically making a new line to walk. Your thumbs meet at the center of the sole, and then slide back to the edge. The butterfly may be done in a specific area or on the entire foot, depending on where you are in the sequence of the treatment. Remember, unless otherwise indicated, the fingers basically slide along with the hands as the thumbs perform.

FACT

As an effective transition tool, the butterfly technique allows for easy movement as you change from one place to another. At times you may move your fingers as well as your thumbs. In this case, all the fingers and the thumbs are moving in concert from the outside of the foot to the middle.

It's Time to Practice

Hold your hands in the air with your thumbs in finger-walking position. The fingers are slightly bent, tips overlapping, as though resting on the top of a foot. Let the thumbs walk toward each other until they touch. Imagine they are sliding on the foot as you pull them back, move down slightly, and thumb walk in again. Your fingers may have to move away from each other a bit to get the full effect. The important thing is to practice, practice, and practice. Now try this on a foot.

You can butterfly an area or the entire surface of the foot. Start at the top of the foot or the bottom and move both thumbs into the center of the foot with a long thumb-walking stride. The fingers are slightly bent and gently gliding along the top surface. As the thumbs reach the center, gently glide them back to the outside edge of the foot and move up slightly. Continue until the hands reach either the top or bottom of the foot, and either repeat or move on to the next segment.

Karate Chops

Karate chops help with circulation, and they are one of the signals that the session is ending. This technique is done by holding your hands with fingers together and using quick chopping motions in a staccato effect. The sides of the hand contact the bottom of the foot and along the edges as well.

Heel pain has many causes, usually connected with repetitive stress to the heel. This repetition may come from constant walking or standing on the feet. Runners often have repetitive stress syndrome from the steady, repeated pounding on their feet. Women in later stages of pregnancy may feel heel pain from the substantial weight gain.

The chopping effect is stimulating, making the receiver feel energized and ready to move. Karate chops are used at the end of the session to help ground the receiver, bringing him or her back to earth. Reflexology allows a person to relax, hovering between dreaming and sleeping. Some do fall asleep! Karate chops bring the receiver back, allowing time and space to reconnect with the present. The tingling sensation often felt as the blood rises to the surface is a lovely wake-up.

This technique is effective in dealing with heel pain. Quick, sharp, repetitive chops, especially around the heel ridge, stimulate the stressed tissue associated with pain in the heel. Repeated chopping over a length of time helps to strengthen the tendons that have been overused.

Tapping

This is done with the tips of the fingers tapping along the bottom, edge, and top of the foot. Gentle, quick tapping movements assist circulation and again signal closure, either of the session or as a transition to the next area. Often one hand taps as the other supports the foot.

Tapping is used up the legs and is very effective on the hands as well. Heel pain generally comes from poor walking habits and long-term use of improper footgear. Tapping along the calf and the sides of the shin stimulates the tissue with increase in blood flow and nerve transmission.

Generally all the fingers are tapping together. The tapping may be done up and down the foot, usually on the sole, in a rhythmic style. When tapping on the top surface of the foot, most reflexologists tap from side to side, again using all the fingers at once.

You can see why short nails are imperative in this work. Imagine using any technique with long nails. Tapping along a person's feet or legs with long fingernails would feel painful and discourage further visits.

Knuckle Press

This is a great move to relax an entire area. With a closed hand, use the length of the fingers in the fist from the second rim of joints to the

FIGURE 6-2
The knuckle press is a kneading movement that relaxes large, tough areas.

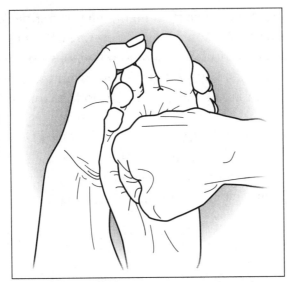

knuckles. Gently press in as though kneading dough. (See **FIGURE 6-2**.) The hand moves over the area in a steady rhythmic movement. As the press relaxes the area, you can gently rotate the closed fist, getting in even closer and deeper. Always use an even, slow motion with a kneading, circular style. Do not move quickly with this technique; take your time.

Let your fisted hands rest down on a tabletop. The fingertips are tucked into the palms, with the second section of your fingers actually resting on the table. Lean your fists up onto the points of the second joints. Now roll from those joints forward, so that the next section of your fingers is now resting on the table. Looking down at your hands, you can see the fingertips bending up toward you. Practice rolling back up on the joints and back down on the fingers. This is kneading.

A gentle knuckle press up and down the sole of the foot brings deep relaxation. The press is affecting all the reflexes, allowing for great release. Each time you press into the foot with the knuckles, the message is clear: You are helping the foot relax, and therefore the receiver lets go.

FACT

The knuckle press is effective in warming up the lung area. Commonly known as the lung press, reflexologists use the flat outside of the fisted fingers and press the entire region. This press is helpful when working on the heel, enabling the giver to relax the entire heel area. Pressing on the heel with the knuckle press relaxes the sciatic line and the lower body as well.

Clapping

Clapping is done with an open hand, actually slapping on the entire foot area. Clap the top surface, the bottom, and the sides as well. The top of the foot is gently clapped and then this is repeated on the bottom of the foot. Both hands can "applaud" the foot at the same time, too. At times you may find it is easier to use the palm of the hand, while at other times, the back of the hand is easier.

There are two important considerations with this technique, really with every technique. First, always use a steady even pressure, not a forceful painful energy. Always work within the comfort zone of your receiver. Traditionally, people have steered away from reflexology because of the misnomer that it has to hurt to be effective. This is not true! Any professional practitioner of reflexology will tell you it's not how hard you push; rather, it is working the reflex areas properly that counts.

Second, see how your hands are feeling as you work on the foot. Does using your palm feel awkward? Try the back of the hand in the area that felt uncomfortable to you. When you clap along the side of the foot, rather than use both hands, let one hand provide support. One hand or both may be used, depending on your comfort with administering this technique.

The wonderful truth of reflexology is that this is a holistic healing art. Within the definitive guidelines is room for growth and creativity. During the relaxation section, you may find you want to do more of a particular style and less of another. Go ahead, experiment, and develop your own pattern.

Feathering

This technique is done as a transition and at the finish (after the karate chops, tapping, and clapping). Using both hands with the fingers moving slightly, gently tap off the feet. The fingers do touch the foot, though the touch is light like a feather. On the top of the foot, use the bottom and tips of the fingers. On the sole of the foot, use the backs of your fingers.

Feathering is a stroking, smoothing technique that can be used on the feet or hands. The effect is a soothing, calm feeling. Let your hands stroke the air for a moment, using your hands, and then use your fingers. Then allow the fingers to move in a gentle vibrating manner, as though moving the air about. Again, let your hands smooth the area. Feathering is a combination of both these movements.

All of these techniques are used during a reflexology session. Different finger procedures are used to work certain areas. The main methods used during any reflexology session are thumb walking, finger walking, hooking, and rotating, though all the techniques are used at some point.

Feathering is used throughout the session when you move from one area to another. As the back reflex is finished and you prepare to work the lymph reflex, soft feather strokes allow you to move easily into the section. The feather technique also helps to sooth the area, further promoting the relaxation effect.

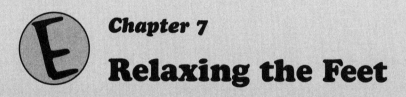

Chapter 7

Relaxing the Feet

Caring for your feet is a relatively easy yet essential exercise. To function at their optimal performance level, your feet need to be treated with respect. The greater care you give your feet, the longer they are able to do their job—the job of balance, support, and shock absorption.

Greeting the Feet

Before you begin to work on someone's feet, you need to greet the feet. To do this, place both open hands on the bottom of the feet, allowing the hands to rest there gently. You will feel the heat begin to flow between your hands and the receiver's feet. This is a quiet and respectful introduction. Move the hands to the outside of both feet, gently holding until you actually feel the feet relax.

The Second Step

The next step is to place both hands on the right foot, holding top and bottom. Again rest the open hands here allowing the rhythm of your breath and that of the person in the chair to flow in tune together. The pulse of the foot beats evenly as the heat from your hands penetrates the foot, encouraging further relaxation. Release this foot and let both hands cup the left foot, repeating the same step.

The Finale

Finally, rest hands on the top of the feet, telling each foot you are ready to begin. Using soft easy strokes, feather off gently and place both hands on the right foot, sandwiching the foot between the hands. One hand is on top of the foot, and the other is on the bottom, with the open palms resting on the foot. Slightly rock your body back and forth as you also push and pull the foot forward and backward. Everything is done with a count of three to five.

Realize that the receiver's right foot is facing your left side and the left foot is facing your right side, which may confuse you at first. An easy way to distinguish is to remember everything begins with the right foot, and you are looking at the bottom of the feet, which makes the feet appear backward. Don't worry; you'll get it.

The left hand is holding the top of the right foot and the right hand is on the bottom of the right foot. Imagine the hands as the bread and the foot as the filling. Rhythmically move in time, pressing forward and back as you begin to relax the foot, ankle, and body. This is called *dorsal flexion* and *plantar flexion,* relating to the dorsal (top) and plantar (bottom) surfaces of the feet.

The top of the foot is pushed toward the body, and the bottom of the foot is pressed away. The hands rest easily, basically guiding the foot as this motion simulates walking. Many of the relaxation procedures copy motions found in walking. Sometimes receivers will automatically try to help by moving their foot with you. Remind them it is their time to unwind and let go; you will do the work.

Turning Feet in and Out

Stay on the right foot, with both hands grasping the sides of the foot. Slowly turn the foot side to side. Watch the ankle turn in and out—this is the movement you are looking for: an in/out turn with both hands gently guiding the foot. The stationary foot is teased to subtle movement by the guidance of pressure from the holding hand. Here you are again mimicking walking, that side-to-side, in-and-out posture of the foot.

FACT

With 26 bones, 33 joints, 12 tendons, 107 ligaments, over 7,000 nerve endings, and thousands of sweat glands in each foot, these incredible structures carry us throughout our entire lives with very little worry or upkeep on our part.

The foot turns in toward the body and then is moved away from the body. The turn is subtle, with the hands positioned to guide the foot in each direction. You will meet with a natural resistance, as the foot can only turn so far in each direction. Let the hands guide the foot as far to one side as is comfortable and then to the other side. The foot will relax and actually feel looser.

Often the person being worked on will try to turn the foot for you. It is easy to feel when this is happening. Reflexologists do not encourage the receiver to help; the receiver is there to relax and release all control.

If your person is turning her foot along with you, gently suggest that she relax, allowing you to do the work. Generally a helper does not realize her involvement, so you may have to repeat the reminder a few times.

Wringing the Foot

The next technique is called *wringing,* which involves wrapping the hands around the foot as though it is a silk shirt that needs to be wrung out. Wringing imitates a delightful massage. This simple yet effective relaxation technique is essentially relaxing the entire body, as the foot represents the whole body.

Beginning from the bottom, move the hands firmly up the foot, and then move the hands steadily down, wringing all the way. As you hold the foot, your thumbs are on the sole and the fingers are on the top of the foot. The wringing motion is firmly applied—meaning the hands hold the foot closely as they move up toward the toes and down toward the heel.

Everyone loves the wringing part of the session! People generally comment at this point, stating how much they like what you are doing. The wringing technique is bringing together the two previous actions as well as preparing the foot for the next delicious sensation.

Imagine you are wringing out a face cloth before you hang it over the tub. Repeat this three times up and three times down with your hands remaining on the foot as the wringing is performed. Hold the foot firmly, but do not squeeze or press with great pressure. This is a steady, even move with a healthy grasp of the foot. You want the receiver to feel complete trust in your work. You are letting the recipient know that you will use a gentle yet strong touch, without deep pressure or pain.

Receivers often experience a feeling of warmth spreading through their body at this juncture. You can see a letting go. Some people may close their eyes and begin to drift, releasing tension. Breathing may become more tranquil as the wringing is repeated.

Relaxing the Spinal Reflex

Spinal relaxation is a two-part technique. Hold the right foot with the left hand while using the right thumb and index finger. Starting from the inner edge of the heel, push with the thumb and then pull with the index finger along the edge of the inner foot up through the arch to the great toe. Continue with this push/pull movement back down to the inner edge of the heel and all the way up again, doing this three complete times. Use your body to give assistance with a rocking motion; this allows for more effective work.

What you will begin to feel is the actual relaxation of the entire inside edge of the foot, known as the *medial edge.* The area becomes more palpable, and the color and temperature may change as well. After three or four complete up-and-down moves, the second part of the technique begins.

Place both hands on the inside arch, one next to the other in a grasping style. Both palms are cupping the arch as the fingers wrap around and rest on the top of the foot. Begin to twist each hand in opposite directions while staying directly on the arch line. Move the hands up the inner line as you continue twisting. The top hand moves right, with the bottom hand following. Wring and twist along this edge to the great toe and down to the heel three to four times.

The receiver will feel warmth spreading up the spine as the twist on the spinal reflex is performed. Give the person you are working on permission to share what is being felt. Throughout the session confirmation is important; the receiver will assist in this process. Watch the person for expression in body language as well.

FACT

Moving the body is essential in providing leverage and allowing strength of position to come from the body, not from the hands alone. Effective pressure is best derived from using the entire body. Pushing solely with the thumbs and fingers does not feel as good to the receiver or to the giver.

Rotating the Foot

Hold the right foot by cupping the ankle with the left hand and firmly gripping the toes with the right hand. The left hand will provide support, keeping the foot steady as the right hand does the turning. The right hand is folded over the toes so that as you turn the foot, this hand can guide the movement. Using the right hand, rotate three turns clockwise and three turns counterclockwise.

The foot will actually move from the ankle—the turning hand is holding the foot straight and tall as the ankle is gently rotated. The left hand is cupping the back of the heel and ankle. The rotation is slow and defined, and you are assessing as you move the ankle. Check with the receiver to gauge the degree of rotation.

Always keep contact with the foot being worked on. One hand will support and provide leverage while the other performs the working movements. By staying connected to the feet the receiver feels a deep sense of safety, further allowing for relaxation.

The range of motion in the foot, especially the ankle area, might be limited. The cause of limited range might be an old injury, chronic joint-related issues like arthritis, or some other systemic condition that may affect movement. Do the best you can—that will be good enough.

With this movement you begin to actually feel and see the foot, ankle, and even the leg sink down and relax. You have allowed the ankle to be at rest, not having to actively support all the movement.

Loosening the Foot

From the rotation of the foot, move on by tucking the heels of both palms up under the right anklebone. Feel how completely natural this hold is. The hands rest on the sides of the foot as the palms hold close to the ankle. The foot is securely supported, cradled by the palms.

Begin to rock the foot side-to-side and watch as the foot actually flops around! The more accustomed you become with this move, the quicker you can rock the foot. This is a real test of how relaxed the person in the chair is: the more flopping you get, the looser the receiver is.

This is a great move to allow people the right to let go. Many times up until this technique, the receiver may have tried to actively help. Gently shaking and flopping the foot encourages the recipient to relax, release, and let go.

Move your hands down now to the heel, still in the same cupping fashion. This time the palms hold the heel as you rock the foot. The side-to-side movement will not be as pronounced; the foot does not move as much from this angle. Still, you can see how the foot and ankle have let go of the control and completely surrender.

Stretching

While your hands are resting at the heel, let the right hand reach under and cup the entire heel. The left hand holds across the top of the foot just at the ankle, securing the foot in a safe grip. Keeping the leg straight and resting down on the pillows, picture the hip connected at the end of the leg you are holding. Using very steady, even, yet light pressure, pull straight toward you to the count of three. Stop and hold for a count of three to five, then release.

This is mobilizing the hip, which in turn is stretching the back. The hip is often a tight, immobile area of the body. Passive stretching is used to release tight areas. For instance, this stretch helps relieve congestion in the joint, People love this technique, as it is relaxing to the entire body. Listen for the groans of delight.

Connected to stretching is breathing. Every good stretch generally includes a deep breath, followed by a long releasing breath. We breathe in as we stretch and exhale as we return from the stretch. Are you getting the picture here? This technique, and all the techniques that you are learning from this book, deal with relaxing, releasing, and letting go.

Be very careful when stretching. Do not overpull, and remember to keep a straight line, with no up or sideways movement in the pulling. The object is to mobilize the hip joint not the knee. Check with the receiver to make sure there is no discomfort in the knee or elsewhere.

Using the Knuckle Press

Here is that press again. With the hand closed into a fist, use the flat ridge of the fingers to press along the surface of the sole. Remember to use your body as you rock forward and back, pressing into the foot each time. Vary the technique between pressing and making a semicircular motion, always with a kneading movement. Using the knuckle press on a foot that has been completely relaxed is the icing on the cake.

Practice Kneading

Imagine again that you are going to knead bread. Use a flat surface such as the palm of your other hand. Begin by closing the hand into a fist. Remember the fingertips are curled into the palm, and the thumb usually rests along the edge of the hand, not inside the fingers.

Now look at the fist so that you become familiar with the position. Notice how the long section of the fingers, between the two rows of prominent knuckles, is fairly flat. This is the section that does most of the kneading work. Hold your open palm up and knead into it with your fisted hand. This means to use the long, flat bones and press into the palm.

Applying the Technique

Begin at the bottom, or heel, of the palm and move the closed fist up and down, almost in a rocking motion. Pay attention to how the backs of the fingers knead the palm. The two rows of knuckles serve as the end lines, where the kneading motion ends and then begins. Rock the fist back and forth, and begin to move up the palm. Once you encounter the fingers, move the fist back down to the heel of the palm, kneading as you go.

A final use of this technique is to hold the fist on the surface you are kneading and gently press with the backs of those same fingers, in a semicircular motion. Move around, across, up, and down the area, gently pressing into the area. This is done easily and slowly, with a very gentle touch. As you are working on the tough skin areas on the heel, ball of the foot, and the palm, this technique allows the area to relax.

QUESTION?

How exactly does one rock and move while giving a session? For years, reflexologists just made sure they moved their bodies. They would check their hands and arms and their posture. If a reflexologist wasn't moving or was holding her hands and arms incorrectly, she would sure know soon enough: her back, neck, hands, and arms would begin to ache. Nowadays reflexologists have discovered the exercise ball, which allows freedom of movement and require one to sit properly.

Greeting the Solar Plexus Reflex

The solar plexus reflex is one of the most powerful reflexes. Whenever a reflex is painful, anywhere on the foot, working the solar plexus reflex may lessen or even alleviate the feeling. It is situated under the ball of the foot, exactly in the center. You will notice that the thumb fits perfectly into the indented space found there.

This technique is used in the warm-up, during the session, and in the cool-down phase as well. Become familiar with this technique and the reflex. As you learn the sequences of a session, the solar plexus reflex is also an area you press as you transition from one section to another.

Hold the right foot with your left hand, bending the foot from the top to create a hollow space under the ball of the foot. Place the right thumb into this space, pressing in firmly and at the same time pulling the foot down over your thumb. Ask the receiver to take a slow, deep breath in and exhale slowly, imagining the breath coming out through the feet. The solar plexus press is used to release pent-up tension. This technique is also used as a transition from one segment to another.

Once the breath is released, let the receiver relax and breathe normally. While he or she is breathing deeply, hold your thumb firmly in place. As normal breathing resumes, slowly remove the thumb. Then repeat these steps on the left foot.

FACT

The solar plexus release is profoundly relaxing. If a receiver is having a hard time settling down during the warm-up phase, reflexologists often will relax the solar plexus reflex a second time. Pay attention to the body language and depth of breathing during this section, as this will alert you to tension still held.

Working Both Feet

There are two occasions when reflexologists work back and forth between the feet. The first is this relaxation sequence and the second is during the cool down. Generally they work the entire right foot and then the entire left foot. Relaxing both feet before beginning the session allows the body, mind, and spirit to become totally involved. In this way, you are giving the message to the receiver that it is time to let go of the control and relax.

ESSENTIAL

Once the treatment portion is complete and the cool-down phase begins, it is fine to move back and forth again. Have fun and remember there is no wrong way, only better ways.

Once the feet are both relaxed, return your attention to the right foot. Most of the body's processes work from right to left; therefore, you will follow the way the body works. Energetically, the right side is the past and the left is the present. Working from right to left allows the receiver to let go of the past to heal the present.

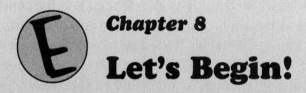

Chapter 8

Let's Begin!

Reflexology is a wonderful treatment modality. When applied correctly you cannot hurt anyone, you can only help. It is a privilege to help others relax and access their own healing ability. Through the steps and guidelines supplied here, you will learn the basics and perhaps even become interested in further study.

Remembering the Imaginary Guidelines

There are a number of imaginary lines that run through the feet. One group of lines is the ten longitudinal zones. Five zones run on each side of the centerline of the body. Each foot is divided into five zones that run through the entire body from head to toe. The great toe represents the major reflexes of the head, so that toe is also divided into five zones.

Zone one begins in the big toe and runs up the body to the brain and then down the arm to the thumb. Zone two runs from the second toe through the body to the head and out to the index finger. Zone three begins at the third toe and runs up the body to the brain and out to the middle finger. Zones four and five are the same with the related toes and fingers. All the zones run right through the whole body and the sections are equally divided.

The right side of the body is reflected only on the right foot and the left side of the body is on the left foot. In the theory of zone therapy, there is no crossing over to the opposite side of the body. The right brain is the right side of the head and body, and the left brain is the left side.

The Meridians

The twelve meridians are another set of guidelines, with six beginning or ending in the feet and six beginning or ending in the hands. The meridians are curved lines running through the body covering different areas. They too are represented on both sides of the body; however, since the lines zigzag back and forth, the reflexes are found on the lines, not in the sections.

The Horizontal Lines

Another set of imaginary guidelines indigenous to reflexology is the transverse lines that divide the sole of the foot into four distinct sections. The first line is found under the toe necks, running from the great toe out to the edge of the little toe. This represents the shoulder line and includes all the body parts from the shoulder up.

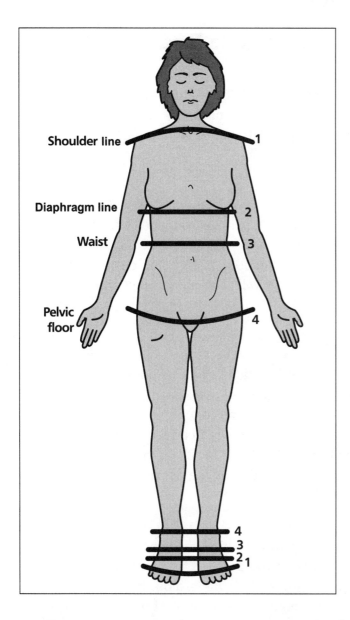

Shoulder line — 1
Diaphragm line — 2
Waist — 3
Pelvic floor — 4

4
3
2 1

FIGURE 8-1
The imaginary horizontal lines separate
the body into sequential working sections.

The next line, which runs under the ball of the foot, is the diaphragm line. The area embodied between these two lines is the thoracic, or chest cavity. The center of the arch is where the next line is found, and this line is representative of the waist and thus is called the *waistline*. The reflexes characterizing the upper portion of the abdominal cavity are contained here.

The last guideline is found in the upper portion of the heel. This line is known as the *sciatic* or *heel line*. The reflexes between the waistline and the heel line are those for the lower portion of the abdominal pelvic cavity. (See **FIGURE 8-1**.)

FACT

The tendon that runs from the diaphragm line to the heel line is another guideline. This line is used to divide the foot in two. As you work, you will often designate areas to either side of this tendon.

Picture the Foot as a Map of the Body

When you look at the feet that are facing you, it is easy to imagine the shape of a body superimposed over those feet. The natural shape of feet resembles the curves and lines of the body. The mirror image found on the feet maps the placement of organs, glands, bones, and muscles.

Reflexology Charts

All reflexologists have a favorite foot chart or map that they use. Often the chart is the one they trained with, perhaps with additions of their own. The reflexology chart, along with the reflexology technique, has evolved. The more that is learned about the body, energy, and other areas of traditional practice, the more reflexology will continue to adapt and change.

Corresponding Body Parts

The feet are a map of the body, and every reflex corresponds to an organ or body part. The toes are all the head reflexes and all the elements involved with the head, including the sensory organs, brain, endocrine glands, and sinuses. Whatever is on your head is found on the toes. The base of the toes equals the neck reflex, including the glands and lymph. The shoulder reflex is found under the toe necks and wraps around from the sole to the top of the foot.

All the guidelines on the foot help you to locate reflex points. These guidelines and referral areas remind you of the structure of the body while you are working on the feet. Reflexologists learn these aids early on, and they become a natural piece of their work.

The ball of the foot, the area that is nicely padded, houses the chest reflexes with all the related organs: heart, lungs, bronchioles, and breast. The corresponding area on the top of the foot represents the upper back. There are more lymph reflexes in this area as well. From the ball of the foot to about the center of the heel is where all the reflexes to the internal organs and glands that relate to the center of the body are found. The remaining top of the foot is the lower back.

The arch line of both feet holds the spinal reflex. The reproductive and pelvic regions are represented along the inside and outside of the foot from the heel up to the ankle. The hip, knee, and leg reflexes as well as the sciatic nerve reflex are found along the underside of the ankle to the outside of the anklebone. More lymphatic regions are found running up the center back of the leg. Along the outer edge of the feet is the area that represents the muscular skeletal system.

A Logical Sequence

Reflexology is a whole-body concept. This means that when you work on a person's feet, you work all of the reflex points, not just the area representing a problem. You will begin at the top and move down the entire body, as it is found on the feet.

QUESTION?

Why don't we work from the bottom of the feet up to the top of the feet?
The mainframe of the body is run by the brain, which is found in the head. So we work the brain first and then follow along in a basic pattern that seems to mimic the order of the body

Once you have created a healing space, set your intention, and relaxed the feet, you are ready to begin. You will first work completely through the entire sequence on the right foot, and then work through the sequence on the left foot. Save the cool-down section of both feet until the end.

Begin with the toes since they represent the head and neck. Working with the head reflex as the beginning focus also allows you to continuously recognize the mirror image of the body represented on the feet. Memorizing the foot map becomes easier if there is a logical sequence to perform. Even though the feet carry around the body, the operating signals come all the way from the head.

As you work your way down, you'll next come to the base of the toes, which are secondary support reflexes. Then move into the balls of the feet, which also include the long bones of the foot. As you work the sole area, you'll also work the top of the foot. From here you'll go to the arch, covering the upper and lower sections and the top and bottom of the foot. The heel area is next and then finally the inner and outer sides and ankle areas.

The Shoulder Girdle

The shoulder girdle is the demarcation of everything in the body from the shoulders and above. The toes are the face, with the big toe reflecting the major reflexes and the other toes offering support with secondary reflexes. The great toe has reflexes for the pineal and pituitary glands, as well as points for the nose, eyes, ears, brain, forehead, and inner ear. All the toes have reflexes for sinus, teeth, lymph, hair, and the back of the head. The toe necks are equally as important as they represent the neck area and the glands found there. Of course, the shoulder is also represented.

The great toe is also divided into five zones, denoting all the zones found on the foot and in the body. Remember, in zone therapy the ten zones run through the body meeting in the head, hands, and feet. The head holds all ten zones, while the feet and hands each have five.

The great toe, also know as the big toe, holds many reflexes. Just as important is the fact that this toe is part of the medial column, a group of sixteen bones that are key to maintaining our balance and providing shock absorption.

There are many key meridian points above the shoulder line as well. The liver meridian starts at the back of the great toe. The gallbladder meridian passes through the body, ending at the fourth toe. The bladder meridian ends at the little toe. The spleen meridian starts at the center of the great toe. Lastly, the stomach meridian ends at the top of the second toe, with branches to the great toe and third toe.

The Diaphragm Line

The diaphragm line runs along the end of the ball of the foot. This line is representative of the diaphragm muscle that runs across the chest. The areas of the body that are between the shoulders and the diaphragm have symbolic reflexes on the foot. These reflexes are both on the top of the foot and on the bottom.

The zone lines run through this area of the foot, connecting with all other areas. Remember, although zone one in this diaphragm section theoretically contains the references to the bronchial tubes, the heart, parts of the lung, and a section of the esophagus, this section can refer to other areas in zone one. All of the zones run through the ball of the foot, so anywhere on the body may be a referral.

Referral Areas

There are a few types of referral areas found on the foot, relating to the body. One type is the references to all areas in each zone. For example, zone two from the second toe runs up through the body into the brain, through the eye, and down the arm to the index finger. The organs in zone two are generally those that are located half a finger's length away from the center of the body.

The organs and other parts of the body linked to this area are sinus, teeth, secondary nose and thyroid reflexes, some of the bronchi, lungs, solar plexus, a section of the thoracic back, and the areas of lymph. However, while working in this zone, the person may state that he or she feels a throbbing pain in the front of the thigh, near the centerline of the body. This is still zone two, which you are stimulating.

This type of connecting will happen throughout the entire body. Perhaps you are reflexing the right shoulder reflex. This time the receiver tells you she is feeling something in her right hip! Here is an illustration not only of zone therapy at work, but also what is called anatomical referral areas. The right side always refers to the right and the left to the left. The right shoulder refers to the right hip and the left shoulder refers to the left hip. The upper arm refers to the thigh and the forearm refers to the calf. Elbow and knee are referrals to each other as are the wrist and ankle. The last referral areas of this type are the hand and foot.

Referral areas allow you to provide assistance to an area that might be too sensitive or injured. For instance, an injury of the foot would refer you to work on the hand, as a hand injury would relate to work on the feet. Understanding these anatomical referral areas helps you to provide the best care. All parts of the body are represented on the feet; stimulating the related reflex of an injury will help to relieve pressure and congestion of that area.

FACT

The solar plexus reflex is found along the diaphragm line, tucked under the center of the ball of the foot. This powerful point is also the beginning of the kidney meridian.

When a Referral Is Really a Meridian

For years, reflexologists believed that everything on the right relates to the right and everything on the left relates to the left. However, there are other times when zone therapy is not the answer. Let's say you are reflexing a person's right hip reflex, and he puts his hand on his left hip as he tells you that warmth is spreading through that hip. The feeling has crossed over. The same meridian runs on both sides of the body, and the gallbladder meridian does run through the hip, so it's possible.

The Waistline

The waistline guideline is found in the center of the arch. The shape of the foot actually helps to locate this line. Look at the outside of your foot. Follow the little toe down the side until you come to a bump. This bump is about halfway down the outer edge; it is the bottom edge of the long bone known as the *fifth metatarsal.*

The parts of the body represented here are everything from the diaphragm to the waist. This refers not only on the front of the body, but the back part as well. The reflexes for the stomach, pancreas, pyloric sphincter, duodenum, liver, gallbladder, spleen, middle back, adrenals, and top of the kidneys are in this center area.

All the zones run through here as well as the meridians, which connect this section with all the other sections of the foot and thus the whole body. The difference with this area is the location of reflexes. Not all reflexes are found on both feet; here, some on are the right foot and some on the left foot. For instance, the liver, gallbladder, duodenum, and pyloric sphincter reflexes are on the right foot. The spleen reflex is found only on the left foot.

Heel, or Sciatic, Line

This line is easily found, as it is located at the top of the heel. Look at the bottom of your foot. Do you notice how the beginning of the heel seems to have a slightly different color? This line becomes the imaginary guideline. In this area are found all the reflexes from the waist to the tailbone.

The Organs Reflected

All the organs below the waist are found reflected in this section. However, this area has reflexes for certain parts on one foot and different parts on the other foot. For instance, the right foot reflects the small and large intestine, as it is found in the right side of the body. The left foot represents the left side of these organs.

This guideline is itself a reflex. When you thumb walk across this line, you are affecting the sciatic nerve. The sciatic nerve is the largest nerve in the body and travels from the sacrum and down the back of the leg to the knee. There it splits into branches running down the leg and into the feet.

FACT

Stimulating a reflex point in any zone in this area will of course simulate the entire zone. The spleen, bladder, kidney, stomach, gallbladder, and liver meridians pass directly through this area.

Heel to Heel

The heel, or sciatic, line brings us to the end of the reflexes found in the abdominopelvic cavity. However, the section between this line and the end of the heel is important. This part of the foot reflects the lower back, legs, feet, and hips. Unfortunately, this secondary access to the lower extremities is an area often forgotten in foot care.

Many people suffer from dry heels with cracked and broken skin, swelling, and/or bone spurs in this section. In a reflexology session, this area of the foot is included, often using this space as a transitional spot. Reflexologists generally use the knuckle press, as this can be a tough section to work.

The Tendon Line

The tendon that runs from the heel to between the first and second toes is used as a guideline. This line helps to divide the foot, offering a landmark to work in toward as you thumb walk across the sole of the foot. This is one of many tendons found in the sole of the foot.

Feel along the sole of the foot, letting your fingers trace a line from the ball down to the heel line. Feel the tautness along this particular tendon; there is actually a line you can feel vertically down the sole surface. Have the receiver flex her toes; you will notice that the tendon actually presents itself to you.

ALERT!

Direct pressure on this tendon line will cause pain and undue stress to the tissue. Always use even, gentle pressure when performing reflexology. The use of undue pressure at any time not only causes unnecessary pain, but also could overstimulate an area.

The tendon is a guideline. There are reflexes that fall on one side or the other with regard to this line. This helps you to find exact points and to remember where you are on the foot in relation to the body. Ⓔ

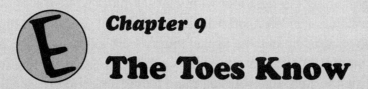

Chapter 9

The Toes Know

As you have surmised by now, every reflex is connected somehow to every part of the body. As you perform reflexology you will assist the body in maintaining a well-balanced level of living. Any situation—physical, emotional, or intellectual—can affect a spiritual response that may manifest into a physical reality. Let's begin and see what happens!

Thumb Walking the Toes

Practice thumb walking for a moment. Walk your right thumb across the back of your left hand from the first knuckle to the wrist; then bring your thumb right back up to the next knuckle and repeat, continuing through all five knuckles. Once you've got that down, it's time to move to the feet.

Start by holding the right foot with your left hand while the right hand does the walking. The left hand will support the foot. Begin with the great toe and slowly take small bites as you thumb walk along the edge of the toe up to the top. Walk across the top of the toe and down the other edge into the toe web. Use your left hand to separate the toes, as the thumb walking down into the web will feel awkward at first. Your right thumb can only go down so far along this first inside edge. When you feel the thumb cannot go any farther, turn and thumb walk up the ridge of the next toe.

Thumb walk up each toe, walk across the top, and walk down the other side to each web. Once you reach the outside of the little toe with your right thumb, you will switch hands. Now the right hand becomes the holding hand and the left hand does the work. Thumb walk back along the ridges and down into the web of each toe until you again reach the great toe.

FACT

When your thumb makes the turn, it feels as though you are swiping in between the two toes. Be patient. At first you will feel like you are all thumbs, but this will pass. View this process as walking up the mountain, across the plateau, and down the mountain into the valley. From the valley it is back up the mountain again.

Walking the Zones on the Great Toe

After you have walked to the farthest side of the great toe, switch hands so that you are working with your right thumb. Use your left hand to support the right foot by holding the top half with your palm and gently wrapping your fingers and thumb around the foot. Now you should imagine the great toe divided into five zones; you will be walking each zone on the big toe.

Start at the base of the great toe and thumb walk up onto the flat sole surface of the toe. This is zone one. Bring your thumb back to the toe neck and thumb walk up in an imaginary line right next to the first walkup. This is zone two. Keep bringing your thumb back to the toe neck and walk up each zone; this will include the side of the toe as well. Do not drag you thumb back to the neck, just take it back smoothly and walk up the next zone. After the last zone, use your thumb to rotate on top of the toe, moving in small circles, as you stimulate the brain reflex.

The Remaining Toes

From the great toe, bring your right thumb to the base of the second toe, the plantar (bottom) side, and thumb walk up to the tip of the toe. Bring the thumb back to the toe neck and walk up to the top again. Rotate and hold on the top of the toe. Remember, rotation is using your thumb in a small circular motion on one area. As you are holding, feel through your thumb how the surface of the toe begins to give, responding to the treatment.

The remaining four toes each have about two lines for you to walk up. These are not zones. Rather, they are imaginary lines you are picturing to guide you through the toes. At the top of each toe, circle and hold, then move on to the next toe, until all toes have been thumb walked in this manner. As you complete the baby toe, switch hands and walk back along each toe, repeating the movements with the left thumb. The right hand becomes the holding hand, giving support and leverage.

Walking the Tops of the Toes

Don't forget the top (dorsal) surface of the foot! The reflexes on the topside reflect the back of the head. Holding the right foot with your left hand, let the right thumb rest along the bottom side of the toes. This thumb will provide leverage while the tops of the toes are being worked. Using your index finger, walk down the top of the toe to the base. Bring your finger back to the top and walk down again. Repeat once more;

then move on to the next toe. Complete this movement on all the toes and then switch and walk back.

QUESTION?

What is the toe neck?
The toes are shaped a bit like our head, with the larger portion of the toe relating to that part of the skull which houses the brain. The head of the toe is bigger than the lower region of the toe, which we refer to as the toe neck.

Working the Necks of the Toes

After walking all the toes along the ridges, the plantar surface, and the dorsal surface, you will now move into the area that represents the neck. With the left hand holding the right foot, use your right thumb to walk the neck of the great toe on the bottom of the foot. Take very little bites from the outer edge of the toe in toward the next toe. Bring your thumb back and repeat with tiny bites along the neck for several swipes across. The toe neck will feel stiff under your thumb, so try walking until this area feels less tight.

Allow your thumb to rest as you walk with your index finger along the neck surface of the toe on the top of the foot. Again, take tiny bites as the finger walks to the edge of the toe and bring your finger back to repeat again.

Finally, with both thumb and index finger, walk together toward the other side of the toe. The thumb is on one side of the toe and the index finger is on the other side. Let the index finger rest at the base on the top of the foot as the thumb actually walks in between the first and second toe, at the base. You have just worked the entire neck reflex.

Thumb Walking the Toe Joint

Each toe tapers into its neck, which connects to a joint at the base of the toe. This second joint of the toe is called the *metatarsophalangeal joint*—whew! Refer to this area as the MTP joint. The MTP joint bends the toes at their base. There are many reflexes in this region.

Hold the right foot with your right hand; you will be using your left thumb for this area. Thumb walk across this joint from the baby toe to the end of the second toe. Bring the thumb back and walk along this joint again. You are walking right in the folded area, where the necks of the toes bend. Switch hands. With the left hand holding, use your right thumb to walk in the joint from the great toe out to the little toe. Repeat this thumb-walking process a few times.

Again with the left thumb, walk into each web starting with the web between the fifth and fourth toes. As the thumb moves into the web, you will feel a hard ridge. Stop here, rotate, and hold gently; do not push. Rotate and hold into each web, ending in the final web next to the big toe.

From the baby toe, thumb walk through again in the ridge with tiny, slow bites, using your left thumb. Then let your thumb begin to move along under the ridge into the fatty part of the foot. This area is directly under the joint, and you will walk here from the little toe to the big toe. Bring your thumb back under the little toe and stay along this region as you walk back to the great toe again. Switch hands and walk back and forth a few times.

Using your right hand as the holding hand, rest your left hand along the outer edge of the foot, with the fingers along the top part of the foot. With your left thumb, walk the space along the outside edge of the foot between the shoulder line and diaphragm line. Then, with your first two fingers, walk on the top surface of the foot from under the little toe to under the third toe. Bring the fingers back to the edge and repeat.

Thumb walking will generally be used over the toes, with the advanced technique coming in to fine-tune certain areas. Remember to walk slowly and steadily with even pressure. Do not push hard; pushing will only hurt you and your receiver.

Hooking Specific Reflexes at the Top of the Foot

The reflected image of the shoulder is on the bottom surface of the foot as well as on the top and side. There are two areas here at the top region of the foot that you will hook. To refresh you on the hooking technique, remember to walk in and hold on the spot. Begin to rotate slowly, staying on the reflex point. As you rotate with gentle, steady circles, let your thumb feel the spot underneath. The area should begin to welcome you. Once you feel you have moved in to a comfortable level, push and turn, using your thumb as a hook.

Place your left thumb along the outside region, exactly where you walked along the edge, between the diaphragm and shoulder line. Push in easily on the side of the foot where your thumb is. The area under the little toe on the bottom of the foot will actually form a small curvy line next to the bone you feel in that spot. Walk gently across this area, and hook into the space the line has made. Your thumb fits cozily into this spot. Hook and hold.

The great toe has a reflex you hook into as well. Look at the great toe and focus on the first joint. This part of the toe seems big and shaped rather like a head. Imagine a line drawn from the center tip of the toe down to the crease where the neck begins. Now picture another line crossing this vertical line a smidgen above the center of this section of the toe.

Place your right thumb on the spot where the two lines cross. Gently begin to rotate on this spot. Sometimes you may actually feel what seems like a small pea shape at this center cross point. When you feel ready, push in at this spot, hold, and turn so you can hook up with your thumb.

ALERT!

You might feel a small pulse as you work this area, especially while you are holding on the reflex. Don't worry! This is great; it is the reflex talking back to you! It's a confirmation of a job well done, letting you know you are on the right spot.

Relief from Headaches

Sometimes a person may come to a session stating that his or her head hurts, either from stress or allergies, or maybe a cold. Whatever the reason, reflexology does help us deal with headaches. A tension headache may result from an upset at work or worry over bills. For some, this type of headache comes after a crisis; the headache is part of the release. Often a headache is a learned response. Whatever the background cause of the tension, reflexology works to bring about balance.

Negative response to tension upsets the natural flow of energy, disrupting homeostasis. A reflexology session helps to restore the vital energy necessary for harmony. The reflexes of the toes contribute to the letting go of tension and the return to whole health.

The toes represent the head. The great toes are the entire head, with all the endocrine glands, eyes, ears, nose, throat, brain, teeth, sinuses, and all the anatomical parts of the head. The other toes support the big toe. Some have secondary reflexes, and all have sinus reflexes as well as lymph, teeth, hair, brain, and neck reflexes.

Whatever the cause, reflexology is an appropriate adjunct in support of pain relief. As you help people relax, they become less fearful and less tense, better able to deal with the origin of their pain.

FACT

Many people suffer from allergies, and headaches are one of the resulting symptoms. The pressure buildup in the sinuses may present itself as a full-blown frontal headache. Everyone knows what it is like to have a cold. Often when a cold settles in, one of the common symptoms is an achy head. Being overtired or not having enough fresh air can also produce a painful headache.

The Toes and Sinuses

The toes are also representative of the sinuses. As you walk along the ridges and up the flat surface of the toes, you are stimulating the sinus reflexes. Thumb walking on the sides of the toes allows you to affect the sinuses in the cheekbones. Thumb walking upon the bottom of the toes affects the sinuses found above the eyebrows, on either side of the nose, and those behind the nose.

There are eight nasal sinuses in the head. These little air-filled cavities help to balance the skull. The neck is small in size compared to our heavy heads. The sinuses reduce the weight of the head. Sinuses also work with the voice dealing with the range and sound that is produced.

The sinuses connect to the nasal passages of the nose, affecting the quality of breathing. If any of the sinus cavities are blocked, the ability to breathe is compromised. While excessive production of mucus can indicate infection within the membranes that line the sinus and nose, not enough can indicate congestion. Reflexology, especially working the sinus reflexes and the reflex for the nose, will assist in opening the passages, allowing the flow of mucus to be discharged or slowing down the manufacture of excess mucus.

Many people will respond with a runny nose during the session. Often these people have been very congested, even uncomfortably so. As you thumb walk along the ridge areas of the toes, you can actually see a change. This is exciting and rewarding—you are involved in helping someone feel better. Because reflexology is holistic, you are working on balancing the whole person, integrating with whatever other treatment may already be in process.

Feel the Neck and Shoulders Relax

Tension is often held in the neck and shoulders. Some people work all day at a computer, drive for long periods of time, or stand in front of a group, making a presentation. Some people carry children, lift packages, build houses, or crawl under or over spaces. Some people bend and turn and lift all day. Whatever people are doing, their necks and shoulders are involved.

The reflexes in the toes mirror the neck, and the guideline of the shoulder mirrors the shoulders. Thumb walking around the entire base of the great toe affects the neck. Walking up the toes from the base also deals with the neck. The entire shoulder reflex, found on the bottom, side, and top surface of the foot, reflects the front, side, and back of the shoulders.

FACT

The neck supports and moves the head. Part of the neck is actually the spine—the most mobile part of the spine. The neck allows you to nod your head up and down, turn your head side to side, and to look up and, to an extent, back. You can jut your chin out and pull it back, which is another function of the neck.

The many muscles, nerves, and blood vessels found in the neck work with the shoulders as well. Tension in the neck may generate from the shoulders or vice versa. Often people hold their shoulders in a state of constant tension. As the shoulder muscles tighten, the neck muscles that are connected tighten as well.

As you reflex the neck and shoulder areas reflected on the foot, you may see a visible relaxation of the body. Generally, the receiver will feel warmth in the neck and shoulder region, and she may actually feel the relaxing effect begin to spread throughout her body. As the giver, you may feel the reflexes in the feet relax as well.

When you begin to reflex these areas on the feet, you may find tension, identified by hard, tight skin or sandy, clicking areas. The buildup of lactic acid or adhesions will often respond with a crunchy, gritty feeling. However, as you continue to reflex these areas, you can truly feel a relaxation response.

FACT

Reflexologists call the adhesions under the skin *crystals*. These crystals feel gritty and crunchy. The tiny, tight knots felt under the skin are actually a condition called *tonus*. Tonus is a mild spasm of muscle fibers that results in a tight, hard area that can be felt when thumb walking.

Circling the Brain Reflex

The brain reflex is found on the top of all the toes. Work this reflex by thumb walking up the toe and stopping at the tip of the top. At this spot, which is one of the main reflexes for the brain, slowly begin to rotate with your thumb. As you continue to rotate on this reflex, you will feel the toe opening to the pressure from the thumb. Keep on working in the circular motion, allowing your thumb to keep rotating in tiny circles.

This reflex is the mirror of the main nerve center of the body, which is housed in the skull. The brain contains billions of neurons and nerve fibers and consists of many parts that receive, store, and transmit messages throughout the body, via the spinal cord.

FACT

The left side of the brain controls the right side of the body, and the right side of the brain controls the left side of the body. The right side is artistic and creative, whereas the left side is logical and analytical.

As you circle on the brain reflex, you are connecting with the twelve pairs of cranial nerves. The nerves in the brain are either motor, sensory, or a mixture of both. These cranial nerves work with the muscles and sensory organs found in the head and neck. You are supporting the homeostasis of this organ. Keeping the brain functioning at the highest level keeps the body functioning equally as well.

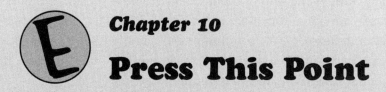

Chapter 10

Press This Point

The great toe is an important toe for walking and standing. This toe is equally as important in reflexology since it holds many reflexes for the significant glands and organs found in the head and neck. The entire big toe area holds reflex points that are integral to the proper functioning of the body.

Reflex Points of the Great Toe

The great toes house the reflex areas for the eyes, nose, ears, inner ear, and sinuses. The mouth, throat, tongue, and teeth are reflected on the great toes. Also, the reflexes for the endocrine glands of the hypothalamus, pituitary, pineal, thyroid and parathyroid, as well as for the cerebrum, cerebellum, and the brain stem are all represented here. As you can see, the great toes hold many reflexes, making them very important to reflexology. As you thumb walk, finger walk, and hook into the reflex points for the sensory organs on the great toes, you are helping to maintain a state of balance within the body.

ALERT!

Reflexes represent the mirrored images of the whole body linked together through zone therapy. You should not treat for a specific condition or single body part or system. Instead, work all the reflexes all the time.

The Eyes and Ears

The main reflexes for the eyes are found on both the great toes. The right eye is on the right toe and the left eye is on the left toe. The eyes function like a camera, responding to light, acting like a shutter lens. Nerve cells receive signals from light, sending messages to the brain where the transformation of these signals into visual data occurs. Reflexology assists in the homeostasis of this operation.

The ear reflexes are also on the great toes, with supporting reflexes found elsewhere. These tiny, complex organs are very simple in design yet powerful in their functions. The ears have a broad range of responsiveness, reacting to sounds as powerful as a rocket or as subtle as an ocean breeze. The sounds can be near or far, yet the ears register the vibrations. Barometric pressure can affect their function pertaining to balance and the ability to assess space.

Within the ear, two other parts exist. The middle ear has three bones known as the *hammer, anvil,* and *stirrup.* These bones, named because of their shape, actually pulse with sound waves and connect with the inner ear. The inner ear has two integral functions: to send signals to the hearing center of the brain and to send signals to maintain equilibrium.

As you reflex the points that affect the ears' function, you assist in maintaining the receiver's ability to hear clearly and to stay balanced, literally. If the receiver is suffering from blocked ears or other such symptoms, reflexology may help clear some of the congestion.

The Nose

The reflex points for the nose are reflected along the inside edge of the joints on both great toes. These bony protuberances are the guideline to find the nose reflex. As you look at both feet, placing them together, the great toes will line up and this joint will be obvious. When you thumb walk up the inside ridge of the great toe, you are moving directly into the nose reflex. As you walk up the toe from the base, you encounter a joint in the center of the big toe. Just above this joint is the nose reflex.

The nose is the transmitter of olfactory senses heading toward the brain. The brain can identify approximately 20,000 different scents. You are able to breathe clean air because of the filters found in the nose and nasal canal. The incredible structure of the nose allows you to filter air, transport and remove dust particles, and enjoy the beauty of scent.

FACT

The feet are small in comparison to the body. There are many organs, glands, and other body parts represented by the reflexes that are mirror images found on the feet. Often one reflex point may overlap another, which is why you take small, tiny bites as you thumb and finger walk your way around the feet.

The Sinuses

The sinuses are found on all the toes, as the four other toes support the great toe. These reflexes are on the tops of the toes, along with the brain reflex. When you thumb walk up to the top of the toe, as well as walk over the toe, you are working the sinus reflex. This is a reflex where you also hold and rotate, thoroughly dealing with the reflection of the sinuses.

Reflexology can prevent blockage. With regular reflexology sessions, you can keep the mucous membranes in the sinus healthy. Once there are issues of impaired sinus function, reflexology can assist in relieving congestion.

The Mouth and Throat

The mouth and throat are mirrored on the great toe, with support on the other toes. The reflexes for the mouth and throat are found along the lower inner edge of the big toe, as well as the edge at the bottom of the toe pad and the toe base.

When you thumb walk around the entire base of the toe, you are affecting the neck, half on the right and half on the left. As you thumb walk up the inner edge, just below the toe joint, you find the reflex for the mouth, teeth, and tongue. Thumb walk in and hold here for a count of three and move on up. Whenever you thumb walk along this toe edge or thumb walk the zones of the great toe, you are affecting these reflexes.

When we refer to the inner edge of the toes or feet, it means those reflexes that are toward the inside edge of both feet. This is reflecting the midline of the body. The outer edges of the feet or toes address the reflexes nearer the outer side of the body.

The Brain

The cerebrum, the brain stem, and the cerebellum are all reflected on the great toe. The cerebrum is the frontal part of the brain with the reflexes located on the entire top of the great toe as well as the other toes. You will thumb walk over this point, thumb walk up to this point, and rotate, push, and hold on this reflex point.

The brain stem holds the medulla oblongata, the pons, and the midbrain. The spinal cord is a continuation of the brain stem. The reflex for this area is found on the top surface of the foot, at the base of the great toe. You will finger walk around the entire neck of the toe, affecting this reflex. You will also finger walk and thumb walk down the top surface of the toe from the tip to the base. When you work these areas, you are working the reflexes for the brain stem as well as the entire back of the head.

The cerebellum is located behind the brain stem in the head. The reflex for the cerebellum is located on the dorsal surface of the toes, especially the great toe. This reflex and the brain stem reflex overlap. As you work on the dorsal aspect of the great toe, with finger walking and thumb walking, you are affecting areas of the brain.

FACT

If you look down at your feet while you are sitting, you are looking at the top surface of the feet. This is called the *dorsal surface.* The soles of the feet are known as the *plantar surface.*

The Hypothalamus Reflex

The diencephalon is the region of the brain that contains the hypothalamus. The hypothalamus is also identified as part of the endocrine system and as such deals with the chemical production in the body. This part of the brain controls many body activities and is a regulator of homeostasis. The hypothalamus is a link of integration between the endocrine and nervous systems. It deals with activities of the autonomic nervous system (ANS). It regulates the heart rate, the contractions of smooth muscle, and the movement of food through the intestinal tract.

There are several hormones produced by the hypothalamus that work directly with the pituitary gland. The hypothalamus is the master controller of the pituitary gland. The pituitary gland in turn influences the production of many of the hormones in the body.

This small section of the brain, the hypothalamus, is the pleasure/pain center. This area regulates your extreme feelings and your behavior regarding these emotions. This is also the area that tells you when you are hungry, when you are full, and when you are thirsty.

Even your sleep patterns have roots within the hypothalamus. Here is where your daily sleep program is established. The temperature of the flow of blood through the hypothalamus regulates your body temperature. When the blood is too hot, the ANS receives information to cool it down, and the opposite occurs if the blood is too cold. The reflex for this part of the brain is essentially the same as that of the pituitary.

FACT

> The hypothalamus regulates many body activities. For instance, it controls the contraction of the heart muscle, influencing the heartbeat. This organ also regulates emotions of rage, joy, aggression, and compassion.

The Pituitary Reflex

The pituitary reflex overlaps the hypothalamus region on the foot. You'll find this reflex on the inner edge of the great toe, just above the center joint, as shown in **FIGURE 10-1**. Thumb walk up from the base of the toe exactly along the ridge from the inside, slightly past the joint. You'll see that the toe has an indentation that receives the thumb. Once the thumb has found the reflex, rotate on the spot and hold. Turn the thumb so the side is in the actual groove, and with a slight back-and-forth motion, work this reflex, moving in more deeply. As the thumb feels the reflex give, stay in this spot and press.

FIGURE 10-1
The pituitary gland reflex is on the inner ridge of the great toe.

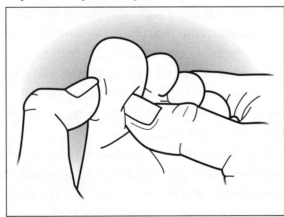

The pituitary is pea-sized. This hormone-producing gland sits in the middle of the brain, behind the nose. It is connected to the hypothalamus, which is the governing agent. The pituitary is called the "master gland," as its job is to release major hormones that will influence the entire endocrine system, in turn affecting the whole body. This gland has lobes that secrete different hormones produced in conjunction with secretions from the hypothalamus.

The Anterior Lobe

The anterior lobe of the pituitary gland produces and releases the following hormones, which affect bodily activities:

- Human growth hormone
- Thyroid-stimulating hormone
- Adrenal gland hormone
- Milk production hormone
- Reproduction hormones

The Posterior Lobe

The posterior lobe of the pituitary gland stores and releases hormones. These chemicals deal with bodily function.

- Antidiuretic hormone for the kidneys—reduces fluid
- Oxytocin for contractions of the uterus—post-childbirth

Reflexology works to establish a dialogue with all parts of the body. When dealing with the pituitary gland, or any endocrine unit, the intention is to assist with homeostasis.

The Pineal Reflex

The pineal gland is a minute structure buried deep in the brain, far behind the eyes. This pinecone-shaped endocrine gland produces melatonin, which affects our sleep patterns. Sunshine helps to balance the flow and production of this hormone. Too little sun releases too much melatonin, which results in excessive sleepiness. During the winter months, some people may need to find artificial sources of light to assist in keeping the hormone level balanced.

Finding the Reflex

The reflex for the pineal gland is found in the central padded area of the great toes, directly in the center, as shown in **FIGURE 10-2**. (This reflex represents the eyes as well.) To access this reflex, first warm up the toe. This is done by thumb walking across the entire toe, up the padded area

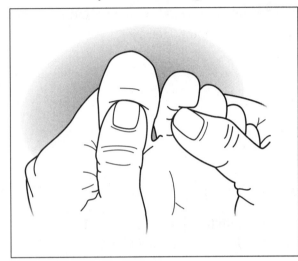

FIGURE 10-2
The pineal reflex is found exactly in the center of the top pad on the great toe.

from the neck of the toe to the top. Continue to thumb walk across the toe, up and down a few times. As the thumb moves back and forth across the toe, feel the entire padded area begin to relax. Look at the toe, watching the color begin to change as well. At times, the pineal reflex will actually pop right out for you!

Stimulation of the pineal reflex may bring about the desire for sleep. Often when you reflex the pineal gland, the receiver will begin to relax deeply. This is a true compliment to the effectiveness of your work. Reflexology does encourage relaxation to the alpha state.

Going Fishing

Above the joint line, which is in the center of the toe, thumb walk into the center of the padded area. Here, imagine X marks the spot. Place the working thumb directly on the center of that X and begin to rotate in small, steady circles. Feel the reflex as it begins to respond to you. With the thumb, circle in to the center, stop, and hold, applying even pressure. Get ready—you are going fishing now! The toe is the bait and your thumb is the fishhook. Holding the toe steady, turn the thumb on the exact reflex, push in, and hook up. The reflex may feel like a little pea under your thumb.

Hold, keeping the hook in place. Working on the pineal reflex allows many receivers to reach a state of deep calm early in the session.

The Thyroid Reflex

The thyroid is another endocrine gland. This gland has two lobes and is found nestled in the base of the neck, just below the voice box, with a lobe on either side of the windpipe. The thyroid is shaped like a butterfly; each wing is on one side of the body.

The thyroid stores its hormones in large quantities, so the thyroid always has a supply on hand, enough to last about 100 days. The hormones indigenous to the thyroid are thyroxine, calcitonin, and triiodothyronine. Thyroid hormones regulate oxygen use, which affects the production of heat within the body. These hormones also regulate the metabolism of the body, affecting all the processes.

FACT

Metabolism is the culmination of all chemical actions within the body. The interrelation of these chemical actions provides the energy and nutrients needed to sustain life.

Aids in Growth and Development

The thyroid gland plays an important role in the growth and development of the body. The thyroid affects the growth of nervous and muscle tissues. This gland helps to control calcium levels, as well as reduce cholesterol. The thyroid deals with glucose conversion; glucose affects your energy level, because as glucose burns calories, more energy is produced.

The element iodine is mainly concentrated in the thyroid gland and is essential to the production of thyroid hormones. You obtain iodine naturally through food. Too little or too much iodine can create a malfunction of the thyroid. Deficiency of thyroid hormones can affect newborns, creating small build, poor development of the brain, and underdeveloped reproductive organs. Excessive production of hormones in this gland results in an overactive thyroid, with accelerated heartbeat and increased weight gain.

Finding the Reflex

The thyroid reflex is found in the neck of the great toe, along the inside edge moving into the joint at the base of the toe. Thumb walk in toward the neck ridge, allowing the thumb to walk over the base of the toe four or five times. As you take small bites on this reflex, walk up from just below the toe neck, in at the edge, and hold. Then finger walk onto the topside of the toe at the base a few tiny steps in. The thumb also takes small circular moves along the inner edge of the toe neck.

Following these tiny moves in and around and up and down, circle on the point and hold, applying steady pressure. If there is any tightness in this area, continue to work on the reflex point. Reflexology helps to move out toxins and break up congestion everywhere in the body. If the thyroid does have blockage, reflexology will help to re-establish homeostasis.

The Parathyroid Reflex

The parathyroid glands consist of two pairs, a superior and an inferior, that sit on the back of the thyroid gland. The parathyroid glands produce the hormone PTH, or parathyroid hormone. PTH deals with the balance of calcium and phosphate in the blood. Under the correct circumstance, the parathyroid hormone absorbs calcium and phosphate from the GI tract, moving these minerals into the blood.

Calcium and Phosphate

Calcium and phosphate are structural components of bones and teeth. Phosphate works within the body structure performing a number of tasks, combining with other minerals to make DNA and RNA. Calcium is absorbed into the bloodstream. This absorption is controlled not only by the parathyroid hormone, but also by vitamin D, which enters our bodies through sunlight and food. If the calcium level drops, PTH increases, allowing calcium to be released from the bones directly into the bloodstream. The opposite occurs if the calcium level is too high. Calcium is essential for many bodily functions, including blood clotting, muscle contraction, normal heartbeat, and nerve health.

FACT

The parathyroid also affects the kidneys. PTH speeds up the removal of calcium from the urine to the blood. At the same time, it accelerates the arrival of phosphate from the blood to the urine. Therefore PTH increases calcium in the blood and decreases the level of phosphate in the blood.

Finding the Reflex

The reflexes for the parathyroids are found to the side and slightly under the thyroid reflex. As you look at the bottom surface of the great toe, exactly at the neck reflex, the parathyroid reflex overlaps with this reflex and the thyroid reflex as well. Thumb walk under the fat pad of the great toe right along the edge near the centerline. The second lobe reflection is found at the bottom of the thyroid reflex, along the base of the toe neck. Thumb walk in and hold, and rotate and hold, letting the thumb stay exactly on the point.

Using Rotation, Holding, Pressing, and Hooking

These techniques allow you to work deeply and more effectively, without having to apply unnecessary force. Reflexology is a loving application; every part of the session is done in honor of the receiver, to assist in his or her empowerment. As the receiver strives toward whole health, you are able to be part of the healing process.

There are many areas of the feet that require an assortment of thumb and finger techniques. It is important to have a working knowledge of all reflexology techniques. The feet have many bony eminences, structural hills and valleys, all of which you can and do reflex.

Rotation

Rotating on a point gives the reflexologist true access. As the thumb circles in, the actual movement encourages the reflex to respond, letting the giver continue to move in more deeply. By staying directly on the reflex, you are continuing the communication with the area represented. Using steady, even pressure, circling in on the reflex point, continue to rotate and then hold, still allowing the point to respond. At times you can use your finger in the same fashion, on specific reflexes. For instance, when you work on the parathyroid reflex, you may use the thumb and also the index finger.

Sometimes you will circle into a point, and as you hold steady, actually rotate the foot around the thumb. The working thumb holds on the reflex point as the holding hand turns the foot, slowly rotating in a circle. Both of these rotation movements allow you to work deeply and effectively, relieving congestion.

Holding

Holding on a point helps to clear blockage right at that point, as well as stimulate the blood flow. Both the thumb and the fingers, depending upon the areas to be worked, perform this technique. Thumbs cannot always reach as effectively as the fingers. The more you practice, the better you will be able to judge this option.

Whether you thumb walk, finger walk, rotate, hook, or press onto a point, holding at the reflex supports the relaxation of that point. Maintaining even pressure allows the reflex to fully open to the work being done. Always hold on the reflex points of the brain and the endocrine points of the head.

Pressing

There are many areas during a session when pressing on a reflex is the coup de grâce. When you work on the pineal reflex after you rotate and hold, press in with your thumb and hold again. Often you will thumb walk across an area and, before moving on, press with the flat of your thumb. This is a way of sealing in the work you have just performed.

Pressing on a point or an area is a calming and reassuring way to move in deeply, without any trauma to the area or the receiver. Always work within the comfort zone of the person receiving the treatment.

Hooking

Perhaps the most advanced technique in reflexology is to hook in and back up. With this technique you can actually pinpoint those specific reflexes that are small and set in, representing areas deep within the body, such as the pineal gland. The hooking technique allows you to stimulate deeply in an area that is too small to effectively thumb walk within.

This technique allows deep penetration, yet there should be no pain, as the process is slow with steps that take the thumb into the reflex area for effective stimulation. The key to any of these steps and points is to practice, practice, and practice. The more people you work on, the more proficient and professional you become.

To apply this technique, move directly to the point and thumb press into the point. As you are pressing, begin to rotate, moving in deeper and deeper. Each circle allows a closer penetration. From this point, push into the area and hold. As you hold on the point, press in with the tip of the thumb, turn the thumb 150 degrees, push in, and pull up as though using a fishhook.

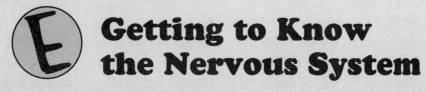

Chapter 11

Getting to Know the Nervous System

The nervous system and the endocrine system are in many ways the lifelines of human whole health—the keys to body, mind, and soul wellness. Reflexology connects with the central nervous system through the nerves running to and from the feet. The connection continues with the nervous system and the endocrine system through the spinal cord and the brain.

The Need for Equilibrium

Homeostasis is the state of normal function for all the various systems of the body. The internal environment of the body is maintained at a precise level at all times. The body is in homeostasis when the systems are responding in balance and operating at appropriate levels. The equilibrium of all body fluids, through the balance of temperature, chemical level, and internal pressure, represents good health for all cells.

You have worked with the reflex points of the head, neck, and shoulders, as well as those that deal with many of the hormone-producing glands of the endocrine system. The reflexes for the brain, the brain stem, and the sensory system are reflected in the toes you have just worked on. However, there are many compartments in the brain, and it's time to become actively engaged in stimulating this network.

The introduction of stress creates an imbalance within the environment of homeostasis. When this happens, the operating systems of the body, particularly the nervous and endocrine systems, promote a return to balance. These two systems share the maintenance of homeostasis, keeping the body functioning at a healthy level.

The Parts of the Brain

The subconscious brain is involved with activities that take no thought, but just are. Different parts of the brain deal with different arenas, as you will soon learn. These parts are:

- Medulla oblongata
- Pons
- Midbrain
- Diencephalon
- Cerebrum
- Cerebellum
- Limbic system

The Brain Stem

The medulla oblongata is found in the brain stem and holds the pathways of communication between the spinal cord and the various sections of the brain. The medulla is used to conduct sensory information from one side of the brain to the other, which in turn influences the opposite side of the body. This part of the brain stem controls the heartbeat and the rhythm of breathing, and regulates the size of blood vessels. Minor operations of the medulla oblongata deal with the functions of swallowing, vomiting, coughing, sneezing, and the hiccups.

The pons is the bridge that connects the spinal cord to the brain and various brain parts to each other. This part of the brain stem works with the medulla to help control respiration.

The midbrain is the final piece of the brain stem. This section deals with motor and sensory nerve bundles. These nerves carry impulses from the cerebral cortex to the pons and the spinal cord. The midbrain also contains nerves that conduct energy to the thalamus.

Diencephalon

This section of the brain contains the thalamus, the hypothalamus, and the pineal gland. It is a transmitter to the cerebral cortex, relaying sensory information from other parts of the brain and the spinal cord. The thalamus portion of the diencephalon interprets and translates sensory messages such as pain, temperature, light touch, and pressure. The pineal gland is that lentil-sized structure that produces the hormone melatonin. Melatonin promotes sleepiness as well as working with the circadian rhythms of the body.

The hypothalamus, although small in size, conducts a major amount of business. This portion of the diencephalon controls many activities related to homeostasis. Some of the functions of the hypothalamus include:

- Regulation of heart rate, digestion, and flow of urine.
- Reception of information from the internal organs.
- Connecting the nervous system and endocrine system.

- Production of hormones.
- Control of the pituitary gland.
- Creating a center to deal with mind over body control.
- Establishing a connection between emotions and behavior.
- Control of body temperature.
- Regulation of food and fluid intake.
- Maintenance of established sleep patterns.

The hypothalamus continuously receives information from outside and inside the body. This tiny area of the brain is a major influence in maintaining balance throughout the systems, keeping you functioning at your highest level.

Cerebrum and Cerebellum

The function of the cerebrum is to deal with the areas of sensory impulses and muscular movement as well as the areas of emotions and intellect. This center of control is divided into four sections, the lobes of the cerebrum. Each set of lobes has a specific function.

- Frontal lobes control muscle contraction, learning ability, intellect, and emotion.
- Parietal lobes control impulses of pain, cold, heat, touch, and pressure.
- Temporal lobes control hearing, smell, and language development.
- Occipital lobes control seeing and recognition of shape, color, and movement.

QUESTION?

Did you ever wonder why certain smells trigger old memories?
The smell of gingerbread permeates the air, and thoughts of winter holidays abound. These sensory memories are stored in the cerebrum, waiting for release.

Areas of taste are also controlled by the cerebrum, as are sensory memories from the past.

The cerebellum is a motor region of the brain, dealing with the subconscious movements of the muscles. This butterfly-shaped section is the second largest area of the brain. The cerebellum deals with coordination, posture, and balance.

Limbic System

The limbic system is the area of the brain that surrounds the brain stem, in a wishbone shape. This system is the emotional and behavioral center, often called the "emotional brain." Certain areas of memory are controlled from the limbic center. Because emotions are connected to the memories, those memories with powerful emotions are clearly remembered.

Connecting the Feet, Spinal Cord, and Brain

The central nervous system is the brain, the brain stem, and the spinal cord. The basic functional unit in the CNS is the neuron. Electrical impulses are chemically transmitted across synapses to other neurons, creating a pathway. The CNS integrates incoming information, generates thoughts and feelings, and stores memories. The impulse for muscles to contract and glands to secrete comes from the central nervous system.

The Peripheral Nervous System (PNS)

Once the neurons move into the peripheral area of the nervous system, they become nerves. The peripheral nervous system connects the CNS to sensory vehicles, muscles, and glands. The peripheral nervous system is composed of cranial and spinal nerves. These nerves carry information in and out of the central nervous system. Sensory neurons carry information from sensory receptors in the body into the CNS, while motor neurons carry impulses out of the CNS to the muscles and glands.

Somatic and Autonomic Nervous Systems

The peripheral system can be further divided into the somatic and autonomic nervous systems. The somatic nervous system (SNS) carries information from sensory receptors in the head, body frame, and limbs to the brain. Information dealing with movement travels from the brain via motor receptors to skeletal muscles. The autonomic nervous system (ANS) conveys sensory information from the organs to the CNS while motor neurons carry information from the brain to smooth muscle, glands, and the heart muscle.

FACT

A further division occurs in the motor section of the autonomic nervous system. These two areas are the sympathetic and the parasympathetic sections of the nervous system. The sympathetic section expends energy, speeding up activities, such as increasing the heartbeat. The parasympathetic component conserves energy, slowing down the heartbeat.

Spinal Nerve

The nerves of the spinal cord connect the central nervous system to the operations of the body. Remember, these nerves are part of the peripheral nervous system. There are thirty-one pairs of spinal nerves emerging out of the bones that house the spinal cord. (The bones form a column called the *vertebral column*.) These nerves travel out over the entire body, connecting with all the operating systems.

One branch of the nerves found in the feet stems from the largest nerve in our body, the sciatic nerve. The sciatic nerve consists of two nerves, the tibial and the common peroneal. These nerves are tied together by connective tissue. The sciatic nerve sends its two branches down the leg into the foot. In the foot these nerves branch out again, with many divisions nourishing the entire area.

7,200 Nerve Endings

Nerves are excitable tissue, covered and protected by connective tissue. Blood vessels within these coverings feed the nerves. Spinal nerves are mixed nerves containing both sensory and motor impulses. As the nerves move out from their attachment to the spinal cord, they branch out into areas of service. These branches are called *rami*. An example is the ramus that attends to the muscles and structures of the limbs; this branch is called the *ventral ramus*.

Dermatomes are identified as an area of skin that gives sensory information to the roots of cranial or spinal nerves. All nerves have dermatome identification. At the same time, skeletal muscles receive motor stimulation from neurons within spinal nerves. A section of a spinal nerve that provides motor information to muscles is considered a myotome. These regions affect the nerve endings found in the feet as well.

While all this may be a little confusing, it helps to have at least a general overview of the nerve structures. All you need to be concerned with is the fact that the feet contain many nerves, providing signals throughout the body, as well as receiving signals from outside stimulus.

FACT

The ventral rami form a network of nerves called a *plexus*. From the plexus, other nerves move out into the body, toward a specific region. Once in the service region, these nerves branch out yet again to innervate specific structures. The sacral plexus is the main provider for the legs and feet.

The Feet as a Post Office

You are sitting at the feet of the receiver, with your foot reflex chart nearby. You have warmed up both feet, and are now preparing to begin reflexing the feet. Look at those feet and see the doorway to the entire body. The nerves are the wires that run into the main column, where cables connect to the mainframe. Within the mainframe are many mailboxes, each with a certain address.

Following the input wires, mail is picked up and the delivery process begins. The mail is carried away along the output wires to the designated addresses. The message being delivered is essentially the same to all addresses: "Please function at your best level and be in a homeostatic state. Thank you." The act of reflexology provides that message. The continued application of pressure to the feet is a constant reminder for the entire body to wake up and smell the coffee.

The nervous system has many parts, most of which are affected by reflexology. As you reflex an area on the foot, you are directly stimulating the sensory nervous system. This message is then relayed to the autonomic nervous system through the spine, on to the brain, and back out the spine to the autonomic nervous system. Both sections of the autonomic system are affected.

The spinal cord reflex also plays an important role in homeostasis. This quick automatic response has no brain thought involved. The spinal cord is a roadway for sensory nerves to the brain, and motor nerves to the body. There are times when the information is exchanged only in the spinal cord, involving activity between a sensory and a motor neuron. This response is called a *reflex*.

Reflex response can be simple or complex, depending upon the nerves involved. Simple reflexes involve one sensory and one motor neuron, while complex reflexes involve a relationship with more than two neurons. For example, the stretch reflex is simple, and the tendon reflex is complex.

Reflexology elicits a reflex response when pressure is applied to the reflex points. Sensory and motor receptors receive information via the nerve pathways from the feet. Whatever may be needed at the time, the reflex response will be activated, releasing chemical and physical results. The feet receive and integrate information throughout the body, working with the nervous system toward homeostasis.

Seeing the Receiver Relax

As a reflexologist, you become aware that each segment of the session provokes a deeper relaxation response. From the moment of arrival, the receiver has begun the process of de-stressing. For some people, just the thought of returning is often enough to activate the relaxation reaction. As you study this technique, you will learn to pick up cues from the receiver. As the receiver is made comfortable, you allow him or her the right to relax. Often your first words relay the message. For many, the permission to relax and let go is essential.

The next important piece in this process is the introduction of touch. The relaxation techniques facilitate not only relaxation of the feet but also of the body and of the mind. By accessing the nervous system through steady, even touch, the receiver is truly able to relax and trust.

Trust is essential in this process. The receiver must feel safe and secure from the beginning of the session. The giver establishes an environment of caring through firm, gentle touch. A quiet, clean ambiance is important; a compassionate, genuine treatment is vital.

Moving on from the relaxation segment, you begin to finger walk the toes. Stay focused on the receiver, being aware of the pressure you use as well as the routine. The face of the receiver is easily read; the more relaxed the person becomes, the harder it will be for his eyes to stay open. The color of the skin will respond, beginning to display a healthy glow.

Alpha is a meditative state that is often entered into through deep relaxation. Freedom from stress brings more relaxed breathing; the receiver generally releases deep sighs signaling a tranquil state. Make sure you have a light cover over the person you are working on, as the body temperature does drop.

Chapter 12

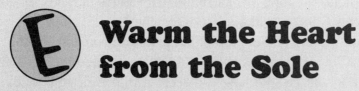

Warm the Heart from the Sole

The next section of the foot is from the shoulder guideline to the diaphragm guideline. Close your eyes for a moment and picture your body. See what organs and parts of the body reside in this area. Now that you have prepared yourself, it's time to move on to this segment.

The Ball of the Foot

This area of the foot is part of the forefoot, housing the metatarsal heads and top halves of the five metatarsal bones. The fleshy section of the ball is located under the joints that bend the toes at their base. This top sector of the ball of the foot contains the metatarsal heads, and the rest of the ball holds the long metatarsal bones. Various muscles, tendons, and ligaments work to hold the bones together.

Let your fingers trace the top of the foot, and you will feel the metatarsals. The first bone is short and wide, and the other four are thin and long. Look at the sole now and see how the entire ball of the foot puffs out, just like the chest region of the body.

If you pull the top of the foot down toward the sole, a natural line will appear under the ball of the foot, which is the diaphragm line. The entire region from under the toes, which is the shoulder line, to this line in the arch is the area we are dealing with now.

This part of the foot holds reflexes for the heart, lungs, trachea, bronchioles, breast, some of the skeletal system, and the upper back. The reflex for the thymus gland is found here as well as reflexes of the lymphatic system. The areas of representation are fairly straightforward, although some regions do overlap. For the most part, the locations of the reflexes are exactly where you would imagine them to be.

FACT

The ball of the foot is the area that we spring off when we walk. There is a point during the cycle of walking when the forefoot bears all of the body weight. These tiny bones do a tremendous amount of work! Often people will have callus, dry skin, even pinched nerves, due to improper shoe gear and walking habits.

Begin with a Knuckle Press

Still working on the right foot and holding with your left hand, prepare to continue on with this section. Your right hand will form a closed fist as you use the outside of the long bones to press into the foot. With your left hand solidly behind the foot, your hand is acting like a cup, letting the fingers provide the support. Another option is to grasp the toes firmly with the left hand, holding the foot straight and tall, as you press into this section of the foot.

There will be times during the session when either the right or left hand may do the work, depending upon the giver. The knuckle press is one such technique. Just make sure you support the foot, so one hand provides leverage and the other is working. Experiment by switching back and forth to see which way works best for you.

Establish a Rhythm

Support the foot as you gently and firmly press into the entire ball of the foot. Begin with the top region of this area and press down and up continuously for a number of presses. Look at the face of the receiver; encourage him to relax and to breathe deeply. This is a relaxing technique that can be used throughout the session, whenever you feel the need for transitional assistance.

Continue to press in and let your body move gently, establishing a rhythm. Press in as you move in. Let the fist rock a bit on the foot, flowing from knuckles to finger joints and back to knuckles again.

FACT

Knuckles are joints, too. The difference between them and the other finger joints has to do with movement. The knuckles are bones that can point and bend, as well as move side to side. The part of the fingers discussed here, the second joints, can only point and bend.

Think of Kneading

Another way to describe the knuckle press is to equate this technique to the motion of kneading. Kneading the ball of the foot is connecting you with all the reflexes found in the chest region. As you knead, let the supporting hand press in on the top of the foot, keeping the rhythm. This provides a comforting feeling to the person receiving the treatment.

The knuckle press is a good technique for large areas of the foot that may have tougher skin, like the ball and the heel. This does not mean you can push heavily! If anything, you need to be more sensitive since the knuckles have no feeling. You need to be aware of how deeply you are pressing, adjusting to the receiver's comfort zone.

ALERT!

Never push in deeply. The foot will open to your pressure as you work. Even if the receiver wants you to push harder, explain you are working at the right level at this time. Trust that when the body is ready, you will have deeper access.

Thumb Walk the Heart Reflex

Now that you have relaxed the chest region, you are ready to move on. Place both feet together for a second so you can see the relationship of the heart reflex in the feet to the position of the heart in the body. Look at the shape of the feet and notice how the swell of the ball is greater on the inside edge of the feet, especially at the base. This reflects the heart; the base of the ball of the foot right at the inner edge is the heart reflex.

FACT

Here it is recommended that you use the left hand to press on the right foot, while the right hand supports the foot. When working this area on the left foot, switch hands. You will see this frees up each hand, allowing the thumbs the ability to work without strain.

Finding the Reflex

Use the knuckle press again to create the flow, and after a few presses, let the second joint of your index finger trace a line. This line will run from the bottom base at the outside edge of the great toe down around the whole metatarsal head, which seems like a continuation of the big toe. Look at the foot again. See the slight crease, or indentation, that runs from the big toe down to the diaphragm line? This is the line you glide your second joint over. Let the joint glide around and down, and the reflex will pop right out. This is the heart reflex, with more on the left side than on the right. You will actually see the skin peek out a bit from the side of the foot.

ALERT!

If the receiver has any circulatory issues, such as high blood pressure, or is on any kind of heart medication, use an alternative technique. Using the left thumb, thumb walk across the diaphragm line from the outside edge of the foot to the inner edge. The heart reflex will still pop right out.

Working the Reflex

Now that you have located the heart reflex, gently use the thumb of the supporting hand to circle on the reflex. The supporting hand is still holding the foot; the thumb is brought to the side to perform the circling technique. Let the thumb softly and slowly circle on this reflex, and soon the area will feel warm.

After making small circles, thumb walk over the reflex as well. Here the thumb of the supporting hand is still doing the walking; essentially, both thumbs have met at the heart. Thumb walk from many different angles on this reflex point, coming in from all sides in small, steady bites. Finish this reflex with small circles and a gentle stroking off.

Caterpillar the Chest Reflex Region

Let the left hand support the foot again, as the right hand will start the sequence. Using the right thumb, you are going to thumb walk the chest region in an inchworm, or caterpillar, type movement.

Beginning at the heart reflex, thumb walk up from the heart reflex to under the great toe, turn, and thumb walk down to the diaphragm line.

Continue to thumb walk in this manner up to the base of the toes and down to the diaphragm line in a curvy line until the thumb reaches the outside edge of the foot. The left hand is holding the foot, gently clasping the toes, as the right thumb walks across the reflexes. The fingers of your right hand may rest on the top surface of the foot while the thumb does the work.

Do not overstretch your hand. If you feel the thumb is pulling away from the fingers, curl the fingers up behind the thumb; the fingers come along for the ride as the thumb works across the ball of the foot. There will be many times throughout a session where you will need to adapt your reach. Always pay attention to your form; if you feel your fingers stretching away from one another, readjust.

FACT

This caterpillar technique is the preliminary walk-through for all the reflexes on the ball of the foot. Each little bite is working on reflexes that deal with the lungs, windpipe, bronchi, bronchioles, breasts, upper lymphatic, thymus, or the heart. Each foot contains the same reflexes.

Once the right thumb has created the curvy path from the inside edge to the outer edge, switch hands. Now the right hand is the supporting hand and the left hand is the one doing the work. Use the left thumb to caterpillar back across the ball of the foot. Take small bites, turning down into the curves each time and walking up again. This movement will bring you back to the heart reflex again.

Thumb Walk from the Inside Edge

Use the left hand to support the foot, either by holding the toes or holding the foot firmly. The right hand is the working hand. Return to the heart reflex and prepare to thumb walk. Look at the foot for a moment, visualizing what you are getting ready to do. Imagine the two guidelines you are working between, the shoulder line and the diaphragm line.

Notice how this section of the foot is shaped, almost rectangular. The two edges of the foot would be the sides, and the guidelines are the top and bottom, creating a rectangle. The heart reflex is located in the bottom right of this rectangular box.

Thumb walk along the diaphragm line from the heart reflex. Stop just over the central tendon line, which is right in the reflex point for the bronchioles. Quickly and smoothly bring the thumb back to the heart reflex. Move the thumb up just a bit above the heart reflex point and thumb walk in again just beyond the tendon line. The reflexes for the bronchioles and bronchi begin to overlap.

Breath: The Vital Life Force

Take a moment now to think about breathing. Breathing is vital to our existence, and proper breathing allows dynamic living. Often people have not incorporated the importance of deep, calm, nurturing breath. The connection between breath and wellness is profound.

Breathing affects the body, mind, and spirit. The more rhythmic and deep your breathing, the cleaner your systems are. The entire respiratory system works to exchange gases between the cells, blood, and atmosphere. The many organs of this system work to keep the body toxin free, utilizing breath as the cleanser.

Continuing On

As you continue to move up this section of the foot, you are working on the lungs and bronchioles. Always thumb walk slowly to the center and bring the thumb back to the inner edge of the foot to follow the next line up. Each line up this side of the ball is working toward the shoulder line. Imagine that this process is like stacking sheets of paper in one side of a rectangular box, continuing to stack until this side is full.

Just before the shoulder line, at the very top edge of the first metatarsal, close to the inner side, is the thymus reflex. Begin by thumb walking the line to the center and bring the thumb back, to rest on the reflex point for the thymus. Place the thumb directly under the shoulder line, just below the neck and thyroid reflex, along that inner edge.

The reflex may feel a bit bony or bumpy under the thumb, but whether it does or not, this is the thymus reflex. Rotate the thumb on this point. Feel the reflex relax under the thumb as you rotate in small circles. Stop and hold on this point, pressing down gently on the reflex.

FACT

The thymus plays an important role in the development of our immune system. It is most active up through puberty; however, it is functional throughout the lifespan. The thymus hormones promote the production of T cells. T cells establish immunity on a cellular level, improving our resistance to disease.

Once you have completed thumb walking up this portion of the rectangle, you will thumb walk down in the same fashion. Starting from the thymus reflex, thumb walk in to the center and bring the thumb back to the edge, just under the thymus point. Continue to walk down this side of the ball of the foot, until the last swipe across comes from the diaphragm line. You will now move over to the left side of this section of the foot.

Thumb Walk from the Outside Edge

The essence here is to complete the other side of the rectangular box that you have created over the ball of the foot. The right hand is now the supporting hand and the left hand has become the working hand. The routine for the reflexes on the ball of the foot are the same on both feet. Begin with the left thumb on the outer edge of the diaphragm line; this will be the left edge of the foot as you look at it.

Thumb walk with slow, small steps to the tendon line, then bring the thumb back to the outer edge. Continue to thumb walk into the center, each time moving the thumb up a bit to create a new line from the outer edge. Again, imagine stacking sheets of paper on top of one another to build the other piece of the rectangle.

As you thumb walk over this region, you continue to work on the lung reflex. Reflexology promotes circulation, and working on reflexes signals the muscles of the body to let go and relax. When the lung region releases tension, the entire chest area settles down and accepts the healing. Often the receiver will cough or sigh, a signal that tension is leaving.

By walking in and out of this side of the chest region, you are also working the breast reflex. Thumb walk the breast reflex and continue up the foot, walking in toward the tendon line and coming back out to the edge of the foot to start a new line. At the shoulder line, repeat the process, moving down the foot to the diaphragm line.

The dorsal surface of the foot reflects the back of the body and the sole reflects the front. Many reflexology foot charts place the breast reflex on the top of the foot. Perhaps this placement mirrors components of the lymphatic system. However, for our purposes, the breast reflex mirrors the breast location on the body.

Butterfly the Area

The butterfly technique is a wonderful transitional move, as well as a smoothing and bringing together of the process. Cup the foot in both hands, with one hand on each side of the foot. Remember to rest the fingers of both hands on the top surface of the foot, allowing the thumbs freedom of movement. The thumbs will walk along the plantar surface, in this case from the shoulder line to the diaphragm line. The thumbs work together, taking small, tiny steps moving toward the centerline of the foot.

Start at the edge of the foot, with the thumbs at the shoulder line. Imagine for a moment the wings of a butterfly superimposed on the ball of the foot. Let the thumbs begin to walk the faint lines that represent the pattern of the wings. As the thumbs reach the center of the foot, bring the thumbs back to the edge and move down a thumb length. Both thumbs are resting on the sides of the foot. Move down a bit and walk in again to the centerline. The tendon that runs down the middle of the plantar surface of the foot divides the foot in half. Continue to butterfly in to the center, bring the thumbs back to the sides, and repeat. When the thumbs reach the diaphragm line, work back up the foot using the same process.

With this butterfly technique, all of the reflexes are affected. By working in this manner, you assure that every point has been reflexed—that nothing has been overlooked. The beauty of reflexology is that many reflex points do overlap; therefore, a technique like the butterfly allows you to effectively contact all areas.

Proper transition from one section to another or from one technique to another is easily attained with this technique. The butterfly movement signals two types of transitions. First, you are leaving the bottom surface and moving to the top for the next segment. Second, you will be using a different technique on the dorsal surface.

Work on the Top Surface of the Foot

The top of the foot represents the back area of the body. There are two divisions, using the diaphragm line to create the separation. Picture your back. Imagine a line representing the actual diaphragm muscle; this will be the line that divides the back into upper and lower regions. The back of the body consists of major muscles and bones, along with the spine. Place both feet together to picture what is represented here.

What's in a Back?

Sit and look at the tops of your own feet. Get comfortable and imagine the back of your body mirrored on your feet. The inner edge of both feet represents the spine. The imaginary guideline of the shoulder represents the shoulder. The two feet house all the bones and muscles of both the upper and lower back.

For this section, you are concerned only with the upper-back reflection. In this upper region of the foot are reflexes for the scapula, which is commonly known as the shoulder blade. The reflex points for the muscles that attach to this bone—the trapezius, the rhomboids, and the levator scapula—are reflected in this area as well. The reflex for the rib cage is also represented here.

Try the Technique

Now that you have a general idea of what is mirrored on the top surface of the foot, try the technique. Again you are working the right foot completely, and then you will work the left. The technique will be the same on the left foot.

The foot will rest comfortably as you position both hands on either side of the foot, at the thoracic region. Rest the thumbs on the plantar surface; they will provide leverage. Begin a slow, steady, even finger walk, all fingers moving together toward the center of the foot. This movement seems as though the fingers are crawling together. Imagine the foot is an accordion; you are playing the notes as your fingers move in between each long metatarsal bone. Keep finger walking until the fingers meet; the fingernails will actually click together, signaling that the fingers cannot move any farther.

Slowly walk the fingers back, letting the fingers inch backward. This is done exactly as it sounds. From the center, pull all the bent fingers back a bit, then straighten out the fingers slightly and then right back onto the tips again. Let the fingers drag slightly. Picture walking between the ribs as the fingers move across the bones.

You are not digging in here, nor are you applying pressure to this bony area. Instead you are inching back, holding, pressing, and inching back again. Continue this move until both hands reach the edges of the foot.

This technique could generate heat in the back area of the body. The receiver may relate an extreme feeling of relaxation, a letting go of the tension held in the back and neck. Perhaps the person in the chair is asleep. If so, good job!

Full-Finger Walking on the Top

The fingers are resting on the sides of the foot, waiting for you to make the next move. Keeping the thumbs on the bottom of the foot, again for leverage, move all the fingers up to just under the toe neck. Tuck the fingers into the little shelf created by the joints that bend the toes in that region. The tips of the fingers are touching and the fingers are flexed, ready to move.

Using all of the fingers at once, slowly finger walk down the top surface of the foot, inching along. Keep an eye on the imaginary guideline. When the fingers reach the diaphragm line, stop. Hold the fingers here, apply light pressure, and with a slight side-to-side, squiggly motion, pull back to the base of the toes. Finger walk back down and repeat.

All of the upper-back reflexes receive attention with this two-part technique. Reflexology does promote circulation, and you have sent communication supporting the delivery of oxygen and blood to the back area of the body. If any congestion by toxic buildup is present, the reflexology will assist in releasing this tension.

The anatomy of the feet seems to support the reflex areas of reflexology. As you prepare to finger walk down the foot, look at the surface you are working on. Ask the receiver to bend his toes down. Notice the tendons that work to extend the bones; they create a path for your fingers.

Lymph Drainage

To review, there are several major components of the lymphatic system. The fluid is called *lymph* and is transported by the lymphatic vessels. The lymph passes from the vessels through lymph nodes back into the vessels and continues on throughout the body in this fashion. A large portion of the 600-plus lymph nodes reside in the breast, armpits, chest, and abdomen, as well as in the groin area. The others are scattered freely throughout the body. Certain organs also have lymphatic tissue: the spleen, the thymus, and the tonsils. Lymph is one of the main defense systems of the body providing resistance to invaders.

Lymph drainage is important, as it allows the flow of lymph to continue unobstructed. The technique for lymph drainage is simple. Both feet have the same reflexes. You are still on the right foot. The thumb and forefinger are used simultaneously for this movement.

Begin with a practice run on your hands. Use your right hand to work on your left. Turn the left hand so that the palm is facing you; the thumb will be closest to you. Place your right thumb at the top of the web between the thumb and forefinger of the left hand, on the palm's surface. Rest your index finger at the top of the web, on the dorsal surface of the hand. Press in gently, feeling contact. Curl the remaining fingers into a fist, so they stay out of the way and can easily move with you.

Using slow, steady movement, inch forward and allow the thumb and finger to walk down the web toward the wrist. When you have gone as far as your hand will allow, press and hold. Gently, with light, even pressure, slowly pull back along the route you just traveled. When the two fingers reach the top of the web, hold and press the two fingers together at the tips, through the web. Gently pull off and move to the next space between the fingers, repeating to the end and back again.

Now, move to the foot. The left hand is supporting the right foot, holding at the heel. Place the right thumb and forefinger at the web between the great toe and second toe. The thumb is touching the plantar surface and the forefinger is on the dorsal side. Close the remaining fingers into a fist, tucked out of the way.

Thumb and finger walk down the foot toward the ankle. Again go as far as your hand will allow. At the end of each walk down, before moving to the next web, gently pull up to the top again. The pressure is steady, but not heavy.

QUESTION?

What if my hand is too small?
Sometimes the hands are too small to use both fingers together. If this is the case, walk down the top surface and pull back, and then walk down the bottom surface. Repeat for each web.

Solar Plexus Reflex

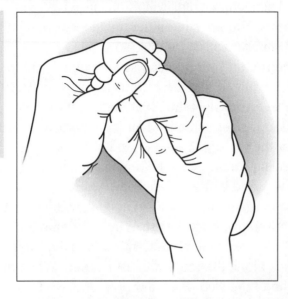

The solar plexus reflex is found directly in the center, just under the diaphragm line, as shown in **FIGURE 12-1**. A plexus is a meeting place for a group of nerves, a vital center of activity. This network in turn relates to specific areas and organs in the body. As part of the autonomic nervous system, the solar plexus has sympathetic and parasympathetic nerve cells.

FACT

The autonomic nervous system regulates the involuntary movement of muscle. Sympathetic nerves speed up action, a response to stress. Parasympathetic nerves slow down action, bringing the body activities back to normal.

Solar Plexus Reflex Connections

The solar plexus seems to be related to emotional and spiritual issues. Its name implies the power of its function. You work on the sole to treat the soul; the solar plexus is the key. The physical organs close to this region are the diaphragm, breasts, heart, and lungs.

This point is perhaps the most singularly powerful reflex, providing relief from painful points, as well as a strong connection to breath. The solar plexus reflex relates to the nervous system, assisting in overall relaxation.

Working the Reflex

This reflex is the same on both feet, though you are working on the right foot at the moment. Cradle the right foot with the left hand; pull the toes down over the shoulder line, and an indentation will appear exactly at the center just below the diaphragm line. This point is aligned in zones two and three and is the beginning of the kidney meridian. Holding the foot steady, the right thumb walks in from the medial edge along the diaphragm line to the point directly under the center at the ball of the foot.

Using the entire flat surface of the thumb, turn the finger slightly sideways, pressing into the depression to identify the reflex. While the right thumb is pressing into the reflex, use the left hand to pull down from the top of the foot, effectively creating an awning over the reflex. Hold here and ask the receiver to breathe in deeply, holding the breath for a count of three and then slowly releasing.

As the receiver relaxes, release the toes while continuing to press the thumb into the reflex. At times the reflex will actually pulse, which is a signal that the reflex is involved with the sense of calmness spreading through the body. Slowly back the thumb out of the reflex, feeling the skin push up against the thumb. This technique is very effective, creating an immediate relaxation response.

This technique will often release congestion felt in other reflexes. As you work, if a reflex is painful, use the solar plexus method to reduce this response. Often, activating the solar plexus is enough to reduce or eliminate the painful response.

Flutter Off

Transitions are important in a reflexology session. As you move from one area of the foot to another, you continue to create a calm, relaxing environment. At the end of this section, use the flutter movement. Place both hands on top of the foot. Using soft, fluttery strokes, move the fingers up and off the foot.

The stroke is performed by gently moving the fingers on the surface of the foot. Act as though the foot is a piano keyboard, with all fingers playing at once, moving up toward the ankle.

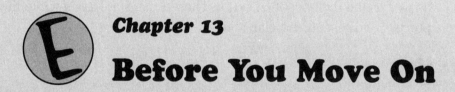

Chapter 13

Before You Move On

Reflexology has many theories. As wide and varied as some of these theories may be, there are constants as well. The divisions of the feet and representation of reflex points are generally similar. More reflexologists today recognize the physical and energetic connection of the work, and understand that footwork encompasses a vast amount of ever-changing information.

Right Foot, Right Side

The right side of the body is in many ways the twin of the left. There are important differences, however. The right side contains the liver, gallbladder, pyloric sphincter, duodenum, jejunum, and ileum. This side also contains the ileocecal valve, cecum, appendix, and ascending colon, as well as the right hepatic flexure. These organs are essential in the process of digestion and elimination.

The Liver

The liver is the largest gland in the body and is located under the diaphragm predominantly on the right side of the body. Its functions are vital to homeostasis:

The functions of the liver are as follows:

- Manufactures bile salts to rid body of fats
- Contains enzymes to transform toxins to usable compounds
- Produces and stores fat and glycogen
- Transforms glycogen, fat, and protein into glucose
- Ingests worn-out red and white blood cells
- Is instrumental in preventing blood clots
- Stores vitamins and minerals, as well as poisons that cannot be excreted
- Works with the skin and kidneys to activate vitamin D

The gallbladder is tucked under the liver, working together with the liver to store bile. The gallbladder holds extra bile until the small intestine needs it.

ALERT!

Some ingested poisons cannot be removed from the body. Such poisons as DDT have been found in the livers of humans and other animals. Fruits and vegetables sprayed with DDT leave high levels of the poison in the liver. At the very least, wash such foods with soap and water; if possible, eat organic.

The Small Intestine

The primary job of the small intestine is to digest food and to pass along the nutrients to the blood and lymph. Between the small intestine and the stomach is a valve known as the *pyloric sphincter*. Food leaves the stomach through this valve, moving into the duodenum, the first segment of the small intestine. The duodenum joins with the jejunum, merging with the ileum. The small intestine is over 21 feet long, allowing lots of space for the nutrients to move into the bloodstream.

The Large Intestine

The large intestine extracts any nutrients that were not absorbed by the small intestine. The ileocecal valve is the entryway into the large intestine. The nonabsorbable substances pass from the small intestine into the colon through the ileocecal valve. Behind this valve is the cecum, which is attached to the appendix on one end and the ascending colon on the other.

Decomposed and undigested waste products are moved through the passageway of the colon, with any remaining nutrients absorbed in the ascending colon. The final push of waste moves across the transverse colon, down the descending colon, through the sigmoid colon, into the rectum, and out of the body. Half of the large intestine is reflected by the reflexes in the right foot, the half that is in the right side of the body.

FACT

Reflexology in part is based on the concept of zone therapy. Whatever is in a zone is found in the reflected zone on the feet and hands. Further, the body is divided in half at the midline—what is on the right side of the body is again replicated on the right foot.

Left Foot, Left Side

The left side of the body duplicates the right in most areas. The differences occur in the left region of the upper abdomen, which houses the spleen, and in the intestinal area. The unique areas of the left side of the body are the descending colon, the sigmoid colon, and the reflex for the rectum.

The spleen is the organ that contains the most concentrated area of lymphatic tissue. The spleen also contains red blood cells. The function of the spleen is to ingest bacteria and old red blood cells, as well as store blood to be released as needed. The spleen is tucked under the diaphragm next to the stomach on the left side of the body.

The transverse colon flows into the splenic flexure, which is the left curve of the large intestine, underneath the spleen. From the left flexure, the colon merges into the descending colon, moving down the left side of the lower abdomen. The descending colon converges with the sigmoid colon, which begins in line with the bottom of the left hip. The sigmoid colon moves toward the center of the body, emptying into the rectum.

As we have discussed, the large intestine deals with the last stages of digestion. Whatever nutrients may remain are converted for absorption and carried to the liver. The remaining waste is transported out of the body.

From our head to our toes, the left and right sides are basically the same, minus these few differences. The reflexology treatment reflects this, as the technique used on each foot is the same, except for the areas that have been discussed.

It's That Mirror Again

The mirror image of the body is reflected on the feet. A picture of the body superimposed over the feet lends credence to this image. The head sits at the toes and the rest of the body basically follows along, with the center of the body reflected on the inner sides of each foot. The outer edges of the feet represent the outside of the body.

The Mirror Is Energetic

Of course the mirror is not only physical but energetic as well. There are many theories connecting the body with the feet. Some have been discussed, such as zone therapy and meridian therapy. We have mentioned the research and discovery of sensory effects and proprioceptive action, and have talked about the concept of repetitive memory.

ALERT!

Never say you can fix someone or some condition; rather, let people know you can help them relax. The very act of setting aside time for a session will allow busy people to begin to feel less stressed. You provide the tools to implement relaxation.

Repetitive Treatments

Repetitive treatments seem to store a memory within the sensory system that quickly comes to the surface as you conduct a session. The first time a receiver is given reflexology he or she has no idea what to expect, yet the understanding that this is a relaxation technique is clear. The person in the chair often cannot keep her eyes open much past the relaxation part of the session. Throughout the treatment the receiver may talk, sleep, remark how relaxed they feel, or any variety of such responses. By the time the session has ended, the receiver is ready to schedule a return appointment.

As you practice you will find that the people you work on will become enamored with reflexology, always eager for you to work on their feet. Remember, the more you practice, the better you become. Some people find relief of chronic pain in their hands and feet through continued reflexology treatments. Although you do not treat any condition, continued release from stress will help manage pain.

Repeat sessions seem to create a pattern within the body that recognizes reflexology as a tension reliever. The mirror here is one that reflects the memory of relaxation due to stress release. The entire body relaxes during a session, even the conscious mind. Generally, the receiver slips into a semidream state, aware yet relaxed. Many people who repeatedly receive reflexology report that they continue to feel relaxed in between sessions. It seems that the effects of this modality allow for long-term, sustained relief.

A Reflexologist's Job

You ever have a day you just don't feel like going to work? The thought of going in to your job just does not appeal to you. Imagine the value of always enjoying what you do, regardless of how you may be feeling personally. The giver of reflexology receives as much as he gives.

A reflexologist's intention is to give the best session, to help in whatever way is appropriate, and to ensure the receiver is safe and secure. He works in a systematic style, allowing for complete relaxation, in an environment that honors the receiver. He listens and respects what they are told, incorporating pertinent information. The person sitting in the reflexologist's chair trusts that the giver is providing what he or she needs.

Total Relaxation

As you work on the receiver, the release of tension is involved in a two-way channel. This is the energetic construct of reflexology. The giver sets the stage for total relaxation, allowing the receiver to release troubling or busy thoughts, permitting the muscles to let go of tension, and creating an environment dedicated to whole wellness.

Whole wellness is the concept of healing the whole person. The giver sets up an energy flow that creates a path allowing unrestricted use of the healing touch he is employing. Well-intentioned touch through reflexology promotes deep relaxation.

Total relaxation allows the nervous system to activate a healing response. This response reaches out farther into the body, affecting the immune system. The process of homeostasis is a constant flow of balanced energy.

A Partnership of Wellness

Remember, you are not treating any specific condition, nor are you diagnosing any illness. What reflexology does, by viewing the receiver as a whole being, is to allow an atmosphere of wellness to become a real concept, incorporating both the giver and receiver in a partnership. This cooperative entity enables the receiver to take charge of his body, mind, and spirit, utilizing the tools the giver has introduced.

The value of wellness is a learned response. Many people do not realize the role they play in this concept. As you encourage the receivers to stand in their own place of power, this value becomes real.

FACT

Psychoneuroimmunology is the study of how the mind and the body affect each other. Studies have proved that a positive state of mind creates a positive emotional environment that will support wellness. Disease is promoted by negative thoughts and emotions. Reflexology helps the receiver establish a harmonious attitude, generating the integration of body and mind wellness.

Expect the Unexpected

Let's say you've begun to practice on others. You have done the reading, and you understand the concept of zone therapy. Therefore, you realize that what is on the right side of the body reflects on the right foot and vice versa. You have relaxed both feet, and you are working on the right foot. As you reflex the shoulder point on the right foot, the receiver relates that he is experiencing a feeling in his left shoulder.

How can this be? Remember, always listen to the receiver; it is his or her body! "But, but," you think, "this is impossible." No, it is not impossible. The person in your chair is affected by the work from the right foot, not only on the right side of the body, but at times on the left side as well. Are you confused?

The Integration of Somatic Therapies

Reflexology is not only zone therapy, but also an integration of many somatic therapies. The concept of meridians is definitely involved. Meridians are reflected on both sides of the body just as zones are; yet the areas are not restricted. Of the fourteen main meridians, twelve connect to an organ while the other two deal with the center of the body. As you work on one side of the body on an area where a meridian runs through, the energy may connect to the opposite side of the body. For example, any of the meridians out of the feet will at some point run near the shoulder and all of the meridians of the hands run through the shoulder.

Another area where you may see opposite areas affected will be the reflex connections with the head. As the right side of the brain affects the left side of the body and the left side of the brain affects the right side of the body, this may be reflected in the session as well.

Basic Guidelines

Whatever the reason for an unexpected response, these basic guidelines will help you to provide an appropriate treatment:

- Trust in yourself.
- Believe the receiver.
- Listen openly and intuitively.
- Know you are helpful.
- Go with the flow.
- Have respect for the work.
- Be patient and keep learning.

The body is an incredible creation, alive with feeling, physical as well as emotional. All areas of the body have sensory receptors, allowing the skin to feel the slightest touch to the heaviest pressure. A soft breeze may often be felt more strongly than a gust of wind. The skeletal muscles also receive sensory input, which allows us to have feeling inside the body as well. All of the body is connected, not just the direct spot you may be touching.

Dermatomes are the sensory lines that affect the skin and are connected with the central nervous system. The discovery of dermatomes brought about valuable research in the field of touch. A light touch is more effective than heavy pressure.

Explanation of Bones as Guidelines

The bones of the feet give the reflexologist clear guidelines to perform their trade. They also work on the lower leg, as the tendons, ligaments, and muscles connect into the foot and are key to movement. The foot contains 28 bones, 4 layers of muscles, 12 tendons, and over 100 ligaments. There is distinct anatomical terminology for the bones as well as terms used to explain direction and movement. The divisions of the bones are separated into three regions. These regions are the proximal tarsus, the intermediate metatarsus, and the distal phalanges.

The Proximal Tarsus

The tarsus consists of seven tarsal bones that form the back and ankle region of the foot, and the lower arch.

1. Talus, the anklebone
2. Calcaneus, the heel bone
3. Cuboid, a cube-shaped bone
4. Navicular, a bean-shaped bone
5. Medial cuneiform, the inside bone
6. Middle cuneiform, the middle bone
7. Lateral cuneiform, the outside bone

The talus bone is actually in between the two bones of the lower leg; this bone is the first weight-bearing bone during the action of walking. The heel bone, or calcaneus, is the largest and strongest of the foot bones. The heel takes half of the weight from the ankle and the other tarsal bones carry the remainder of the weight during walking.

These bones are the guidelines for the lower-body reflexes. The heel represents the lower back, especially the sciatic reflex. A part of the intestine reflexes are housed in the heel. The talus has access reflexes for the fallopian tubes and the vas deferens and reflexes for the lymphatics.

The navicular bone sits on top of the foot sandwiched between the talus and the three cuneiform bones. The reflex for the lower back does reach this bone, as do the reflexes for the lymphatics. The cuneiforms come along the top of the foot from the inside edge, representing the lower back.

The Metatarsus

The metatarsus is made up of five metatarsal bones. These bones are known as I through V, with number I being the metatarsal bone near the inside edge. These bones have three parts: a base, which touches the tarsal bones; a shaft, which consists of the length of the bone; and the head, which touches the bottom of the toe digits. The reflexes involved with the metatarsal bones are all those found from the diaphragm line to the sciatic line, whether these points are on the top or bottom of the foot.

The Phalanges

There are five phalanges of the foot also known as I through V. Four of these toe bones, numbers II through V, have three parts: the base, which touches the metatarsals; the middle bone; and the head, which is the beginning of the toes. The big toe, also known as the *hallux* or *great toe,* has two phalanges. The bones of the great toe are heavier and bigger than the other toe digits. The great toe contains a base and a head. The reflexes dealing with this section of the foot are those found from the shoulder line up to the tips of the toes.

FACT

Two small bones, the sesamoid bones, are connected to the first metatarsal head. These bones are actually in the tendons and sit on the underside of the metatarsal. Sesamoid bones seem to appear in areas that take a great amount of pressure. Some people have sesamoid bones in their little toe as well.

Arches of the Foot

There are two arches of the foot, formed by the bones. The arches give the foot the ability to support and balance the body. Leverage for walking comes from these arches as well. Although these structures are called *arches,* these formations are not immovable. The action of walking produces an application of weight and then a lifting off of this weight. The arches act like a spring, providing shock absorption.

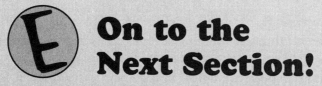

Chapter 14

On to the Next Section!

By now you are probably seeing that this reflexology stuff is actually pretty good. You have learned to relax people. Perhaps you have witnessed a stuffy nose run or an achy shoulder feel less tense. Whatever outcomes you have observed, you have more amazing routines to learn.

Diaphragm Line to Waistline

Remember, you are still working on the right foot. After the warm-up, always complete the routine on the right foot before moving to the left. Look at the sole of the foot and trace the diaphragm line, which runs from the outside edge of the foot to the inside edge, right along the fold of the ball of the foot. Remember, this is where the chest reflexes end. Now look at the inside edge of the great toe from just above the base, where the ridge from the second joint bulges out. This is the beginning of the esophagus reflex. Trace that down for a moment, to just below the diaphragm line, along the inside edge. The esophagus reflex will flow into the stomach reflex.

The Middle of the Arch

You are looking at the section of the foot between the diaphragm line and the waistline. Both sides of the foot represent the lines to create a new box, a rectangular shape that will hold the reflexes between the diaphragm line and the waistline guideline. The waistline coincides with the center of the foot, in the middle of the arch. Follow the little toe down into the fifth metatarsal; this long bone actually ends with a slight protuberance along the outside of the foot. Place your finger or thumb across the sole coming from this bone. Notice how the thumb is almost exactly in the middle of the arch.

Terminology

Anatomically there are names for the positions and directions dealing with areas of the body. These directional terms are used when any section of the body is discussed.

- **Superior**—toward the head
- **Inferior**—toward the lower part of the body
- **Anterior**—front of the body
- **Posterior**—back of the body
- **Medial**—middle of the body
- **Lateral**—outside of the body

- **Proximal**—near the point of origin
- **Distal**—farthest from the point of origin
- **Superficial**—surface of the body
- **Deep**—far from the surface

Any discussion of the feet may incorporate most of these terms as well as a few terms specific to the feet:

- **Plantar**—bottom of the foot
- **Dorsal**—top of the foot

Think about the Foot

The area you are working on now has the five shafts of the metatarsal bones, which are used as guidelines in your work. The diaphragm line begins just under the metatarsal heads and the waistline comes at the ends of the metatarsal bones. It often helps to feel your own foot first, tracing the bones that are the guidelines of this section.

Feeling the Foot

As you hold your foot, let your fingers move across the bones, feeling the muscles as well. Walk your fingers down, up, and across, identifying the metatarsal bones. The bases of these bones are enlarged; feel across the bottom of the foot and then the top. Once you feel comfortable identifying this area, try this on the receiver. Hold the foot with both hands and feel the metatarsal heads on the top of the foot. This will give you an idea of where the diaphragm line begins. Use the thumbs to walk down the bones to the base, feeling how the base of each bone enlarges slightly. The waistline guideline is here. Thumb walk in between the bones to feel the connecting muscles.

Hold the foot with the fingers on the top surface and the thumbs on the bottom. Let your thumbs feel the bones, as you did when you felt your own. Become familiar with the bottom surface, understanding where the bones end. Feel on each outside edge, the lateral and medial sides, finding the ends of the bones. These bones represent the end lines for the imaginary waistline.

FACT

The first metatarsal is a bit shorter and wider than the other four bones. The base of this bone broadens when it touches the medial cuneiform, which is the bone that follows right behind. Many times the point where these two bones touch forms a bump on the top of the foot, which may cause irritation from ill-fitting shoes.

What the Feet Do

The feet hold all of your body weight, carry you wherever you wish, and perform many other activities. The section of the foot you are now dealing with is also part of the two arches, the longitudinal arch and the transverse arch. These arches provide leverage and support. The medial longitudinal arch is an area where ligaments and tendons may weaken, resulting in a fallen arch or flatfoot.

The upper half of the instep also helps with balance whether you are standing still or walking. Picture the footprint you leave on the beach. Generally the ball of the foot is clear and the instep is not readily available. The center of gravity for the body is located in the arch.

Picture What Corresponds in the Body

You will be working on the reflex for the mouth and esophagus first. As you look at the feet, superimpose the idea of the mouth over the great toes, directing your gaze to the lower medial edge, just above the necks of these two toes. The mouth reflex is found on both toes just above the bottom inside edge of the toe bone. The reflex for the esophagus runs along the medial edge from the bulge of the bone along the inner edge to just below the diaphragm line. The esophagus moves right into the stomach reflex.

Again, look at both feet and imagine that part of your body from the diaphragm to the waist. This is the upper abdominal area, housing many organs and structures. Rest your hands on this area of your body; your thumbs naturally rest on the edges of your ribs as your fingertips touch in the center. A strong casing of muscles protects the organs within. The stomach is the next organ you encounter. The stomach is **J**-shaped, with most of the fatty part of the letter in the left upper portion of the abdomen. The reflex for the stomach is reflected on both feet.

The lower portion of the stomach moves toward the intestines. A valve at the end of the stomach keeps the processed food from re-entering the stomach. This valve is known as the *pyloric sphincter.* The reflex for the pyloric sphincter is found only on the right foot, as the curve of the stomach moves into the right side of the body with this part of the organ.

The Deep Organs

Move in deeper as you begin to picture the organs that sit behind or below the stomach. The pancreas lies behind the stomach and like the stomach connects with the small intestine. This gland is an accessory structure situated outside the gastrointestinal tract, yet it is integral to digestion.

ALERT!

Remember, reflexes are not body parts. A reflex is a point that energetically reflects the area of the body that it represents. One way reflexology connects to areas of the body is through the nervous system. When you reflex points, you are sending energetic and electric messages to encourage homeostasis.

The liver lies completely on the right side of the body and the gallbladder is tucked in under the liver. These two glands deal with bile, which is important for digestion. The stomach, pancreas, liver, and gallbladder all empty into the duodenum, the piece of the intestines that connects with the pyloric sphincter just about right of the center of the waistline.

The reflexes for these organs or structures are reflected on the coinciding feet. The liver and gallbladder are only on the right foot, whereas the pancreas is on both feet, just as in the body. The duodenum is found on the right foot.

The Spleen

Another organ that is found in the upper abdomen is the spleen. The spleen sits behind the larger portion of the stomach, completely on the left side of the body. This organ is important as a storage site of plasma, red blood cells, and lymph. The spleen eats old red blood cells and delivers recycled iron to the liver. This organ helps the immune system with the production of disease-fighting B and T cells. The reflex for the spleen is found only on the left foot, tucked under the outer ledge of the sole, along the diaphragm line.

The Adrenal Glands

The adrenal glands sit on top of the kidneys, one on each side of the body, behind the liver and the stomach, tucked up under the last set of ribs. These tiny bean-shaped glands produce important steroidal hormones. The adrenals secrete mineral hormones essential to the homeostasis of water, sodium, and potassium. The reflexes for the adrenal glands are found just above the waistline guideline in the center of each foot.

FACT

Another group of hormones from the adrenal glands deals with metabolism and stress. These hormones work to produce enough energy in the body. The adrenals secrete estrogens and androgens, which are male and female sex hormones. Two other important secretions produce the fight-or-flight response.

The Middle Back

Think about your middle back, that area that begins just below your shoulder blades and ends at your waist. The ribs and the muscles that cover the ribs form the midback region of the body. These protect the inner organs and the spinal column. Many people have back pain in this region often from improper standing, sitting, and walking. Of course, for some people the pain many generate through repetitive movement. The reflexes for this section of the body are found on the top of the foot, from just below the toes to the center of the top where the metatarsals end.

The Lower Back

The back does continue down into the sacral and coccyx region of the body. In reflexology, this section of the body is represented on the dorsal surface of the foot and again when you work with the spine reflex. If you continue on the top of the foot when you are working the middle-back reflex, you will walk right on into the lower-back reflex. This brings you to the bones behind the metatarsals just in front of the ankle.

Understanding Digestion

Most people forget that digestion begins with sight, smell, touch, or sound. We see food that we love and the gastric juices begin making our stomach growl.

Once the food has found its way to your mouth, the process of digestion continues. The tongue and teeth are involved, as well as saliva. The teeth chew and grind the food, mixing it with saliva, as the tongue moves it to the back of the mouth. Some of this process is voluntary. You are actively involved, while the autonomic nervous system covers the involuntary stages.

Moving the Food

As you begin to swallow, the food moves from the mouth to a structure called the *pharynx* and from the pharynx into the esophagus. This process is controlled by the nervous system, as breathing stops to allow swallowing, preventing food from entering into the respiratory tract. As the food moves into the esophagus, breathing resumes.

The involuntary muscles in the esophagus contract, moving the food down the column into the stomach. A sphincter at the entrance of the stomach prevents food from backing up into the esophagus. Once in the stomach, hydrochloric acid and the enzyme pepsin process the food and move it on to the duodenum, through the pyloric sphincter.

FACT

The smell emanating from the cooking of apple pie, lasagna, turkey, or whatever the favorite that was cooked in your home, triggers a response in the brain. The sound, sight, smell, even the touch of food being prepared stimulates stored memories. The impulses sent by the brain activate the salivary glands, implementing digestion.

Pancreas, Liver, and Gallbladder

The pancreas is instrumental in digestion, as it produces enzymes that digest carbohydrates, fats, and proteins. The liver produces bile, a compound that breaks down and absorbs fats and processes cholesterol. The gallbladder stores bile until the small intestine needs it for digestion. All three of these organs unite at a common duct to empty into the duodenum.

The Duodenum

This small structure holds a great deal of power. This tiny segment of the small intestine begins at the pyloric sphincter of the stomach and moves out to another portion of the small intestine. Most of the digestion takes place in the twelve inches of the duodenum.

Almost every organ of the digestive system seems to have a connection with this small curve of the intestines. Some of the digested food from the stomach comes into the duodenum. The pancreas sends enzymes while the liver sends bile. The main process of digestion has been completed in this section. The remainder of the work to be done is absorption and elimination, which is performed by the rest of the intestines and the colon.

Thumb Walk the Esophageal Reflex

Now that you know the workings of the digestive system, it's time to begin the process for this next section. Working on the right foot, begin by holding the foot with your right hand, using your left hand to perform the first sequence. The right hand cradles the foot for support and leverage.

Working the Reflex

Bring the left thumb to the inner, lower edge of the great toe, just above the second joint. This is the mouth reflex. Position the thumb so it is facing down and rotate on the reflex. Rotate in a circular motion, press, and hold. Very slowly using a firm, gentle touch, thumb walk down the inner edge of the foot, from the great toe. Thumb walk over the medial edge of the metatarsal head moving down the foot. This area may feel like a bony ridge, or may have a little padding, depending on the shape of the foot. The thumb is walking on the exact medial edge; this is the reflex for the esophageal tube.

Continue thumb walking down this edge past the metatarsal head to just below the diaphragm line. Bring the thumb back up and walk down again. Feel how the reflex begins to relax under the thumb.

Try this move on yourself. Thumb walk along this reflex and see how your foot feels. Are there any tender spots; do you need to ease up the pressure? This is a great way to find out how your technique feels—always try any of the segments that are possible on your own feet.

Be Aware of Your Body

Let's try something. Hold the right foot with the left hand and use the right thumb to walk the reflex for the esophagus. Notice how awkward this is. There will be many times during a session when using the opposite hand or using the fingers instead of the thumb will make sense.

The rule of thumb is, do what feels good and you will be right. It is important to have your body feel relaxed while working, not awkward or painful. Giving reflexology feels as good as getting if the giver is using good body mechanics. Be aware of your arms, hands, and fingers, as well as the rest of your body.

The arms should generally be relaxed, slightly bent at the elbow, with your fingers moving easily and freely. If you can see your elbow out of the corner of your eye, it is too high, and you should lower the arm. If your fingers or thumbs become too tired too quickly, stop pressing so hard. Remember, move your body; let the pressure come from the movement, not the hand.

Three Fingers Mark the Spot

The left hand is the holding hand. Hold the right foot by the toes or cradle the foot in the palm. The left hand will provide support and stability as well as leverage. Look at the plantar surface of the foot, visualizing the two guidelines. Find the centerline of the foot and place your first three fingers to this line from the inside edge of the foot. The fingers look like three stacks of wood piled up, one on top of the other.

When holding the fingers to the centerline, the second knuckles seem to rest at the inner edge of the foot. The index finger is lying on the waistline, the middle finger is lying just above the index finger, and the ring finger is lying just under the diaphragm line. These fingers are holding the place of three reflexes, marking the spot.

FACT

The ring finger is holding the area of the stomach and pyloric sphincter reflexes. The middle finger is marking the area for the pancreas reflex. The index finger is lying on the area of the duodenum reflex. All three fingers give you a clear vision of the reflexes held in these areas.

Proceed with Thumb Walking

Now remove the fingers. Beginning at the top area, where the ring finger was, thumb walk slowly across this line to the center mark. Feel the foot under your thumb as it begins to relax, as the reflex responds to the pressure. Thumb walk along the next reflex, that of the pancreas. Move slowly, taking tiny bites as the thumb walks in toward the centerline of the foot. Thumb walk the last line, which is the reflex for the duodenum. Again, using small, slow moves, let the thumb walk along this reflex into the tendon line.

Bring your thumb to the end of the waistline at the inner edge of the foot, the outside edge of the duodenum reflex. Turn the thumb and walk up in a straight line to the diaphragm line. Bring the thumb back, moving in a bit along the waistline, and thumb walk up again to the diaphragm line. Repeat this movement until the thumb reaches the centerline.

Switch Hands

Switch hands and use the right hand to hold the foot while the left thumb walks from the centerline out along the reflex for the stomach. Bring the left thumb back to the tendon line and thumb walk along the pancreas reflex out to the inside edge of the foot. Lastly, thumb walk along the waistline from the center of the foot to the inner edge, reflexing the duodenum reflex. Switch hands again, and, using the right thumb, repeat the thumb-walk technique from the inner edge of the foot to the centerline for the three reflexes. Walk each one slowly, feeling how the area has changed under your thumb.

When you move back to an area already worked, you'll likely see that the initial stiffness or tightness has disappeared; the area is much more giving now. It's as though the foot has let its guard down, trusting you. This is body wisdom, recognizing the reflexology as a good thing.

Liver and Gallbladder Reflexes

The liver and gallbladder reflexes are easy to find. Place the three fingers back across the areas you have just worked. The area of the foot still showing is the liver reflex. Yes, it is that big; don't forget that the liver is the largest gland in the body. Notice how the area is shaped a bit like a slanted triangle, with the point tucked under the breast reflex. The reflex stretches over behind the stomach reflex and down to just below the guideline for the waist, along the outside edge of the foot.

Don't take those fingers away yet. Using the middle finger as a guideline, place your left thumb one joint in from the outside edge, in line with that finger. Press in slightly, feeling the depression; this is the gallbladder reflex!

ALERT!

Use the reflexology foot reflex chart as a reference, a backup to confirm the reflex position. It is a good idea to keep the chart out and visible while you are learning the routine. Practice is the only way to become a good reflexologist. Practice the technique and practice learning the reflex points. You can do it!

Walk the Reflex

Support the foot with the right hand. Use the left thumb to walk over the entire liver reflex. This is done by thumb walking each section, bringing the thumb back to the outside edge of the foot, then moving along the next section. Walk the reflex completely, from the edge in.

Now bring the thumb to the corner of the waistline guide, along the outside edge. Turn the thumb toward the diaphragm line and walk up the reflex. Keep bringing the thumb back to the waist guideline, and, each time, move in a bit toward the center before walking up again. These two moves look like you have just created a grid of lines, sideways and up, crossing over one another.

Move your thumb back to the gallbladder reflex. Let your thumb drop right into this recess and rotate on the point. As you feel the thumb moving in deeper, hook into the reflex. Hook here by pressing in and pulling the thumb back toward the edge of the foot, while still in the reflex. Hold on this point, waiting to feel the gentle give of the reflex, then release.

Be Gentle

This area is often a tender spot for people. The tenderness could be the entire liver reflex or the gallbladder reflex or both. Be aware and remind the receiver to tell you if the pressure is too hard or the reflex is too painful.

The reason for the pain may be any number of causes. It is not your job to identify why the area is painful. Rather, it is your job to continue to work within the comfort level of the receiver. If the question does arise, simply state that you do not know why it is painful and move on.

QUESTION?

What do I do if the receiver has pain?
Always stop reflexing a painful area. Suggest that you will work lighter in that region. If the recipient agrees, try again. If the area is still too painful, move on. You can come back later.

Spleen Reflex

You are moving into areas where the reflexes are different on the two feet. Until now, the sequence has been the same, as the reflection of the body is similar. With the introduction of this section, however, you will see the divisions. The spleen reflex is found in the far left corner of the left foot, tucked under the outside end of the diaphragm guideline. This reflex is on the plantar surface of the foot and is fairly easy to identify.

Although you are not finished with the right foot, look at the left foot for a moment. Hold this foot in your left hand; the spleen reflex is accessed with the right thumb. Remind yourself of the diaphragm guideline, and as you do so, place your thumb one digit in from the outside edge, just under the line. Interestingly, the thumb will drop into a dip here, as there is a slight giving of the tension of the skin at this point.

Press the thumb into the reflex and hold. Firmly rotate on this spot, feeling the thumb move in deeper. As the reflex relaxes, hold the thumb on this spot, press, and hook back toward the edge of the foot. Allow the thumb to stay in the reflex, holding the hook in place.

This is another reflex that may be sensitive. The area of the foot where the spleen reflex is located is part of the lateral column. This is the section of the foot that is used for support, which could cause tenderness. Again, it is not your job to find the cause of the tenderness; you just need to be aware and continue on.

Gallbladder Meridian

Rest the left foot for now, covered and relaxed, and go back to the right foot. The gallbladder reflex, which is tucked up under the liver reflex, has another access point. The gallbladder meridian is one of the meridians that travel through almost the entire body. This meridian begins in the head, at the outside corner of the eye. It moves up into the head in a meandering pattern, covering a large area on the side of the head. Imagine holding the sides of your head with both hands; this is similar to the pattern and area covered by the meridian.

The meridian continues flowing down the body in this zigzag manner, branching in at the diaphragm, waist, groin, and hip. From the hip this meridian travels through the leg and knee, close to the lateral edge. The gallbladder meridian ends at the fourth toe, with the line coming across the surface of the foot.

FACT

The gallbladder is a storage container for bile, essentially holding a concentrate used for digestion. Ancient Chinese believed the gallbladder to be the originator of energy for all organs, transmitting a purity of use to the other organs. Because the gallbladder does not transport or store waste, bile is considered a pure essence by this ancient culture.

Here is where it gets really interesting. The gallbladder reflex is one thumb joint in from the lateral edge of the right foot. The gallbladder meridian line runs right through this reflex to terminate at the fourth toe. Here is a clear joining of two modalities, connecting with the same organ. The meridian shows a pathway of energy, which when blocked may cause certain disorders. The physical gallbladder helps with digestion and the energetic pathway deals with keeping the process clear.

Don't Forget the Adrenals

The adrenal glands sit on top of the kidneys, one on each side of the body. The reflexes reflect these glands on both feet. You are working on the right foot at the moment. Place those three fingers back on the reflexes they represent. The finger you are interested in is the index finger, which is resting on the waistline guide. The padded section of the first joint in this finger is resting on the adrenal reflex and a portion of the kidney reflex as well.

The left hand is holding the foot, with the thumb resting on the sole, ready to move. Using the left thumb, walk along the waistline from the outside edge of the foot. Keep thumb walking right under the index finger, so that the tip of the finger is resting at the edge of the thumbnail bed. Remove the index finger, move the thumb up a bit toward the diaphragm line, then pull the thumb back slightly; this is the adrenal reflex.

Don't be discouraged if at first you do not feel the pushing back or letting go that often comes with the release in a reflex. The release is happening whether you feel the slight change or not. As you practice and trust your work, you too will feel the giving of the reflex.

Another way to check the location of this point is to line up under the solar plexus reflex. The adrenal reflex and the solar plexus reflex are not in a straight connecting line; the adrenal may be a bit more toward the inner side of the foot, along the tendon line. Whichever way you choose to find this reflex point, when you think you have found it, rotate on the spot. You will feel a slight swell or bump on the reflex, indicating you have found the point.

Continue to rotate on the adrenal reflex, applying light pressure. When working on the adrenal reflexes, use a gentle touch, with no undue pressing. Now hold on the spot while gently pressing in. The reflex may push back, indicating it is time to move on.

Finish with Four-Finger Walking

Move to the top of the foot now. Imagine the entire back, as this is the area of reflection you are looking at. Your hands are resting on the edges of the foot, with the thumbs on the sole. You are starting just before the anklebone, where the foot bends. Walk all the fingers in slowly, feeling in between each bone. (See **FIGURE 14-1**.) The fingers look and act as though they are playing an accordion.

Continue to finger walk in toward the center until the fingers meet. Move up slightly, bring the fingers back to the edge, and walk in again. Each time your fingers meet at the center, shift up slightly, bring the fingers back to the edge of the foot, and walk in again. Follow this procedure up to the base of the toes.

At the base of the toes, turn all the fingers down toward the ankle. The palms of the hands are at the top of the foot. Finger walk down the foot; again, this is in between the toes, just from a different angle. Walk all the way to just before the ankle and slide back.

FIGURE 14-1
To work the back reflex, walk with all four fingers on each side of the foot across the surface until the fingers meet in the center.

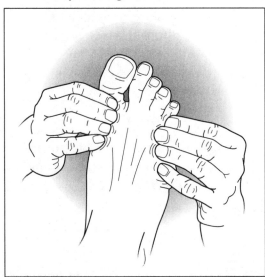

The Muscles and Bones of the Back

The bones involved are the lower ribs and lower vertebrae. The muscles are extensive. There are muscles in between the ribs, known as the *intercostals.* The latissimus dorsi, the oblique muscles, and part of the trapezius are found on the back. The muscles deep to the spine are also in the back.

The reflexology techniques employed to work the back reflexes are working on reflex areas that are representative of this region of the body. As the circulation improves throughout the body, often the muscles in the back area do relax. When someone has a horrific backache and cannot stand to be touched, reflexology is a great tool.

Solar Plexus

You have reflexed a number of areas on the foot, and pressing into the solar plexus lets you bring a conclusion to this segment of the treatment. Working the solar plexus reflex is a reminder to the receiver and to the giver to breathe and flow with the movement of the work. Press your right thumb into the solar plexus reflex. Pull the toes down toward the thumb; ask the recipient to take a slow, deep breath, and hold. Keep pressing as you instruct the receiver to release the breath slowly. Gently remove the thumb and let the toes relax as well.

Butterfly and Flutter

As you prepare to move on to the next section, a transitional move is used. Using both hands, walk the thumbs and fingers together toward the center of the foot, working up and then down the foot. All the digits are involved in a butterfly movement. If you find this too confusing, work the top surface and then the bottom surface.

Once the butterfly has been employed, use the tips of the fingers to make fluttery movements on the top surface of the foot. Move from the ankle area to the toes, repeating this technique.

You have worked the upper portion of the foot, reflexing points connecting to the body from the waist up. The receiver is relaxed, and you are ready to move on. Ⓔ

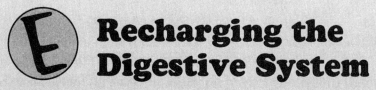

Chapter 15

Recharging the Digestive System

The digestive system is a two-part mechanism. First, we eat food and assimilate the nutrients. Then we need to eliminate the waste. It sounds simple, but there is an incredible amount of work involved in this entire process. So let's get ready to recharge the digestive system!

From the Waistline to the Sciatic Line

The waistline is the guideline in the center of the arch, as you discovered in the last segment of the session. The sciatic line is found in the top section of the heel bone. Look at the bottom of the foot; you are still on the right foot. The instep is shaped like an arch, with the waistline running through the center.

Trace the heel bone, which begins at the end of the arch and ends at the back of the foot. The heel is covered with protective connective tissue and muscle. This covering gives the heel the puffy, fatty feeling as you push on the bone. The sciatic line runs about a finger joint down from the beginning of the heel. Another way to picture the sciatic line is to draw an imaginary line from the bony protrusion of the anklebone down to the heel and across to the other side.

You now have two lines marking the section we will be working on. The waistline is one line and the sciatic line is another. Draw an imaginary line along the inside edge from waistline to the sciatic line and draw another on the outside edge. Again you have made a long rectangular box, which will contain many reflexes.

Another name for the sciatic line is the heel line. The term *sciatic* designates the area of the body where the imaginary line is drawn. The term *heel line* denotes the area of the foot where the line is drawn. Either one serves as a line of guidance and separation.

Discovering Landmarks

In anatomy there are many surface landmarks, and a number of them are found on the feet. The bony bump at the end of the fifth metatarsal bone is such a landmark. Remember, this is the bone that helps to determine one edge of the waistline guideline. When you put your thumb across the bottom of the foot from this bony protuberance, you divide the arch, creating the waistline.

Some of the landmarks deal with muscles—the placement of muscles in relationship to their function. Some are the bony points that muscles attach to. Other landmarks deal with blood supply, marking the area of primary flow. Still other landmarks represent nerve placement. Some landmarks denote direction or movement. There are many such landmarks on the feet and ankles.

Locating the Landmarks

Some of the landmarks are on the top and sides of the foot:

- The medial malleolus is the high spot on the inside of the anklebone.
- The lateral malleolus is the high spot on the outside of the anklebone.
- The great saphenous vein is on top of the foot.
- The great sphenous nerve is on top of the foot.
- The extensor digitorum brevis are muscles on top of the foot.
- The dorsalis pedis artery is on the top of the foot.
- The dorsal venous arch is on top of the foot.

Some of the landmarks are on the bottom of the foot. These are bony protuberances with odd shapes for connective tissue attachment:

- Sesamoid bones, under the head of the first metatarsal
- Base of the first metatarsal
- Head of the fifth metatarsal
- Tuberosity of the navicular
- Tuberosity of the fifth metatarsal
- Tuberosity of the calcaneus

Some of the landmarks are on the back of the foot:

- The peroneus longus and brevis are muscle and tendons from the leg.
- The small saphenous vein is on the back of the ankle.
- The sural nerve comes in on the back of the ankle.
- The tendo calcaneus is connected to the heel.
- The flexor hallicus longus is a muscle to the great toe.
- The posterior tibial artery is on the back of the ankle.
- The posterior tibial nerve is on the back of the ankle.

These landmarks might be used to explain a direction for a reflex technique. At times, these landmarks remind you of the movement the foot can make at these areas. These landmarks may denote the placement of a reflex point. For example, the area of a sciatic reflex point is connected to the actual nerve placement. Often you will notice this link between reflexes and landmarks. What came first?

An Explanation of Some of the Terms

Some of these names may sound familiar to you now. Great! You are paying attention. A term used before is *tuberosity*, which means bony, large protrusion. Tuberosity of the fifth metatarsal is the bony bump at the end of the last metatarsal. This bump pops out on the outside edge of the foot; it is greater on some than on others, but everyone has this bump. In reflexology, this landmark helps you to find the outside end of the waistline guideline.

Malleolus is a large bony formation at the end the shinbone, also known as the *tibia.* There is a malleolus on either side of the leg: one at the end of the shinbone on the inside of the leg and one at the end of the fibula, the smaller bone on the outside of the leg.

FACT

Two landmarks, the medial and lateral malleolus, form the bony area called the ankle. The true anklebone actually sits in between these bony ends of the lower leg. It is known as the *talus.* The ankle area consists of the seven tarsal bones plus the two malleolus.

The Ileocecal/Appendix Reflex

You are beginning with the lower portion of the digestive tract, the reflexes that reflect the areas that deal with absorption and elimination in the body. Look at the feet for a moment, placing them together with the soles facing you. Let yourself imagine the entire body superimposed over the feet. Take a moment to picture the head at the toes and slowly move down, seeing the different parts of the body as your eyes travel down the feet.

Stop just below the waistline. Imagine the waistline going right across the two feet. Move down from the waistline and feel along the outside edge of the foot. Look at the tuberosity of the fifth metatarsal; this is the bump at the bottom outside edge of the long bone that follows after the little toe on both feet. This bony landmark will guide you to find certain points in this next segment. Cover the left foot, as you will deal with the right foot first.

The techniques in this chapter may seem confusing at first, but don't give up! Stick with it and the routine will become second nature with practice.

Hooking the Reflex

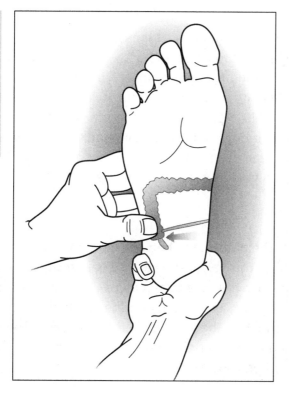

FIGURE 15-1 Pinpoint the ileocecal reflex with the hook in–and–backup technique.

Hold the right foot with the right hand; the left hand gently cups the foot, with the thumb resting on the sole surface. Find the bony protuberance of the fifth metatarsal. Place the left thumb at this tuberosity and turn the thumb slightly down and in, preparing to thumb walk. Only the first digit of the thumb is actually in use at this moment. The rounded beginning surface of the heel is touching the edge of this thumb. This section of the thumb is in between the outside edge of the foot and the rounded edge of the heel on the bottom of the foot. The tip of the thumb is dropping into the reflex for the ileocecal valve.

Once you have pinpointed this reflex, which represents the ileocecal valve and the appendix, push in and gently rotate. Continue to rotate as the thumb moves in deeper; then gently push and hold on the point. The fingers of your working hand are being used as levers, supporting the back of the foot as the thumb pushes in. The right hand continues as the holding hand.

With the thumb pushed in and holding, pull back a bit toward the edge of the foot in the hooking technique. Push in a little more if possible while hooking. (See **FIGURE 15-1** on page 181.) This reflex is important as it represents the beginning of the large intestine. You work the large and small intestines together in much of this segment, as these areas of the body overlap.

The Gatekeeper

This reflex may be reflexed a number of times, as it represents a structure that is a gatekeeper. Throughout the body, there are various small structures that hold positions of great functional importance. In the digestive system alone, there are five such structures. In this system, these are valves that allow materials to pass along the roadway of digestion. Sphincters are generally tight rings of muscle that permit passage in only one direction. As gatekeepers, these valves do not encourage any materials to back up in the body; rather, the movement is a continuous flow in one direction.

FACT

The ileocecal valve is the gatekeeper between the small intestine and the large intestine. This valve lets material pass from the ileum of the small intestine into the ascending colon. Connected to this valve are two other regions, the cecum and the appendix. These structures are reflexed when the ileocecal reflex is worked. The cecum and the appendix filter undigested waste material, beginning the absorption process.

The Ascending Colon Reflex

The left thumb is hooked into the ileocecal valve in a horizontal position. Turn the thumb up toward the waistline and begin to thumb walk up toward the waist guideline. Take small, slow bites as the thumb walks up, creating a line close to the edge of the foot. The thumb is on the bottom surface, but near the outside edge.

This is the ascending colon reflex. The colon is divided into four parts: the ascending, transverse, descending, and sigmoid areas. Waste is passed from the ileocecal up along the ascending colon. The colon begins to churn, contracting and expanding, pulling out all essential material and passing the waste farther along. The ascending colon terminates at the hepatic flexure just under the liver.

The right foot holds the reflexes for the ascending colon and half of the transverse colon. Bring the thumb back to the ileocecal reflex and thumb walk up the edge again. Feel how the foot responds. The more the reflex is worked, the softer the skin will feel. The more relaxed the receiver, the easier it is to work the reflex.

The Flexure and Transverse Colon Reflexes

The reflex for the colon is broken up into parts. The next part is started at the outside edge of the waistline as you begin to thumb walk across this line to the inside edge. Let the thumb work at the outside edge first, with rotation and circling on the area. This is the hepatic flexure reflex. Thumb walk on the point in three directions, after the rotation and circling is completed. The thumb will take one or two tiny bites up, across, and down on the area of the flexure reflex.

FACT

In the body the ascending colon ends, becoming the hepatic flexure, which is a curve in the large intestine. The flexures are pockets formed by a sharp bend in the colon, where waste material may become caught. During a reflexology session, extra attention is directed to the reflexes of these areas.

Thumb walk across the bottom of the foot, along the waistline guide. This is the transverse colon reflex. At the inside edge of the foot, turn the thumb down, just a bit. The area where the thumb has stopped will pop out slightly. Use the right thumb to circle gently on the part of the skin that has pushed out. This is the top of the bladder reflex. You will be working on the entire reflex later.

Peristalsis is a function controlled by muscles. It is an involuntary movement of contraction and relaxation that pushes food through the gastrointestinal tract during the various stages of digestion. The movement is in a wavelike motion that is either slow and controlled or very fast, like a tidal wave.

The transverse colon reflex is on both feet, as the piece of the colon it represents moves across the body near the stomach and the spleen. As part of the large intestine, the transverse colon is involved with all its functions. One major function of the large intestine is to absorb vitamins. The mucus also helps to balance the water level and the sodium and electrolyte levels.

A movement specific to the transverse colon is known as *mass peristalsis*. This occurs in the transverse colon as a great wave sending the contents of the colon into the rectum. This reflex occurs three or four times a day. Mass peristalsis generally takes place following a meal.

Working All the Right Angles

From the ileocecal valve reflex, up the ascending colon reflex, across the transverse colon reflex, and all the secondary reflexes, this walk is reflecting half of the large intestine. At the same time, the small intestine in the body is intertwined with its larger counterpart, allowing for the overlapping of reflexes. Whew, what a mouthful, or should we say bellyful!

This first walk-through has created a different shape than those you have previously drawn. Look at the foot and imagine a line from the ileocecal reflex up and across the transverse colon reflex. This line would look like a right angle. Keep this image in mind as you move forward in this complex area.

FACT

While the large intestine is only 5 feet long, the small intestine is about 23 feet. However, the diameter of the small intestine is only about as round as a half dollar, while the large intestine is roughly the size of a small soup can. The small intestine appears outwardly smooth and the large intestine is rather rough.

The Second and Third Angles

Bring the left thumb back to the ileocecal valve reflex; rotate on the point and hold. Walk the thumb in two tiny steps away from the ileocecal reflex, toward the inside edge of the foot, and then turn and thumb walk up to the waistline. Just below the waistline guide, turn the thumb, moving toward the inside edge of the foot. Thumb walk across, making a line to the medial edge. This is now the second right angle, stacked under the first.

Bring the thumb back to the ileocecal valve point to begin a new right angle. Walk the thumb in from the valve reflex to just past where the last segment began. Thumb walk up toward the waistline again, stopping right below the line that was created by the last walk-through. Turn and work toward the center of the foot again. A third right angle has been created, tucked just inside the previous one.

Right Angle Finale

Depending upon the size of the foot, the next right angle may be the last. Starting at the ileocecal valve reflex, thumb walk across the other lines to begin a new section. Turn and thumb walk up, turning again just below the last line across. Thumb walk to the inside edge of the foot, completing the final right angle. Notice that each time the pattern becomes smaller, as the area involved is less.

These stacked right angles have worked the areas of the large and small intestines as reflected on the right foot. It is the small intestine that plays the major role in digesting the churned food from the stomach and absorbing nutrients and water. The large intestine assumes the role of absorbing the remainder of the fluids and salts, as well as putting potassium into the body.

QUESTION?

What is churned food?
The food we eat sits in our stomach anywhere from one to five hours, depending upon an individual's metabolism. During that time the solid food is churned into a liquid called *chyme.* When the stomach empties into the duodenum, it is emptying liquid, not solid, material, for further digestion.

Create a Fan with Thumb Walking

You have worked the section relating to the small and large intestines on the right side of the body as you built the series of stacked right angles. Now you will work the area again, as this represents part of the system that rids the body of waste, supporting homeostasis. Also, since this area of the foot is often neglected, reflexology improves the tone, restoring much of the vibrancy to the skin and muscles.

Start with the left thumb rotating on the ileocecal reflex, move in, and hook. Gently turn the thumb and walk up the ascending colon reflex. Bring the thumb back to the valve reflex, hold on the point, and then thumb walk up again, next to the ascending colon reflex, to the waistline. Return the left thumb to the ileocecal reflex and hold; visualize the next line up, and thumb walk it.

Imagine a dancer holding a closed fan. The dance begins with the fan closed. With each twirl around the floor, the dancer opens the fan a little more. The base of the fan is constant as the patterns on the pieces of the fan tell a story with each opening.

The reflex for the ileocecal valve is the base of the fan and each line up and out is a strut of the fan. Each time the line ends, at the waistline, return to the ileocecal reflex and thumb walk another line out, opening the fan wider each time. Every thumb walk out will bring the thumb farther along the waistline, closer to the inner edge of the foot. Eventually the line will no longer go to the waistline but out to the inside edge of the foot. Ultimately the last line of the fan will end with the thumb walking away from the ileocecal reflex along the sciatic line to the inner side of the foot.

The fan has effectively worked the section of the foot between the waistline and the sciatic guidelines. The steady, gentle thumb walking has allowed this part of the foot to feel relaxed and renewed.

The Small Intestine Reflex Box

You have built a stack of right angles and created and opened a fan, techniques that relate to both the large and small intestines. The outside areas of the right angles dealt with the large intestine, as did the fan before it opened. You also have a reflex specific to the small intestines.

Look at the right foot and imagine the ileocecal valve reflex. Imagine, too, the ascending and transverse colon reflexes. There is an empty, open boxlike space to the inside and under these reflexes. Now imagine the box filled with squiggly lines, running in from the medial edge of the foot. Switch hands; you will be using your right thumb now.

Start thumb walking just under the waistline from the inside edge of the foot. Walk in to the hepatic reflex. Bring the thumb back to the edge and down a bit, and thumb walk back in again to the ascending colon reflex. Keep bringing the thumb back to the inside edge, a little lower every time. Continue to thumb walk, making imaginary lines and filling this box to the sciatic line.

Once the sciatic line has been thumb walked, fill the box in from the bottom up. This reflex for the small intestine can be worked from the top to the bottom, from the bottom to the top, and diagonally, too. Imagine the 200 some-odd inches of the small intestine. Think, too, of all the work the small intestine does.

Kidney and Bladder Reflexes

There is one more area to complete: the reflexes for the urinary system. On the bottoms of both feet there are reflexes for the kidneys, ureters, and bladder. The reflex for the kidney on the right foot is slightly lower than on the left. In the body, the kidneys are attached to the back wall of the abdomen, sitting just about at the waistline.

The Kidney Reflex

You will work on the right foot, as the technique is the same on both feet. Refresh your memory on the location of the adrenal reflex. Hold the foot with the right hand and thumb walk toward the adrenal reflex with the left thumb. Work on the waistline as you thumb walk toward the centerline. Stop at the adrenal reflex, letting the thumb sit on the reflex and the waistline.

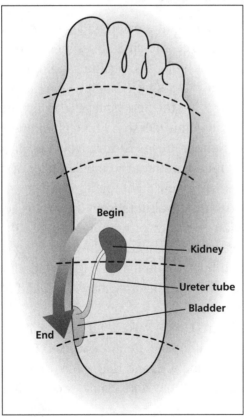

FIGURE 15-2
Thumb walk across the waistline into the kidney reflex, and rotate on the point before thumb walking down to the bladder reflex.

Begin

Kidney

Ureter tube

Bladder

End

Imagine the little kidney-bean shape superimposed on the foot, some above and some below the waistline. Keep cupping the foot at the heel with the right hand. Free the fingers of the left hand, as they are going to move over and around the foot. Keeping the left thumb on the reflex, swing the fingers over the top of the foot.

The fingers have moved from the dorsal surface, over the toes, to gently grasp the inner side of the foot, from the plantar side. You are now looking at the top of the palm of the left hand. The fingers are wrapped around the toes, resting on the dorsal surface, so you cannot see them.

The left thumb is flat on the sole, resting completely on the foot. The kidney reflex is this entire area under the thumb, above and below the waistline. (See **FIGURE 15-2**.) Gently rotate the thumb in, press, and hold. Do not apply excess pressure, as this is a sensitive area.

People are many sizes and shapes, so people have slightly different areas for placement of internal organs. A tall, slimly built person may have a greater portion of the kidneys below the waist, whereas in a short, tiny person, the kidneys may sit above the waist. The body is the same yet individually unique.

The Bladder Reflex

The ureter is connected to the kidney; it is a passageway for urine to the bladder. The thumb is gently resting on the kidney reflex. Look at the foot for a moment, visualizing the path the next reflex will take. From the kidney reflex, thumb walk down diagonally to the lower inner edge of the foot, by the sciatic line. Watch as the area here begins to pop out; this will tell you that you're working the reflex correctly! When the thumb reaches the edge of the foot, there is a slight bulge of the fatty tissue area; this is the bladder reflex. Using your right thumb, gently circle and thumb walk on this region. Thumb walk gently in all directions on this reflex, then softly flutter off.

Waste Management

The containment, recycling, and elimination of waste is a cooperative effort within the body. The kidneys, skin, lungs, liver, gastrointestinal tract, and blood share in the function of waste management.

Nephrons are the functional units of the kidneys. Each kidney holds approximately a million of these filtration units. Nephrons deal with filtering, reabsorbing, and secreting blood and blood plasma.

Proper disposal of waste substances promotes balance in the body. The kidneys and other supporting structures of the urinary system are crucial in maintaining homeostasis, and are responsible for the following functions:

- Maintaining correct water balance
- Maintaining correct mineral balance
- Regulating blood pressure
- Filtering the blood
- Regulating extracellular fluid

The Heel in Transition

You have worked the reflexes of digestion, absorption, and elimination on the right foot. You will now begin to work on the finishing touches, which will complete the main portion of the session on the right foot. Either hand can be used as the working hand, with the other hand holding the foot for support and leverage. First, you want to work the sciatic line, as this is one of the areas of reflection for the sciatic nerve.

The sciatic nerve is the largest nerve in the body, and the extensions from that nerve are found in the feet. The medial calcaneal nerve supplies the heel, as does the lateral plantar nerve. These nerves serve the muscles and skin of the heel. Two dermatomes are also part of this area. Remember, dermatomes are the sensory areas of the skin that are connected to the nervous system.

Learning reflexology is a new function for your hands. The techniques employed require new and different uses of the muscles in the hands. At times the hands may feel tired as the muscles are strengthening. If a working hand is tired, transitions are a great time to give the hand a rest.

Heel Press

Holding the working hand in a fist, press into the heel, as though kneading dough. Press over the entire heel area, back and forth and up and down. This area may be tough and have hardened skin. As you press on the heel, you can feel the toughness beginning to relax, responding to the work. Continue to press on the heel until the response is felt on the entire area.

Thumb Walk the Sciatic Line

The sciatic line has been relaxed with the heel press, ready for a deeper technique. Using either the right or left thumb, walk across the line, starting from either edge. Thumb walk slowly, feeling the area respond. When the thumb reaches the end of the imaginary line, either switch hands and walk back or bring the thumb back to the beginning edge and walk across again.

Reflexologists often thumb walk and heel press, using both techniques interchangeably here. Allow yourself to see what works for you. Try doing each separately and then switch off.

Moving On

As you complete this section, flutter off in transition. Let the hands rest for a moment on the entire foot, cupping both sides. With soft movements, allow your hands to gently stroke or flutter off, giving the signal to rest. In a complete session, you would continue on with this foot. However, this is a learning session, so cover the right foot, and get ready to go over to the other side. (E)

Chapter 16

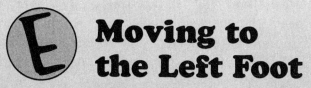

Moving to the Left Foot

The last section may have proved challenging. Any modality worth studying does have sections of ease and areas of complexity. However, reflexology becomes less demanding with practice. Let's go ahead and move to the left foot, and you can practice along the way.

The Left Foot

You have steadily been working on the right foot, with the exception of the warm-up routine and the examination of the spleen reflex. Now it is time to deal with the left foot as you approach the left side of the body. Energetically, the left side of the body represents the sunny side of the slope. The concept of yin and yang can be equated with the concept of homeostasis. One deals with energetic balance and the other deals with physical balance. The combination of the two will create the perfect setting for spiritual balance. A smooth flow of chi along the energy channels in the body creates good health. To achieve this flow, we must operate in harmony.

Much of the flow of movement in the body is from right to left. The digestive system moves the waste out from right to left, and the left foot holds the outward flow reflexes of this system. The lungs oxygenate the blood as it flows from the right side into the left.

FACT

The left side of the brain deals in logical and rational thinking, such as when you play chess or express your thoughts. This side is the predominant side for scientific excellence as well as mathematical genius. The study of languages may come from this side of the brain.

Placement of Organs

The left side of the body holds the larger portion of the heart. This side also has a greater piece of the stomach. The pancreas in some people has a bit more on the left side. One half of the transverse colon is on the left side of the body. The descending colon and the sigmoid colon are found on the left side as well. The rectum is in the center of the body; however, the reflex is generally located on the left foot, in line with the sigmoid colon.

The Gastrointestinal Tract

The gastrointestinal tract (GI tract) has been discussed briefly during the discussion of the digestive system. This section of the reflexology session deals with the lower part of the gastrointestinal tract. Working this area will continue to support the work of this piece of the digestive system. The GI tract is that passageway from the mouth to the anus. Daily volumes of fluid and solids are ingested, secreted, absorbed, and excreted through the GI tract. Eating well assists in keeping this tract functioning well. Eating fiber, either as bulk or roughage, will keep the passageway clear. The fiber is indigestible and comes from plant substances found in vegetables, fruits, grains, and legumes. Insoluble fibers come through the tract relatively unchanged, pushing other material through the tract rather quickly.

FACT

Insoluble fiber doesn't dissolve in water. It comes from the skins of fruits and vegetables as well as the bran coverings on grains. Soluble fibers obviously dissolve in water, forming a gel-like substance. The soluble fibers are connected with grains, broccoli, citrus fruits, and prunes. The gel of this fiber slows down the material moving through the tract.

Structures in the Left Foot

The left foot mirrors the right foot, with the same structures in the same places. You have five toes on the left foot. Each of the four small toes has a front, middle, and end bone, in the phalange aspect. The great toe has two phalanges, the front and the end bone. You have five metatarsal bones, each with a bony head at the beginning and a large base at the end. The first metatarsal head has two sesamoid bones embedded in the tendons.

The left foot also has three cuneiform bones behind the first three metatarsals and a cuboid bone behind the last two. There is a navicular and a talus as well as a calcaneus. All the bones are the same, as are the entire accessory structures connected with the feet.

Creating the Outside Box

Look at the foot and picture the waistline running across the center. Find the tuberosity of the fifth metatarsal, that bony bump at the outside edge, and place your thumb in from here across the center of the foot. There is the waistline guide for this foot. Look at the heel and feel that area of the foot. Grasp the heel; become familiar with the feel on all sides. Feel your own heel and feel the heels of others as well.

Use all your fingers and walk all over the heel. Extend the foot away and feel the tautness. Flex the foot in and notice how the top end of the heel relaxes somewhat. The end of the heel is at the back of the foot; feel from the back along the bottom surface to the beginning of this structure.

Let your fingers move down the heel on the plantar side, toward the back just a bit, perhaps a joint length. Here the heel is puffy and tight, yet the area does respond. This is the sciatic line region. Begin at the outside edge of the foot and thumb walk across the heel, making an imaginary line. Bring the thumb back and walk again.

Now begin to practice on a receiver. The left hand is holding the foot and the right hand is walking. Switch hands and let the left thumb walk along the sciatic line from the inside of the foot. Bring the thumb back to the inside edge and walk along the line again. Always be aware of the response from the foot, checking to feel if the foot is relaxing.

Observe the receiver as you thumb walk as well. This is an area where you may use more pressure, but always check that the pressure is within the comfort zone of the receiver. Remember to move your body, letting the movement of your body apply the pressure, not your fingers.

Thumb Walk the Transverse Reflex

Hold the left foot with the right hand as you use the left thumb to walk along the waistline. The fingers of the left hand may be tucked in a loose fist or rest on the top surface of the foot, whichever works for you. Begin at the inside edge of the waistline and, using small, slow bites, thumb walk across the transverse colon reflex.

Continue to thumb walk along this line, tilting up a bit toward the spleen reflex. As the left thumb reaches the outside edge, you will feel a slight indentation. Switch hands now; the right thumb will take over. Using the right thumb, move into the area that is slightly up from the waistline in the outside corner. This is where the indentation is.

This slight depression represents the splenic flexure in the colon. A flexure is an area of the colon that bends, creating a pocket or reservoir where waste may become stuck. This side of the body has two such flexures.

Using the right thumb, hook into this reflex. Remember to rotate on the spot, press, and hold, feeling how deeply in the foot is allowing you to go. Then hook in and pull back, as though the reflex was the fish and the thumb the fishhook.

ALERT!

Please make sure to check your nails before applying these techniques. Reflexologists must have short, clean, smooth nails. Some reflexologists like to receive manicures, ensuring their nails are short and their hands are well cared for. Whether you take care of your own nails or receive professional care, keep them short and clean.

Thumb Walk Down the Descending Colon Reflex

The descending colon reflex moves from the splenic flexure down the outside edge of the foot, past the bony tuberosity of the fifth metatarsal. The reflex continues to the sciatic line where the descending colon reflex ends.

You are now working with the last stages of digestion. Bacteria that live in the colon contribute to the final digestive process. The remaining chyme is fermented, which produces gases in the colon. Carbohydrates, proteins, and fats are broken down even further, some into feces and some into urine. Any vitamins needed for metabolism are absorbed at this time.

With the right thumb already in position, turn slightly and thumb walk down the descending colon reflex. This may seem awkward at first since you are using the tip and the inside edge of the thumb. The inside edge here means the edge farthest away from the index finger.

Take a look at what has happened so far. You have walked across the transverse colon reflex, which turns up a bit just under the spleen reflex. Under the spleen reflex is the reflex for the splenic flexure; here the techniques used were rotation, press, hook, and hold on the point. From the splenic flexure reflex, you turned the thumb to face downward and used the thumb-walking technique, this time down the descending colon, ending at the sciatic guideline.

ALERT!

The medial side of the thumb and great toe are actually the sides that touch each other. This means that what looks like the outside edge is really the inside edge. Let your arms hang down at the sides of your body. The inside edge of the thumbs, the medial edge, is the edge closest to the body.

The Bony Landmark

The fifth metatarsal on the left foot is used as a guide along much of the process on this foot. The descending colon reflex runs to the end of this bone, where we meet the tuberosity of this fifth long bone. Just past this bony landmark, there is a depression in the bottom surface of the foot. The small space, which feels like a tiny gap, is a reflex.

Trace your finger down the fifth metatarsal bone. Press in and feel the bone, letting your finger come to the end and feel the bumpy protrusion. Feel past the tuberosity and discover the depression just in and under that bone. The fifth metatarsal is in front of the cuboid bone. The cuboid bone is also behind the fourth metatarsal. The muscles and tendon that are connected to the cuboid and these metatarsals are interwoven like a wicker chair. The space that represents a reflex is part of this area. The crisscrossing of the muscles, tendons, and ligaments has left a slight depression that you can feel.

The reflex is the sigmoid colon flexure. This small area reflects the final turn in the colon. Once the waste matter reaches this juncture, it has begun to solidify, moving into position to be expelled from the body. Humans have the ability from an early age to voluntarily control the removal of the undigested waste.

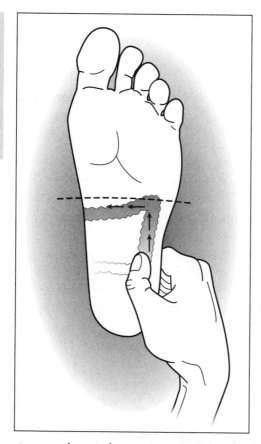

Thumb walk across the transverse colon with the left thumb. Switch to the right thumb and hook into the splenic flexure. Thumb walk down the descending colon. Allow the right thumb to walk into the slight depression under the bony landmark. With the right thumb, rotate on this point, press, and hold. Use the thumb to hook in and pull back, hooking into this reflex. (See **FIGURE 16-1**.)

Rotate on the Rectal Reflex

Thumb walk across the left foot, from the last flexure reflex, over the fleshy top part of the heel, just above the sciatic line, to the inside edge. Take small steps, using a slow, even motion with the thumb-walking technique. Feel the foot responding to the pressure. Walk completely across the foot, over the edge, into another slight depression. This small space is just past the ridge on the inside of the foot, about at the tuberosity of the navicular.

This depression is the rectal reflex. The right thumb walks into the space first, presses in, and holds. The left thumb will move into the gap and take over. Feel how the thumb dips in a bit, as this area is flexible. Use caution here; do not press too hard, as this reflex point is often sensitive. Rotate on the reflex and hold.

The Box Is Complete

Look at the bottom of the foot where you have just worked. In essence you have created another box, an odd-shaped rectangular box.

Using the two imaginary guidelines along with the reflexes, you can imagine this irregular box shape:

- Waistline guideline
- Transverse colon reflex
- Splenic flexure reflex
- Descending colon reflex

- Sigmoid flexure reflex
- Sigmoid colon reflex
- Rectal reflex
- Sciatic guideline

This represents the first complete walk-through of the left segment reflecting the large intestine. Of course, the small intestines are also represented, which will receive attention in the next segment.

The body and its structures are sensory receptors. The foot is part of the body and as such is a sensory receptor as well. Beyond this fact, the foot is connected to the entire body through the sensory system. How we walk, what we wear on our feet, and our overall foot care affect our whole health.

More Right Angles

Ready to have some fun! With this technique, you will alternate using both thumbs. Hold the foot with the right hand, bring the left thumb to the waistline, and close the left hand in a loose fist or let the fingers rest lightly on the top of the foot. Thumb walk across the center of the foot, along the transverse colon reflex.

At the splenic flexure reflex, switch hands. The left hand holds the foot steady while the right hand works. Using the right thumb, with the fingers closed in a loose fist, turn and thumb walk down the descending colon reflex. Leave the right hand there for the moment holding the foot, and return to the left thumb.

Begin with the left thumb just a bit under the transverse reflex at the inner edge of the foot, and walk to the outside edge again, across the foot. Stop just before the splenic flexure reflex. Let the left hand hold there, as you will use the right thumb now.

Using the right thumb to do the work, walk down the foot, alongside and just in from the descending reflex to the sciatic line. Again leave the right hand there, returning to use the left. Bring the left thumb down slightly, and, starting at the inner edge, thumb walk across, stopping at the line just inside the descending reflex. Using the right thumb, walk down from this point to the sciatic line. Look at what has happened. You have created a group of stacked right angles again, one inside the other. Generally three to four little stools are what you can construct on the bottom of the foot.

Washable markers are great tools. Use these markers to draw the shapes on your feet. Or, you can trace your feet, your children's feet, or anyone's feet, and draw these shapes on the tracings. Then hang up the drawings as reference.

Draw Another Fan

With the last sequence you worked the reflexes for the large and small intestines, but you aren't finished yet! The receiver might be reporting grumbles and gurgles emanating from the belly and intestinal regions. You may even hear these sounds. This is an affirmation that you are doing a great job, working to relax the recipient.

The Fan's Base

Begin by using the right thumb, and walk down the descending colon reflex, stopping at the sigmoid flexure reflex. At this juncture, let the thumb slip into the slight depression, rotate to move in deeply, hold while pressing, and hook this reflex. The left hand is holding the foot. The right thumb is doing the reflexing; the right fingers are either coiled in a loose fist or resting on the top surface of the foot. Hold on this point for a moment, really pinpointing the reflex. You are going to build another fan; however, this fan will be slightly different from the one on the right foot.

Fanning Out

Look at the area you are working on. Imagine a line drawn from the sigmoid flexure reflex diagonally across the foot up to the inner waistline. The line will come across the inner arch, reaching up to find the beginning of the transverse colon. This will be the first swipe of the fan—when the dancer is holding the fan closed, waiting to proceed.

Return your gaze to the sigmoid flexure reflex and again imagine a line, this time going across just under the first line. Here the fan would begin to open. If you were drawing this, you would continue to return to the flexure reflex and keep drawing lines out until eventually the fan would be completely open, with the open end terminating on the length of the sigmoid colon reflex along the sciatic line.

Thumb walk the reflex now. Begin at the sigmoid flexure reflex with the right thumb, using the left hand as the holding hand. The left hand will be supporting the foot either by holding the toes or with the hand firmly across the center dorsal surface. Press in and rotate on the flexure reflex. Then slowly thumb walk diagonally across the instep toward the beginning of the transverse colon.

Imagining the sequence before you actually perform the work is always a good practice. Feeling the area of the foot, drawing on paper, or drawing on the foot makes it a natural progression from our imagination. It's much easier to perform if you give yourself the image to work with.

Return to the flexure reflex and repeat this process, following just inside the diagonal line as the thumb moves across the foot. Each time, the thumb returns to the flexure and works diagonally across, reaching the inner edge of the foot as the lines of the fan open. The last line begins with the sigmoid flexure reflex and the thumb walks straight across the sigmoid colon reflex.

A Box for the Small Intestine Reflex

You have worked on the reflexes that deal with the large and small intestines, but now it's time to deal specifically with the small intestine reflex. These are the same on both sides of the body. Recognizing these reflexes lets you put a finishing touch on the digestive segment.

Building the Box

You have a built an odd-shaped box that reflects the large intestine. Within that box is an open area that serves as the small intestinal reflex. Starting at the inside edge of the foot, from just below the waistline, walk in slowly toward the outside edge of the foot. You are using your left thumb, taking small, deep bites across the foot. When you reach the descending colon reflex, bring the thumb back immediately to the inside edge.

Again thumb walk in, this time starting slightly lower, just under the line you just created. Continue to walk in with the left thumb, moving down each time until eventually you stop just above the sigmoid colon reflex. Generally you can make three or four lines before you reach the sigmoid reflex. Switch hands and with the right thumb walk back up and across the area you just worked.

You are creating a pattern across the foot on the small intestine reflex, like the lattice topping of a pie. Either or both thumbs may move around in this reflex, until you feel a softening of the skin. This softening is a signal that the foot has relaxed in this area.

The Jejunum and Ileum

The reflex of the small intestine on the left side holds more of the latter two parts of the small intestine, the jejunum and the ileum. The duodenum digests, while the jejunum absorbs the useful nutrients and the ileum moves the remaining waste and liquid into the ileocecal valve. The jejunum actually allows the nourishment from the food to be absorbed into the blood. The food passes from the jejunum into the blood and is processed by the liver for reinstatement into the blood.

The ileum is the last stop before the colon. This is the largest part of the small intestine and its job is to drive out the remaining food. The ileum also contains a great concentration of lymphatic nodules.

FACT

The duodenum deals with the hydrochloric acid mixture that arrives from the stomach. The glands of the duodenum contain an alkaline juice that neutralizes the arriving acid. However, the high concentrate of acid is constantly burning out the cells of the duodenum. The body replaces duodenal cells every hour. Still, this is where most ulcers occur.

Revisiting the Kidney and Bladder

The body has two kidneys that both empty into the bladder. To access this reflex on the left foot is fairly straightforward. Begin at the transverse colon reflex, and, using the left thumb, thumb walk in to the tendon line near the center of the foot. The kidney reflex sits on, above, and below this line, which is located directly under the solar plexus reflex. Remember, the adrenal reflex will sit on top of the kidney reflex, which helps in finding the point.

Working the Reflex

Once the thumb is on the reflex, switch hands, since you will be thumb walking back toward the inside of the foot. Let the left hand hold the foot now, while the right thumb settles on the reflex. Turn the right thumb; the entire thumb will rest on the reflex, facing down toward the heel. Bring the fingers across the top of the toes and gently grasp the foot. The fingers will hold around the toes as the top of the hand rests on the bottom of the foot.

Turn the thumb slightly in toward the lower inner edge of the foot. Thumb walk down from the kidney reflex, along the ureter reflex, until the thumb reaches the edge of the foot. Walk just a bit farther, and the thumb will push out the bladder reflex. Use the left thumb now to gently circle on the reflex. This is a very soothing technique, allowing for deeper relaxation connected with calming touch.

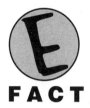

FACT

The kidneys filter, absorb, and secrete blood as well as other fluids. The kidneys generally contain about a quarter of the body's blood, at all times. Every minute the kidneys clean about four ounces of blood. About forty-eight gallons of blood flow through the kidneys every day. Daily the kidneys excrete at least three pints of urine.

What Is Urine?

Urine is actually a byproduct of the work performed by the kidneys. The kidneys work constantly to use the nutrients of the body to regulate the blood. Thus the makeup and amount of blood in the body is brought to homeostasis by the kidneys. Waste material is removed from the blood by the kidneys in the form of urine.

Urine is composed of water, organic wastes, and salts. The waste compounds are the end result of metabolism and other sources such as medicines. Urea is one such compound that is toxic to the body. Urea is removed in the urine. Ammonia, uric acid, and creatinine are also found in the urine. Sodium, potassium, magnesium, calcium, phosphate, and chloride are in the urine. There may be other substances found in the urine, depending upon diet. The better our diets, the better our systems operate. Homeostasis depends heavily on our input.

Ahhh, Knuckle Press the Heel

To perform the knuckle press, use either hand as the working hand. Hold the foot steady and press the flat surface of the closed fist on the heel. Let the knuckles knead the heel, moving back and forth across the entire area. Feel the skin soften and the area become more giving.

Using the heel press is a terrific way to close this section of the treatment. The heel will always welcome and thank you for paying it extra attention. So many of us abuse our feet, particularly the heel area. Walking incorrectly, made worse by ill-fitting shoes, is one of the causes of heel pain. The heel generally supports 25 percent of your body weight.

ALERT!

Never say you have to break in shoes! If they don't fit, if they cause blisters, or are uncomfortable in any way, return the shoes. The rule of thumb when shoe shopping is always ask to have your feet measured. Everyone's feet continue to grow; whether longer or wider, or both, feet grow!

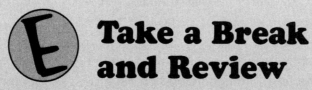

Chapter 17

Take a Break and Review

It's time to come up for air! We have discussed and practiced the techniques for most of the treatment, but we haven't worked completely on both feet. Before we move on, let's practice on the left foot and review what we have learned so far.

Review with the Left Foot

You have relaxed both feet, but it is good practice to greet the left foot again. Cover the right foot, moving it over a bit near the outer edge of the pillow. This will give you room to work without bumping. Do not be afraid to move the feet, gently of course. Often people hold their feet and legs close together; they may even hold their entire body close to their center. This is a natural form of protection. As people relax, their bodies will relax as well.

Cup the left foot, allowing the warmth of your hands to permeate the foot in a gentle greeting. The right hand becomes the holding hand, as the left hand will begin the work. Starting at the inside edge of the great toe, thumb walk slowly up the side, across the top, and down the other side to the web. Using your right thumb, separate the toes, allowing the left thumb to turn and begin walking up the side of the second toe. Continue to walk up the mountain, across the plateau, and down the mountain into the valley along the remaining toes. When you reach the outside edge of the little toe, switch hands. Walk back in the same manner using the right hand.

FACT

This technique may still seem awkward to you. Using the fingers and thumbs in this manner is challenging. Remember to take your time, don't be afraid to separate the toes to accommodate your reach, and practice. In the case of reflexology, practice does make perfect!

Walking the Zones

Using the left hand, walk the zones of the great toe, as the right hand again supports the foot. Move on to walk the imaginary lines of the other four toes. As the baby toe is completed, switch hands and repeat the process. Thumb walk back starting at the toe necks, moving up to the top of the toe, working along the bottom surface of the toes. Upon reaching the great toe, use the index finger of your left hand and walk down the top surface of each toe across to the little toe; switch hands, and walk back.

Working on the Great Toe

Concentrating on the great toe now, you will use your left hand. Begin with the neck of the great toe, and thumb walk with small, slow steps across this base. Repeat until the toe neck feels less tight. Using the index finger, walk the top section of this toe neck, finishing with both thumb and index finger working together at this reflex. The thumb walks the bottom neck area and the finger walks the top section at the same time.

Thumb walk up the flat undersurface of the toe, halfway between the upper joint and the top of the toe. Find the pineal gland reflex, rotate, and hold on the point, pinpointing the area. Turn on the point, hook in, and pull back, holding on this reflex and feeling the pulsing response.

Move from this point back toward the inside edge of the toe, in line with the reflex just worked. The left thumb is looking for a spot that feels like an indentation, where the actual bone dips in. Once it's found, rotate on the spot, turning the thumb sideways, then press and hold. This is the pituitary reflex. Hold on this point. Bring the right thumb in to the other side of the toe, exactly in line with the pituitary reflex. The right thumb will rotate, press, and hold on this point, which is the inner-ear reflex.

You now have the left thumb holding the pituitary point and the right thumb holding the inner-ear point. Both hands are gently holding the foot, as the thumbs of each are out in front doing the work. Bring the right index finger to the inner-ear reflex, taking over for the thumb. The right thumb moves in to the pineal reflex. You now have three points reflexed simultaneously. Imagine how good this feels!

Tinnitus is a constant noise in the ears. The sound may be a ringing or a roaring noise that is continual. This condition may be the result of damage to the hair cells of the inner ear. Whatever the cause, reflexology often does help by lessening the sound.

Brain Reflex to the Shoulder Reflex

Thumb walk up the great toe and stop at the center tip on the top. Rotate the point with the thumb, creating small circles. Circle on this area, press in, and hold. Move to the next toe and circle the top, repeating this process on each toe. Feel the toes opening to you, allowing the fingers greater access.

Circling on the last toe, switch hands and prepare to thumb walk the shoulder reflex with the right thumb. Find the area just under the toe necks and thumb walk in, stopping at the second toe. Bring the thumb back and walk into each web, rotating and holding on each point. The index finger will walk along the top surface of the foot, just under the toe necks.

Move on to the fifth metatarsal head. Using the right thumb, walk in to the reflex, just on the inside of the metatarsal head. Rotate on this spot, press in, and hook. Pull back while hooking, allowing for deep penetration.

Sections of the Body Reflected in the Work

While working on the left foot, another aspect to review is the connection between the reflexes and the body. The toes reflect the head area and the components involved with the head. The physical features include the face, with the eyes, ears, nose, and mouth, as well as other structures related to the head. The brain is reflected in the great toe, along with the reflexes for the endocrine glands of that region. Toes are the area of thoughts, past and present, as well as the reflexes for intuitive creation. You will work reflex points in and under the toe necks that deal with the physical neck, the endocrine glands, and the shoulders.

FACT

Remember, always work both feet first, as reflexology is a holistic experience. During the presession interview, the recipient may discuss areas of the body that hold stress. Only after you have completed both feet will you go back to reflex an area of difficulty.

Shoulder to Diaphragm Reflexes

The ball of the foot represents the chest area, while the top of the foot in that section represents the upper back. The reflexes on both feet are the same. You should start with a lung press, using the knuckles of your right hand to knead the entire ball area of the foot.

The ball of the foot holds the reflexes for the heart, lungs, bronchioles, and bronchi. The reflexes for the breast are also in the ball of the foot. To work this area in the left foot, proceed from the lung press using your first right knuckle to gently trace a line from the first web. Trace around the first metatarsal head to the edge of the diaphragm line, pushing out the heart reflex. Gently stroke the small region that pops out.

Thumb walk the entire chest reflex region using the caterpillar technique. Follow the caterpillar by working both sections of the reflex separately before you use the butterfly technique.

The next reflex represents the upper back. Here you use both hands together as you walk in from the sides, as though you are playing an accordion. Always walk slowly and gently on this reflex, allowing the fingers to move up on the tips and down on the pads. People may actually feel a warming and relaxing sensation through the body during this move.

ALERT!

When a receiver has indicated the use of blood pressure medication or any heart-related conditions, work the heart reflex differently. Beginning at the outside end of the diaphragm line, thumb walk across to under the first metatarsal head. The small area of skin that pushes out here is the heart reflex. Gently stroke as described previously.

Lymph drainage is the same on both feet. Remember the lymph reflexes are scattered around the feet, as they are in the body. However, a great concentration of lymph is found in the chest and upper-back region. The thumb and forefinger move down the foot, in between each web, walking slowly, pressing gently. Go as far as the foot will let you before pulling back along each line, with a slight fractioning type of movement. Finish this section with the solar plexus reflex.

The Next Section of the Body

The section of the body reflected next is between the diaphragm and the waist. The imaginary lines in the foot help to make the division. Some of the reflexes represent the same structures on both feet. Look at the left foot for a moment. Imagine the diaphragm line. Place three fingers from your left hand on the instep of the foot. This time the fourth finger is on top.

- The fourth finger holds the reflex for the stomach.
- The third finger is also over the stomach reflex.
- The third finger points to the spleen reflex.
- The index finger is placed on the pancreas reflex.
- The index finger points to the adrenal reflex.

To work this section of the left foot, use thumb walking on all areas. Remember to hook into the spleen reflex. When working on the adrenal reflex, line up under the solar plexus. The left thumb will walk in from the inside of the foot, across the diaphragm line, stopping just under the solar plexus reflex. Rotate, press, and hold on the adrenal reflex, until the area pushes back.

The reflex on top of the foot reflects the entire back region of our body. As you work this area, let the fingers walk slowly in between each metatarsal bone. Don't forget to walk all the fingers down the top of the foot as well.

Reflections of the Lower Abdomen

You have already worked both the right and left foot in this section. The areas reflected are different on both feet. The right foot holds the reflexes for the ileocecal, the ascending colon, and the transverse colon. The left foot contains the transverse colon, the descending colon, and the sigmoid colon reflexes. The left foot also has the reflex for the rectum. Both feet have reflexes for the kidneys, the bladder, and the small intestines. This section ends for both feet at the sciatic line.

FACT

The solar plexus reflex may be used many times during a session. If a receiver has indicated an area of tenderness, press into the solar plexus reflex and hold, asking the recipient to breathe deeply. Now return to the painful area; if the pain is relieved, work the reflex— if not, move on. Either result is useful.

Systems Affected

The imaginary lines in reflexology divide the foot into sections that reflect the body. This type of division can be related to the anatomical classification of the body. Physiology divides the body by systems, which are also reflected on the feet. The reflexes found on the feet connect to structures within the body. These structures are all part of the organic system that allows the body to function.

Every system of the body is affected by any stimulus to the body. Depending upon the stimulus, the stress can be effective or detrimental. Reflexology teaches the body to resonate with positive energy, giving the receiver the potential to react with a vital and creative approach to stress. Our ability to cope coincides with our ability to relax. As we release stress we learn to manage our lives productively, using vital survival mechanisms to achieve our goals.

Holistic wellness incorporates body, mind, and spirit. These principles are all related, as even medical schools today can attest. Research has shown that 58 percent of the medical schools in the United States now offer courses on spirituality. The systems of the body work more efficiently when all aspects of healing are involved. Reflexology integrates these beliefs, involving the recipient in every part of the process.

What the Systems Show

Reflexology works with the musculature of the body, allowing the muscles to relax and let go of stored tension. The skeletal and muscular systems often show direct results as aches and pains in the body may begin to dissipate with continued reflexology sessions. Rather than working directly on an affected area, reflexology stimulates the systems from within, promoting healing. As muscles relax, the nervous system and circulatory system become more involved in releasing blockage and constriction.

The nervous system is affected directly and indirectly through reflexology. The nerve pathways found in the feet are stimulated through the actual work on the reflexes. These nerves are involved with communication to the greater system, establishing direction to and from the central nervous system.

The circulatory system becomes stimulated, as reflexology affects the blood vessels directly through working on the feet and indirectly through further nerve stimulation. Of course, the sensory system—the skin and other sense organs—are also affected. Every reflex is touched directly, which sends signals from the skin to other systems in the body. The feet themselves could be considered a sensory organ, as they transmit so much information.

ALERT!

Remember, you are not working on the systems of the body directly. As you work a point, that point reflects an area or structure of the body. Always be clear, you are working on a reflex, not the body part. Reflexes work with the systems of the body, assisting in the process of homeostasis.

Every system in the body is affected through reflexology. Some of the systems are affected by touch, which then stimulates the sensory effect through the nervous system. The nervous system deals with every part of the body, so through this system, reflexology has a pathway to all of the other systems, helping to restore homeostasis.

Functions of Reflexology

Through the systems of the body, reflexology is able to activate the vital force of energy, allowing an individual's body to function appropriately for that person. Reflexology has many functions:

- It regulates the body's functions.
- It increases well-being.
- It stimulates circulation.
- It encourages a state of relaxation.
- It provides relief from physical and emotional pain.
- It reduces the body's reliance on medication.
- It supports an internal dialogue.

The functions of reflexology produce reactions. As the functions of reflexology stimulate bodily reactions, you are able to see the positive effects. And as the body improves so does the mind. When you begin to think positively, you begin to feel better emotionally. An improved emotional state encourages laughter, joy, and a surge of gratitude for life. Increased happiness supports an increase in spiritual contentment.

Reactions of the Systems

While reviewing the systems, take a look at the reactions of these systems as well. The link between the organs and other structures of the body is further encouraged through reflexology. Circulation is directly improved through reflexology; this can be observed as the complexion of the receiver improves even before the session is complete. With the improved circulation comes the removal of toxins from the body. Again, this may be observed during a session as a recipient's nose may begin to run, or there may be an increase in perspiration. Often at the conclusion of a session, the receiver will need to void.

Reflexology works to bring balance to the receiver, a state of harmony and of wholeness. As circulation is improved, other areas of the body react positively. With toxins leaving the body naturally, all the systems work more effectively, requiring less dependence on artificial means. A feeling of well-being becomes constant. There are many different developments that may surface. The following are some of the after-effects of a session:

- A feeling of renewal; feeling refreshed and energized
- A feeling of calmness and harmony
- An altered sleep pattern
- A sense of relief
- A regulation in body temperature
- Reduction of aches and pains
- A renewed sense of self
- An increase in nasal discharge
- A new awareness of surroundings
- An increase in release of undigested waste
- A release of water retention
- An increase in lung function

Reactions generally produce a change in overall body function. As the body, mind, and spirit evolve, this becomes apparent on the feet as well. The feet root us to the ground, yet connect us with the universe. The essence of our being is often mirrored in the condition of our feet.

Comfort of the Receiver

The process of reflexology is compassionate and healing. Sensitive, gentle, yet firm touch creates an environment of peace, encouraging deep relaxation. The act of reflexing points on the feet promotes a deep state of alpha. Alpha is the first level of soothing relaxation. In this state, a person is not asleep but is relaxed deeply enough to remove conscious thought. Conscious thought may at times interfere with our innate ability to assist in our own healing.

As the mind is free to "shut off," so then can our intuitive self open to allow natural healing to transpire. The muscles begin to release their rigidity, freeing the blood vessels to promote proper circulation. This discharge of tension allows the nutrients to feed the cells of the body. As the nutrients reach all systems, the release of toxic waste stimulates the body to renew the cycle, creating a continuum of wellness. Homeostasis is perpetuated.

Throughout the session, you should continuously check with the receiver. The comfort of the person in the chair is your only goal. As you work, it is important to assess the continued response of the recipient to the stimulus.

Always suggest to the receiver at the beginning of the session that his or her input is welcome. "Your job is to relax, letting your mind and body slow down. If you feel any discomfort, please let me know." Give the recipient the ability to let go, yet stay in control at the same time.

Expressed Tension

There will be tenderness and sensitivity in the feet, due to tension and foot pain. It's a good idea to be aware of the expressions of tension and to know what they mean. Tension may be expressed in a number of ways during the session as reflexology allows for the release of this stress:

1. A jumping or twitching of the body
2. A sharp, pricking sensation
3. A warm, tingling feeling
4. A floating, euphoric feeling
5. A dull ache, especially in the legs
6. A rush of energy
7. A cramping in the toes

Twitching or Pricking Feeling

The body and feet may twitch or jump as energy begins to circulate. Areas that were deprived of blood and nerve stimulation begin to "wake up," responding to this flow. This is often accompanied by a feeling of warmth as the circulation picks up. At times a rush of energy may spurt through the body, and the receiver will actually glow with renewed color in the face.

The sharp, pricking feeling seems as though you are sticking a pin into the foot of the receiver. The sensation is immediate, not prolonged. This generally indicates a congested area of the foot and some blockage along the energy pathway. This painful sensation indicates the need to move away from the reflex for the moment, but to return later. Usually the pain will not reoccur when the area is again reflexed later in the session.

People who live high-stress lives, without meditative breaks, often feel a dull ache in their legs. This ache is a good thing. The presence of aches in the legs generally indicates the tension is leaving the body. As the session progresses, the dull ache is usually dispelled, leaving a relaxed feeling, which the recipient will learn to identify.

ALERT!

If a receiver has a history of vascular distress, or any cardio-vascular issues, pains in the legs may indicate an underlying situation. Always make a referral. Recommend that the receiver check in with her or his physician to relate what may be symptoms. The doctor will thank you.

Cramping

Cramping in the toes or legs is generally a release of lactic acid, a natural compound in the body. Overproduction of lactic acid can cause accumulation in the blood and muscle tissue. Reflexology releases this buildup as the circulation of blood and oxygen is promoted during the session. The cramping does go away.

Often physically active people may have cramping. Make it a practice to ask if they warm up before exercise and most important, if they stretch after. Stretching after exercise is key to body performance. Learn basic leg stretches to teach to your receivers.

Floating, Euphoric Feeling

The floating and euphoric sense of well-being that comes during the session is the most frequent response. All recipients of reflexology do reach this state. As a sense of trust is established, the receiver is willing to let go and relax completely. The greatest compliment a giver may receive is for a person to fall asleep. When a receiver begins to snore and drool, you know you've done a good job!

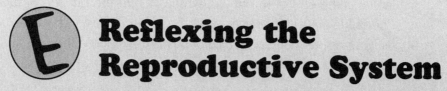

Chapter 18

Reflexing the Reproductive System

The reproductive system is an incredible piece of symmetry. The areas reflected on the feet for this system are the same on both the right and the left foot. Both sexes are represented on the feet, as the structures and organs of this system are placed in very similar locations in the body.

Bony Landmarks—the Ankles

The bony landmarks that represent the ankles are actually the ends of the two lower leg bones, the tibia and the fibula. The bony protrusions are called the medial and lateral malleolus. The medial malleolus is the end of the tibia, which sits on the inside of the foot. The lateral malleolus is the end of the fibula, which sits on the outside of the foot.

The ankle actually consists of all the tarsal bones. (These seven bones were discussed earlier.) The talus is considered the real anklebone and is the initial weight-bearing bone during the action of walking.

Joints

Another area of importance in dealing with the ankle is the joint involved with the movement of this area. A joint is a point of contact between bones. There are different classifications for joints depending upon structure or function.

Structural classification depends upon the presence or absence of space between the bones that are touching. The joints you are dealing with have a cavity, known as a *synovial cavity,* between the touching bones. This classifies these joints as synovial joints.

Functional classification deals with the degree of movement the joint allows. A diarthrosis is a freely movable joint, which is the type of joint you are involved with at this time. These joints have a variety of shapes and allow a range of movement. They are covered with a protective cartilage that allows for freer movement and provides shock absorption.

FACT

Flexion happens when we bend at a joint, like bending a knee or an elbow. Extension often happens when we return the arm or leg to its original position after flexing. Some hinge joints can hyperextend; that's how our heads can bend backward.

The ankle joint is also known as the *talocrural joint.* It is between the end of the malleoli and the talus. This joint is classified structurally as a hinge joint. Part of the classification stipulates that the surface of one bone fits into the surface of another bone, which does happen in the ankles. The movement of the joint is like a door on a hinge; in anatomy this movement is generally flexion and extension. When you flex a joint, it is as though you pull the door in; when you extend, you open the door.

Special Movements

The synovial joints have a subgroup known as *special movements*. These movements are part of the biomechanics of the feet. Every time you walk, you perform these special movements. Six of these special movements deal specifically with the feet and hands:

1. Inversion moves the soles inward, so they face each other.
2. Eversion moves the soles away, so they face away from each other.
3. Dorsiflexion bends the foot up.
4. Plantar flexion bends the foot down.
5. Abduction moves the foot away from the center of the body.
6. Adduction also moves the foot toward the center of the body.

Although not special movements, there are two others that are key to some of these movements: supination is a three-point movement of inversion, plantar flexion, and adduction; and pronation is a three-point movement of eversion, dorsiflexion, and abduction.

Reflexes on the Inside Arch

Moving on, let's pick up with the last section. You will work on the right foot first, of course. Hold the foot with the left hand and knuckle press the heel. Press with a kneading movement; don't forget to move your body. Let the press relax the heel. Move up and down the plantar surface of this foot, using a gentle pressure and allowing the knuckles to relax the entire foot.

Turn the foot out slightly and move your body so that you are looking at the inside edge of the foot, without twisting your neck and back. The reflexes found on the inside of the foot, in the lower arch and heel region, represent the reproductive system. The human reproductive system produces, stores, and transports cells specific to reproduction.

It is in the reproductive system that human life is conceived. Upon conception, this system supports the development of the cells that form the fetus. Another function of this system includes the birthing and nurturing of the child. There are a number of structures involved with this system.

ALERT!

Always position yourself to see the area to be worked and to have easy access. You need to place yourself so you are using your body wisely. If you are sitting on a ball or a rolling chair, moving is simple. If not, get up and move so that you can easily see and reach the area.

Main organs of the female:

- Ovaries
- Fallopian tubes
- Uterus
- Vagina
- Vulva
- Breasts

Main organs of the male:

- Scrotum
- Testes
- Epididymis
- Vas deferens
- Seminal vesicles
- Prostate gland
- Urethra
- Penis

Thumb Walking a Triangle

Look at the inside of the foot and use the bony malleolus as a guide. Place a finger from the very edge of the heel up to just under the outside edge of the ankle. With the other hand, place a finger from the inside edge of the malleolus back toward the upper arch. Let the thumbs join each other along the inside edge of the foot. The shape between these fingers is a triangle.

Working the Reproductive Reflexes

Within this triangle are most of the reproductive reflexes. Some of these reflexes you will pinpoint, others you will include in the thumb-walking technique. Look at the shape once more and remove the fingers, preparing to thumb walk. Begin with the right thumb and thumb walk up from the back of the heel to the outside of the malleolus. Keep moving the thumb in a bit and walk up so that the line continues to come from the inside edge of the foot up to the malleolus. Eventually using the right thumb becomes awkward, which is a sign to switch hands.

The left thumb walks the imaginary line that begins along the edge of the foot at the waistline. Thumb walk along this line to just under the upper edge of the malleolus. Continue to bring the thumb back to the edge and walk with small, slow bites up to the ankle, but not on the bone. Soon the entire triangle is filled.

The line that runs from the edge of the heel to the waistline is next. Thumb walk between these two points. Return to the edge of the heel, move the thumb in a bit, and walk again. You are filling in the area from the heel to the bone on the side of the foot, the tuberosity of the navicular.

The Reflexes of the Inner Triangle

There are many reflexes within this triangle. This area reflects the pelvic region of the body, including all structures found there. The area along the back edge of the heel has reflexes for the testes and lymph. Moving in a bit—just up from the inner edge but still close to the back—are two reflexes: one for the vaginal area and the other for the pelvic bones. The entire triangle is the reflex for the uterus.

ALERT!

Stimulation of the pelvic zone is not recommended until the end of the pregnancy. The mother-to-be's doctor should be aware of the treatment as should her midwife and any other medical professionals involved with her care.

The reflex for the rectum is a thumb joint in from the edge along the sciatic line. Thumb walking the triangle, from the heel, from the waistline, and filling in the whole area allows for complete coverage of all the reflexes. Other areas reflected here are the prostate gland and the urethra.

Press and Hold Behind the Ankle

Look at the inside of the foot for a moment. Focus on the medial malleolus. Feel around this bony area on your own foot. Become familiar with the dips and curves. Flex and extend the foot and move the foot in a circle while your fingers are palpating around this bony section. Place a fingertip in the space just behind the ankle. The finger slips into this small space easily. With the finger in this tiny section, turn the foot toward the finger and feel the finger press in.

You are using the body to work the reflex as the finger holds on the point. What you are feeling is the stimulation of the tibial nerve and the pulsing of the tibial artery. The tibial nerve is a main branch of the sciatic nerve. Surface veins are also in this area.

The sciatic line along the plantar surface of the foot is a reflex for the sciatic nerve. The reflex point just behind and below the malleolus is the sciatic point. Look at the receiver's foot and examine around the inner malleolus. When you are ready, thumb walk in from the edge of the foot, walking with small bites to just behind the inner ankle. Let your thumb fit into the small depression and hold there. Pull the recipient's foot in to the thumb. This is a sensitive region, so be easy and do not apply pressure; the foot will do the work.

Reflexes on the Outside of the Foot

Now you're ready to move on to the outside region of the feet—the right foot first, of course. There are many reflexes found here. Beginning with the heel area along the lower edge is a reflection found for the lymphatics. This runs around the entire region of the foot from the lower edge of the outside heel, up and across the navicular and talus on the top of the foot, and down to the lower edge of the inner heel. Connecting with this line is the reflex for the fallopian tubes as well as the vas deferens.

Reflexology causes people to relax. As relaxation becomes a habit, so does a better lifestyle. Reflexology helps build a bridge of interest. People who begin to relax begin to desire other changes, changes of improvement on all levels.

Becoming Familiar with the Reflexes

At the lower, back edge of the heel on the outside is a reflex for the ovaries; the finger can generally fit right into the groove. Behind and below the outside malleolus is the sciatic point again. Let your fingers explore around the malleolus on this side, slipping into the sciatic reflex, then walking all around the bony protrusion of the ankle. This outer anklebone is the reflex for the hip, the entire hipbone, and the hip joints. The pelvic bones are around this area, too.

Slowly feel along the outer edge, moving up the foot. Your finger will find the bony bump of the tuberosity of the fifth metatarsal. Keep moving up. The next bony bump is the fifth metatarsal head. The first indentation, under the tuberosity, is a secondary access for the hip, knee, and leg. The next indentation is just before the fifth metatarsal head. This point is a secondary access for the shoulder, elbow, and arm.

Move back and look at the area below the malleolus. Place a finger from the back edge of the heel up to the ankle. With the other hand, place a finger from the waistline to the ankle. Using the thumbs, connect the triangle by placing the thumbs along the edge between the waist and the end of the heel. This is the primary access to the hip, knee, and leg.

Technique for Lymph and Reproductive Reflexes

To work the lymphatic reflex, you will use both hands. Place the thumbs on the edge of the heel, one on each side of the foot. Fit the thumbs as far back as possible, touching the tuberosity of the heel on both sides. Begin thumb walking diagonally up and across the heel, still under the malleolus. Continue to walk up, past the malleolus to the center top of the foot. The thumbs will pass over many landmarks as they walk to the top. When the thumbs meet, gently press in and hold. Begin moving the thumbs backward, following the path just drawn. Let the thumbs rotate slightly as you bring them back to the heel. This also represents the fallopian tubes and vas deferens. These reflexes and the lymphatic reflex overlap.

Once this reflex has been walked, imagine a line from the bottom of the malleolus drawn straight down to the heel. Thumb walk halfway up this line, and the finger will fit into a small dent. This is another reflex for the ovaries and fallopian tubes. Rotate in gently, hold, and press on this reflex.

The sciatic nerve reflex is in the same spot as on the inside of the foot. Thumb walk in horizontally, from the edge of the heel to behind the bottom edge of the malleolus. Sure enough, there is that slight dip, waiting for your thumb. Press in and hold, pulling the foot toward the thumb.

There are spots where fingers work as well as thumbs. Pay attention to any outside area that may cause overstretching of the thumb. This is your body's way of telling you to readjust. Remember these are guidelines. Experiment and find what works for your hands.

Begin to thumb walk up the outside edge of the foot. As the thumb walks into the groove before the tuberosity, turn the thumb slightly and hold. Pull the foot in toward the thumb; the body will use the thumb to press the reflex. Continue on from here to the next tiny spot, just below the metatarsal head. Turn the thumb just a bit, holding there, and pull the foot into the thumb. Again, the body is applying the pressure to the reflex.

Another Triangle

This triangle is the one you previously traced on the outside of the heel. Let's review. Put your two thumbs and index fingers together in a pyramid or triangle shape. Move your body so you are at the side of the foot you working on. Place these fingers over the side of the foot, with the peak coming to rest under or on that protruding anklebone.

This outer triangle represents reflexes for the hip, knee, and leg. The entire area is a reflex. Thumb walking this region will reflex the leg and feet, as well as the knee and hip. Using the right thumb, walk up the edge of the foot to the waistline. Bring the thumb back and over a bit and walk up again, this time moving into the imaginary triangle. Continue in this manner, filling the triangle from the heel edge.

When the thumb cannot go any farther, you have hit the underside of the malleolus. Start to walk down with the left thumb. The left thumb will walk from the waistline down, essentially repeating the technique from another direction.

Lastly, thumb walk with the right thumb from the side edge up toward the malleolus, filling in the area. Let the thumb walk all over this section, using gentle, small steps. This area may be painful, so always check the comfort zone of the receiver.

Reflexing the Hips

The reflection of the hip, the hip joints, and the bones of the hip is found around the lateral malleolus. This is the big bumpy bone that sits on the outside of the ankle, the one most people call the anklebone. You have felt around this area before and know how sensitive it can be.

Start at the lower end of the bone and thumb walk toward the back, turning and thumb walking up behind the ankle. Generally the thumb and hand begin to twist awkwardly at this point. Switch thumbs and walk down toward the front of the foot, around the malleolus. The turn of the thumbs will be a bit awkward; this is one time when the body doesn't completely adjust. Pay attention to any areas of puffiness or tautness, as you will need to thumb walk carefully in these regions.

Reflexology and hip pain is quite extraordinary. Generally, a person would try to walk off a pain in the hip, which might or might not work. A better solution would be to make sure there is no internal, symptomatic reason for the pain. Once you have determined through professional consultation that the pain is muscular, go for a massage. Massage is wonderful—the hip feels better, and you can go on your way.

FACT

The sciatic reflex is so close that it may overlap at times. We have found this is not uncommon in reflexology. The body has many areas that are reflected on the feet. Just as internal organs in the body may sit over one another, reflexes may overlap in reflexology. This allows some areas to be reflexed more often, areas that innately need more attention.

Well, if that hip pain is caused by your biomechanics—how you walk—you will not be enjoying the benefit of the massage for long. An overuse condition specific to the feet, yet generating pain in the hip, is the piriformis syndrome. The sciatic nerve runs from the lower-back region of the spine, across the buttocks in a diagonal line toward the back and outer edge of the leg.

There are many muscle layers involved in the buttocks. One of the deeper muscles involved with moving the thigh at the hip joint is the piriformis muscle. This band of muscle sits on top of the sciatic nerve. Another function of this muscle is to keep the upper leg bone from rotating too much in one direction or another. You can turn your hip out and in and the bones do rotate, but if they over-rotate you can strain the muscles.

Chapter 19

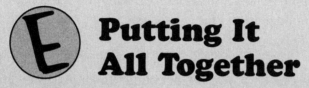

E Putting It All Together

One of the most important systems of the body is the nervous system. When your nervous system is functioning in homeostasis, all of your systems are operating in balance. Every nerve, cranial and spinal, affects the body directly. Each nerve has an area, organ, or structure for which it is responsible. Reflexology works to support this system.

The Spinal and Brain Reflexes

The reflex for the spine runs along the entire inside edges of both feet. Look at your own feet first. Become aware of the natural curves, feel where the bones end, and touch each ridge. Notice the great toe, how it pokes out a bit and then curves in at the joint and curves out at the ball of the foot. The first metatarsal head is the beginning of the ball of the foot. Feel along the edge of the first metatarsal bone; notice as it flows into the medial cuneiform bone.

It is the cuneiform bone along with the navicular bone that forms the arch. Continuing up the arch you will encounter the talus bone. Let the fingers follow the natural decline in the arch. This decline will bring you right to the heel. This area is the reflection of the spine, the spinal reflex. The bones are covered with muscle and connective tissue, forming a protective cushion as well as a container for lymph and blood vessels along with the nerves particular to the feet.

There are no lymph nodes in the feet. There are many spidery thin lymph vessels, aligned with the arteries and veins. These lymph vessels drain the lymph of the foot to either the nodes behind the knee or to the nodes in the groin.

You already know the great toe represents the brain, including the twelve cranial nerves housed in the upper skull. The central nervous system is the brain and the spinal cord. The peripheral nervous system consists of the nerves that come from the brain and the spinal cord. Information is carried to and from the brain cells via the nerve impulses.

The twelve cranial nerves that are part of the peripheral nervous system are either sensory or mixed nerves. The cranial nerves have names and numbers. The numbers are roman numerals that indicate the order of the nerves. The names describe the function:

I. Olfactory is for smelling.
II. Optic deals with vision.
III. Oculomotor is for moving the eye, eyelid, and constricting the pupil.

IV. Trochlear controls movement of the eye.

V. Trigeminal has to do with chewing.

VI. Abducens also moves the eyeball.

VII. Facial deals with facial expression as well as saliva and tears.

VIII. Vestibulocochlear deals with hearing and equilibrium.

IX. Glossopharyngeal is for taste and the secretion of saliva.

X. Vagus deals with smooth muscle contraction in the upper abdomen.

XI. Accessory controls swallowing and movement of the head.

XII. Hypoglossal moves the tongue during speaking and swallowing.

Three Times Three

Three is a very powerful number. Three is the flat dimension of the shapes of a diamond, a pyramid, and a tepee. Many sacred symbols consist of three shapes, colors, or sizes. The number three has many meanings: harmony, completion through harmony, and the birth of harmony. The number three also stands for the beginning, the middle, and the end. In reflexology, you will often do each move within a technique three times. With the application of three, you are sure each movement in the process is complete.

Using Three as a Guideline

Reflexology is an energetic touch therapy. Many people receive comfort and relief through healing touch. Each move within the techniques is applied with compassion. You reflex an area until you feel a response from the recipient. At times you may feel the reflex "give" as the skin beneath your finger or thumb relaxes. Sometimes there is a pulsation from the area of reflex. Or a reflex may "push" you away, a statement by the reflex to move on.

A thumb or finger walk of an area is usually repeated three times. As you become more proficient, you will not need to use the three, but in the beginning the number three is a great supporting guide.

Feeling these responses comes with practice. The better you become with the art of reflexology, the easier it is for your hands to read the feet. As you are learning to intuitively connect and communicate with the feet, you need a guideline for the number of times to reflex each area. For instance, you will generally hold the areas you hook into for a count of three.

Demonstrating the Power of Three

The spinal reflex demonstrates the power of three perfectly. Look again at the foot. Imagine a line running straight down the edge of the foot from the toe to the heel. Do not curve the line; let it be straight. Now imagine another line lying on top of this line, running from the toe to the heel. Then imagine another line on top of these two lines. You have created a stack of three lines.

The bottom line runs straight to the heel. The next line has a slight curve to it. The third line follows the arch and then arrives at the heel. Each of these lines is part of the spinal reflex. As you learn the technique for this area, repeat each step three times, which will make it three times three.

Thumb Walk the Spinal Reflex

Beginning on the right foot, hold the foot with your left hand; the right hand will be the working hand. Position yourself so that you can work comfortably on the spinal reflex area. Hold the foot either by the toes or by cupping at the heel. Whichever hold you prefer, let the left hand give support and leverage, too.

Begin thumb walking on the first line, the one that runs straight along the edge from toe to heel. Thumb walk from either end in small moves forward, working toward the other end. Bring the thumb back to the beginning and walk along the edge again. You may switch hands walking back and forth along the line, if you prefer. Whichever way you choose, thumb walk slowly and rhythmically three times along this edge, from toe to heel or heel to toe.

Bring the thumb back to the heel, or toe, and move across it just a bit. You are now going to thumb walk the next line in the stack. This line has a slight curve. As you begin to thumb walk on this line, feel the curve at the ball of the foot. When you thumb walk over this region, often the receiver may feel a slight discomfort at the metatarsal head. This is the reflection of the beginning of the thoracic area of the spine.

Again, walk this reflex three times with slow, steady movements. The thumb takes little bites as it walks along this section. Begin either at the heel or toe and walk back and forth or walk three lines in the same direction, whatever works for you.

The last line in the stack will follow the bony ridge from the toe to the heel. Thumb walk this line three times as well.

FACT

As you walk the spinal reflex, the receiver may become aware of aches and pains in the foot. The pain may generate from the plantar fascia, the layer of thin connective tissue that runs from the heel to the ball of the foot. When this tissue is inflamed, the condition is called *plantar fasciitis.*

Rotation on the Reflex

The spinal reflex is the reflection of the chakra system as well. Chakras are the energy centers of transformation and transmutation. The nervous system communicates with the various systems of the body and the systems respond by furthering the communication with one another. The nerves stimulate all areas of the body. The endocrine system is stimulated by the nervous system to produce and release the hormones essential to homeostasis. The chakra centers are reflected on the spine and the spine is reflected on the feet.

The interconnection between the chakras, the endocrine system, and the nervous system is not a new concept. All areas of energy work understand and embrace this connection. As you work on the physical level, you affect the mind and spirit simultaneously. Rotating on the spinal reflex allows the energetic link to continue. Releasing energy blockage is as important as releasing physical congestion.

Disease comes from a dysfunction of the mind, body, and spirit relationship. You can contribute to the prevention of congestion and blockage in the body by becoming more positive in your thoughts and feelings. When you believe you are healthy, you are able to release old patterns of illness, reconditioning your beliefs with the concept of whole-health wellness.

Chakras

It is believed that chakras absorb the energy of the environment and bring this energy into the body through the endocrine glands. The endocrine system controls the hormone balance in the body, so if chakra energy is out of kilter, perhaps hormone production is as well. Chakras may affect the endocrine glands, as well as some organs and the nervous system. Every chakra is important, relating to certain functions, emotions, and elements.

Functions Ruled by Each Chakra

Root deals with survival issues, center of abundance, vitality, and the life force.
Sacral deals with sexual and sensual energy, and is our emotional center.
Solar plexus is the center for wisdom and personal power.
Heart is the center of love and compassion.
Throat deals with communication and self-expression.
Third eye is the center of intuition and clairvoyance.
Crown is the connection with our higher self and the divine.

Imagine the base of the spine where the root chakra is reflected. The energy from this wheel spreads out, connecting us with the physical earth. The element earth represents stability, strength, and being grounded.

The sacral chakra is connected with the element of water. Your emotional center flows with the rhythm of water, easy like a bubbling brook or roaring like an angry ocean. Think about how your feelings can sit in the pit of your stomach. That is the sacral chakra center.

The solar plexus chakra is associated with the element of fire. This is your place of power, where you hold firm in the face of adversity. A storm can blow all around you, and you can remain calm, the coals of your fire burning strong and true. With wisdom you have protected the energy source. This represents the essence of the solar plexus.

The element of air governs the heart chakra. As you gain control over your pattern of breath, you are able to regulate a balanced heartbeat. The throat chakra relates to the element of sound, the communication center. To speak your truth is a goal of this chakra.

The third eye is the area that allows you to trust your intuition. We all have experienced times when we felt a situation, an action, or a conversation was a repeated memory, that we have been there before. The chakra that governs our intuitive self assists in these areas.

FACT

Each chakra spins along the spinal cord, moving up to the crown chakra. The crown chakra is reflected at the top of the brain, connecting us with the heavens.

Working the Chakra Reflex

The spine holds the reflections of the chakras. The foot holds the reflection of the spine. If you look at your feet, you can actually imagine the shape of the spine on the inner edges of your feet. The great toe is the brain, the brain stem would be the neck of the toe, and the spinal column runs clear down to past the sciatic line.

Holding the right foot with the left hand, cupping at the heel and outside edge, use the right hand as the working hand. With the right thumb begin to rotate lightly on the spinal reflex, starting at the bottom and slowly working to the top of the great toe. The tip and outside edge of the thumb do most of the work; your fingers are tucked into a loose fist, coming along as the thumb works up the foot. As the first rotation along the edge is complete, come back and repeat.

The three stacked lines of the spine are included in each circle as the thumb rotates up along the reflex. Work up along the edge of the toe neck, continuing up to the very top of the toe, where you rotate on the brain reflex. Of course, repeat this process three times. The response is often heard as sighs of satisfaction.

Zigzag Thumb Walk

Think about the spine for a moment. The cord is covered and protected by the bones of the vertebrae, connective tissue, and fluid. Thirty-one pairs of spinal nerves emerge from the spinal cord. These nerves are the pathways of communication between the body, the spinal cord, and the brain.

The reflexology technique that deals with the reflection of these nerves is a zigzag type of thumb walking. This technique resembles the pattern made by pinking shears when cutting out a hem. Think about the nerves emanating out of the spine; picture the flow as the nerves move into the body.

Begin at the base of the heel using the right thumb and slowly thumb walk diagonally across all three lines of the reflex, turn, and thumb walk back. Continue with this motion up the foot along the entire edge, stopping at the base of the great toe. The movement of the thumb is slow, steady, and even, taking small bites back and forth. At the top, either switch hands and walk down or bring the thumb back to the heel and work up again.

This movement stimulates the nerves, sending messages for the muscles around the spinal column to relax and balancing the nerve function. Working in this manner also helps the fascia of the plantar surface, since part of the area is connecting in to the fascia.

Each time you walk across the lines of the reflex, you are working on the reflection of the nerves coming out of the spine. Imagine the thumb moving across the nerves, and across the bony vertebrae, connective tissue, and cerebrospinal fluid. Let the thumb walk gently, effectively applying a steady, easy pressure.

Walk the zigzag motion three times, allowing for the reflex to relax. With the last walk up the reflex, use your fingers to gently stroke off the edge of the foot.

Walking the Zones

Bring both thumbs to the center of the foot on the bottom surface. The fingers of both hands will support the foot. Begin at the centerline and thumb walk up from the heel to the tops of the second and third toes. Bring the thumbs back, place them on the outside of these two lines, and thumb walk up again, this time to the tops of the big toe and the fourth toe. Again let the thumbs start at the heel, at the edge of the surface, and thumb walk up to the tops of the little toe and the great toe.

Start at the center of the edge of the heel at the back of the foot and thumb walk along the edge of the entire foot, including the edges of the toes. From the top of the foot now, bring the thumbs to the shoulder line and walk in horizontally, using the butterfly technique. Butterfly down the entire bottom of the foot, bringing the thumbs to the edge each time as you move the lines down. This brings it all together, every zone, every meridian, every chakra; you have covered all the bases. Repeat these on the left foot, after you have worked the entire right foot.

The Lymph of the Leg

A reflexology session isn't complete without working the lymph reflexes on the legs. The feet have no lymph nodes, but the lymph vessels of the feet empty into the nodes of the legs.

Begin with both thumbs placed on either side of the foot, in front of the malleolus. Thumb walk up to the top surface; the thumbs will meet. You have worked this reflex before—it is the secondary access to the fallopian tubes. This is also a lymphatic reflex. Gently slide the thumbs back to the heel; this time thumb walk up around the back side of the malleolus, again meeting at the top of the foot, just at the ankle joint. Turn both hands to face the leg and place all the fingers on the top of the leg. Using all the fingers (the thumbs stay quiet), walk up the leg to just under the knee, and gently glide the fingers back and repeat.

Bring both hands to the back of the heel and cup the heel with the palms. Finger walk slowly up the back of the leg, all fingers moving together, again stopping just below the knee. Gently glide back and walk up the back of the leg again.

The Thread of the Tapestry

The brain and the spinal column are the central nervous system (CNS). This control center unscrambles all the messages that arrive via the peripheral nervous system (PNS). Any changes within or on the surface of the body are reported by the peripheral system. Once the CNS has responded, the peripheral system carries the response back to the body. In essence the nervous system weaves throughout the body, creating balance and harmony. The nervous system brings the body to order, connecting the functions of each system and allowing the complex working of the body to operate efficiently.

The two cells of the nervous system are neuroglia and neurons. Neuroglia cells support the neurons, while the neurons deal with the special functions of the nervous system. Nerve cells communicate among themselves and to muscle and gland cells.

FACT

The special functions of the nervous system consist of sensing, thinking, remembering, controlling muscle activity, and regulating glandular secretions. Some neurons are tiny while others seem endless. Motor neurons that wiggle the toes extend from the spinal cord to the feet, while sensory neurons can extend from under the foot to the brain.

The Neuroglia

The neuroglia cells are those cells within the nervous tissue that support and protect the nervous system. The neuroglia cells make up half of the CNS and can multiply, unlike neurons. There are six types of neuroglia cells, four in the central nervous system and two in the PNS.

- **Astrocytes** assist in metabolism, balance potassium, help in brain development, and help with the blood-brain barrier.
- **Oligodendrocytes** produce the myelin sheath.
- **Microglia** protect the CNS from disease by destroying germs and clearing out dead cells.
- **Ependymal cells** line the cavities in the brain and spinal cord and form cerebrospinal fluid.
- **Schwann cells** produce myelin sheaths around peripheral neurons.
- **Satellite cells** support clusters of neurons in the peripheral nervous system.

The Myelin Sheath

The myelin sheath covers most cells, providing insulation and assisting in impulse conduction. The sheath shields the electricity so that the nerve can send the impulse quickly. Cells that do not have the sheath conduct impulses slowly.

Myelin increases as we mature, increasing the ability of the nerve to conduct impulses quickly. Destruction of the sheaths on the neurons can lead to multiple sclerosis. As the myelin sheath is destroyed, the nerve impulses are weakened, causing systemic weakening with progressive loss of function.

QUESTION?

What if a nerve is out of place?
The vertebrae that cover the spinal cord and house the nerves can move, becoming dislocated. A subluxation results, affecting the nerves coming from the particular vertebra. A chiropractor adjusts subluxations. A reflexologist supports and integrates the work the chiropractor does.

The Spinal Nerves

The spinal nerves are part of the peripheral nervous system. These nerves connect the central nervous system to muscles, glands, and other structures. The nerves are divided by vertebral structure. Nerves coming from a vertebra affect certain parts of the body. The nerves not only affect the surface areas and structures but the function of the internal organs as well.

The cervical nerves affect:

C1: The deep muscles of the head, the brain, the pituitary, and the inner ear
C2: Eyes, sinuses, tongue, and skin of the scalp
C3: Facial muscles, outer ear, teeth
C4: Nose, mouth, lips
C5: Vocal cords, pharynx, rhomboid muscles
C6: Neck muscles, shoulders
C7: Thyroid gland, biceps, pectoral muscles
C8: Palm and fingers

The thoracic nerves affect:

T1: Arms and hands
T2: Heart
T3: Lungs, bronchials
T4: Gallbladder
T5: Liver
T6: Stomach

T7: Pancreas, duodenum
T8: Spleen
T9: Adrenal glands
T10: Kidneys
T11: Ureters
T12: Small intestines

The lumbar nerves affect:

L1: Large intestines
L2: Appendix and thigh
L3: Bladder and hamstring muscle

L4: Lower back muscles and prostate
L5: Thigh muscles

The sacrum nerves affect:

S1: Upper leg
S2: Inner thigh muscle

S3: Buttock and hip
S4: Reproductive organs

The nervous system is key to the operation of the body. Reflexology works closely with the nervous system, through the actual nerves in the feet as well as the reflections of the body found on the feet. (E)

Chapter 20

Close Down, Cool Out

You have thumb walked the zones and reflexed the reflexes. You've used the hook-in and pull-back technique to pinpoint certain areas and finger walking to work into particular vicinities. You've had to rotate, circle, press, hold, and butterfly different reflexes during the session. The reflexology treatment is coming to a close, and you want to allow for a harmonious transition.

Close Down

As you prepare to end the session, it is important to allow the receiver the time and space to become grounded and incorporate what has just transpired. First, go back to each foot and work any reflex points that need more attention. These would be the reflexes that called to you during the session.

Perhaps an area was extrasensitive. Or a point resisted your fingers. Maybe another area was too pliable. The more you practice reflexology,

FIGURE 20-1
As you close down, walk the zones on each foot one last time.

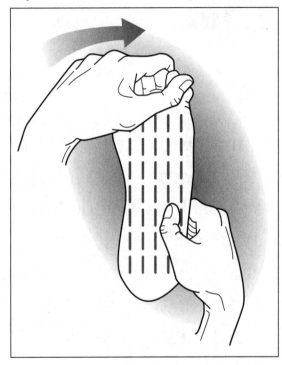

the more aware and alert your fingers and your senses will become to the underlying tensions found in the feet.

Make a practice of gently walking the zones on each foot one last time (as shown in **FIGURE 20-1**), to ensure all reflex points have been properly worked. Walk your fingers down the tops of the feet and in between the metatarsal bones as a final walk-through. This is a gentle cradling of the body, sewing together any loose ends.

Cool Out

Move from working the zones and place your hands gently on the soles of both feet. Allow the heat from your hands to flow into the soles of the receiver's feet. Recommend that the recipient take a deep, slow breath, and you breathe as well. Let your rhythm and the receiver's resonate in a soft, gentle flow of energy.

Hold the right foot, gently moving the foot from side to side; then rotate, changing directions after three turns. Wring the foot from the bottom to the top, and back down again, three times. You are employing the relaxation techniques as a way to bring all the work together.

Hold the left foot and repeat the gentle movements of turning the foot in and out. Rotate the foot in each direction, turning three times in and then three times out. Wring the foot completely. Bring your hands to the Achilles tendon and the back of the leg, just above the heel. Let one hand cup this area and the other hand firmly hold on the top of the foot. The hand holding the top of the foot is wrapped right over the anklebone and is holding gently but firmly.

Imagine the hip and with a steady, even, yet gentle pressure, pull the leg straight back toward your chest. You will feel a slight answer of pressure flowing back toward you through the leg. As you become aware of this pressure, stop and hold the position. Count to three slowly and release, letting the leg gently relax.

After placing the foot down, move to the right foot and gently cup the heel and hold firmly on the ankle. Again imagine the hip, think of the hip relaxing, and gently pull the leg straight out toward you. Hold once you feel the leg resist, count to three, and release. You'll move on from this to the karate chops. The receiver is aware, on some level, of the transition.

ALERT!

Remember to apply this technique gently. Never pull the leg straight up or too forcefully. This is a loving move that allows complete relaxation of the entire leg and hip. If you do not feel comfortable performing this technique, don't do it.

Karate Chops

The close down can be started on either foot. Most begin on the foot they finished last, which in this case is the left foot. Remember, on the warm-up and cool down, you have the freedom to move back and forth.

The karate chop technique is first. Hold both hands horizontally to the bottom of the foot; the outside edges of the hands come in contact with the sole. Moving the hands back and forth rapidly, chop from the heel to the toes and back down the foot. Repeat this chopping motion, up and down the bottom surface, in a steady, rhythmic beat.

Let the fingers of the hands flop loosely against one another. The fingers relax as the chopping motion begins to ground the receiver. This procedure is stimulating and refreshing, announcing to the receiver, "It is time to come back."

Karate chops stimulate the feet and the entire body. As you perform this technique, you are bringing the receiver's consciousness to the feet. This method relaxes the connective tissue, stimulating the fascia protecting the layers of muscles.

Karate chops are highly effective in assisting the repair of plantar fasciitis. The quick invigorating movement creates a healing environment for the stressed tissue. An inflamed heel bursa will begin to find release as well.

Tapping and Clapping

The tapping technique is another method involved with the close-down routine. Steady, rhythmic tapping, with all the fingers, results in a warm feeling on the sole's surface. You may actually see the skin pink up. Using both hands, tap gently and progressively along the surface of the foot, top and bottom. Tap along the sides as well, letting the entire foot feel the sensation.

Of course, this technique—in fact, all close-down techniques—is applied to both feet. Here is a section where moving back and forth is acceptable. Feel free to work these methods as you wish. Tapping allows your fingers to relax; as you freely tap along the surfaces of the feet, your fingers are loosely grouped. This is an area where you receive as well as give.

Use both hands on the foot you are working on. With the foot sandwiched in between the hands, clap. The full hand claps on the foot's surface. The foot feels protected and stimulated. Repeat this on the other foot. You are applauding the feet for receiving the treatment.

Double Solar Plexus Press

Using this powerful technique in closure covers many arenas. Press into both solar plexus reflexes, at the same time. Using your fingers, reach up to the toes and gently pull the toe tops down toward the thumb. As the toes pull down, press in farther at the reflex.

Ask the receiver to take a slow, deep, and full breath. Remind the recipient to hold the breath for a moment, and then to slowly release the breath. Let the person imagine the breath flowing down the legs and out of the feet. Instruct the receiver to relax and breathe normally.

Press in again, asking the recipient to breathe in slowly, this time attaching her favorite color to the breath. Let the person imagine the breath coming up to the top of her head. You are steadily pressing into the solar plexus reflexes. Now let the recipient slowly release the breath, imagining the color washing down the body and out of the feet. After a second of relaxing, follow this procedure once more.

This process allows the receiver to fully embrace the relaxation. This also encourages the receiver to recognize that the session is ending.

FACT

Sensitive reflexes indicate congestion, in the feet and in the body. The receiver may feel a sharp pinprick or a sore spot as the giver reflexes the feet. Pay attention to the recipient's body language; a sudden muscle tension is a signal of a painful reflex.

Quiet, Please

The session is complete, the receiver is relaxed, and the music is playing quietly. Adjust the cover on the recipient, making sure she or he is comfortable. Dim the lights or alter the window shades as you leave the room to wash your hands. It is important to allow this quiet moment. All stimuli has been removed, nothing within this energy can create tension. Balance and harmony is restored and remembered. The receiver will keep this stress-free memory, recalling this moment again and again as needed.

Reflexology gives the body, mind, and spirit a feeling of renewal. The recipient is calmer, stronger, and more energized by the treatment.

Always include a time of quiet at the end of the session to bring together the substance of the treatment.

After you have washed your hands, it is time to sit the receiver up in the chair. Let the receiver sit for a bit, becoming centered and focused.

ALERT!

Do not let the receiver get up immediately. Create an atmosphere that encourages the recipient to enjoy the rest time. A progression from total relaxation back to reality must be allowed. Help the receiver to become grounded before leaving the chair. A glass of water in an upright position usually is effective.

Congratulations!

Reflexology is everything to everybody. The surprising and delightful plus to this work is the empowerment of the receiver. You have just finished a relaxing and refreshing reflexology session. The person in the chair is better equipped to deal with life's journey than when she or he walked in. The actual reflexing has allowed the receiver to de-stress and recharge. Congratulations, you have completed the reflexology session! This is a joyful work we do!

Reflexology and Other Modalities

Reflexology works well with other holistic healing techniques. Reiki, an energy-healing technique, and reflexology make a dynamic combination. Reiki technique increases the effect of reflexology, supporting the balance and harmony achieved.

Acupressure, shiatsu, and acupuncture are all complemented with the addition of reflexology. Any massage session is more dynamic with reflexology included. A pedicure combined with reflexology keeps people coming back!

Reflexology in hospice is a compassionate and sensitive addition when touch is so important. Any inclusion of reflexology with contemporary treatment is a supportive addition. People recovering from surgeries, cancer treatments, or any other severe conditions report the use of reflexology as a welcome supplement.

The Minisession

Many times you will find yourself in situations when the full session may not be appropriate. You would like to practice on your aunt, who is bedridden. Perhaps there is a new baby in the family. Your little sister has watched you practice on people and wants you to work on her. Trades with family members are great. Go ahead, work on your younger sibling or your mate or your child, and then ask them to work on you!

Benefits of a Minisession

A minisession is relaxing and balancing, without working all the specific areas. You can use this type of session when you are under time constraints, such as at health fairs or community centers. The minisession is also used with people who have a short attention span, such as infants and children. Infants love to have their feet touched, as long as it is not for too long a span of time. Children of all ages love reflexology; once children receive a treatment, they always want more.

FACT

Reflexology minisessions work all the zones of the feet, allowing the practitioner to provide a soothing treatment. Comprehensive coverage of all reflexes and points is completed in the longer, full session. The shorter version is a successful means of demonstrating the techniques, while providing a service.

A minisession is a good marketing tool as well. Once a consumer has received a smaller, less labor-intensive session, they want the whole deal. Learning a short session is achieving another technique in this journey of healing.

In the Beginning

Always ask the person or the caretaker of the person for information about any key health issues. Ask the potential recipient if she or he has any health concerns that you need to be aware of. People will share their pertinent information as they hear that you genuinely wish to know.

After listening for any current complaints, move on to clean the feet. Disposable sanitary wipes, the kind used for babies, are a good cleansing tool. Use alcohol and fragrance-free wipes, and clean the feet, at the same time assessing for any open cuts, or areas that need to be covered, such as plantar warts.

What Is Included

Keep in mind that you should always begin the mini with the complete warm-up. Begin on the right foot and use all the warm-up methods. Push and pull the foot in a gentle motion, once or twice. Turn the foot in and out and move on to wringing the foot, moving up and down the foot once. Rotate the foot clockwise and counterclockwise once or twice and then warm up the spinal reflex by twisting the reflex with both hands. Gently use the push and pull, walk up the reflex and down, and, cupping the heels of the palms under the ankle, shake.

Let the foot completely relax with this shaking, moving down to shake from the heel as well. A gentle, deep solar plexus push will allow the recipient to begin to relax fully. Complete this warm-up on the left foot. Return to the right and thumb walk all the toes, to the edge of the foot and back to the center, once through. Knuckle press the entire bottom of the foot a few times.

Thumb walk, circle the chakras, and zigzag on the spinal reflex. Perform each technique twice. Heel press along and thumb walk the sciatic line; then heel press the heel and move on. Thumb walk the zones, and you have finished the right foot. Repeat this process on the left foot, ending with the zones.

Karate chops will announce the end of the session. Notice how relaxed the recipient is. This minisession does relax and balance the receiver. Once the close-down series is complete on both feet, don't forget the solar plexus press.

Chapter 21

When Is Reflexology Not a Good Idea?

Reflexology is always a good idea; however, there are times when a referral to a medical practitioner may be appropriate. Certain conditions require medical assistance as well as complementary treatments. It is essential for a reflexologist to know when to work on a person and when not to.

Overall, Reflexology Is a Safe Technique

Reflexology can never hurt anyone. A practitioner of reflexology always takes a medical history, enabling the receiver to receive the best, most productive, and safest treatment available. Before a person receives reflexology, the practitioner spends a good amount of time discussing the health and well-being of that person. They ask many questions about overall health, about medical care, and about the tension and stress in the life of the person to be treated. If you were seeing a professional reflexologist, you would be asked to provide your name, mailing address, phone, and date of birth. The reflexologist would also ask you certain key questions about your life, such as:

- What causes stress in your life?
- When did you last see your doctor? What for?
- Do you have any current health issues?
- Are you on any medication? If yes, for what?
- Do you visit a chiropractor? How often?
- Do you receive any other adjunct therapies?
- Have you had any past injuries, accidents, surgeries, or ailments?
- Do you have any allergies?
- Do you exercise? How often?
- Are you pregnant?
- What areas of your body hold tension?
- Do you have any discomfort in your feet? If so, describe.
- Have you ever had reflexology before? If so, describe.
- What are you goals in seeking reflexology at this time?

Once a receiver has answered these questions, the reflexologist has a clearer idea of the needs of the receiver. The practitioner can assess the level of comfort the receiver feels as well as understand the person's expectations. The giver will know of any contraindications as well as the amount of pressure to use. The reflexologist will also have knowledge of areas of tenderness on the feet as well as reflex areas.

Professional practitioners of reflexology provide a disclaimer and consent form for their recipients. These forms succinctly clarify for the receiver what the reflexologist is and what the reflexologist is not. Use of these forms allows the receiver to become actively involved in his or her wellness.

A consent form gives the practitioner permission to work on the receiver. At the same time, the receiver is responsible for following through with any and all plans of treatment from other providers. The receiver keeps the reflexologist apprised of any change in his or her health.

FACT

A reflexologist never tells a receiver what to do with regard to any medical treatment the receiver may be receiving. A reflexologist supports and encourages the recipient's journey toward wellness, accompanying the receiver along the path. The receiver's medical doctor will change or adjust the medical treatment as necessary.

It's Not Appropriate When . . .

Under certain circumstances a reflexologist will not even consider working on a person. Deep vein thrombosis is a blood clot, and if a receiver has this condition, the reflexologist would not work on the feet. Often people are treated for this with wonderful clot-preventing medicines; a detailed receiver history will tell of this. This is a condition where a doctor's permission is necessary.

A condition called *compartment syndrome* is painful and progressive. Often caused by the repetitive motion of athletic running, this increased pressure and swelling is usually found in the muscles of the lower leg. Pain or loss of feeling in the toes will indicate this condition is acute! Immediate referral to the emergency room is required.

Avoid These Reflexes

Pregnant women benefit from reflexology, as does the growing baby. The short method described in the previous chapter would be most beneficial during the first three months of pregnancy. Following this, full sessions are acceptable. The professional reflexologist may work through the entire pregnancy, even to being present in the delivery room.

Any bleeding during pregnancy is an immediate referral to the receiver's physician. Many reflexologists find it is best to avoid pressure to the uterus reflex during pregnancy, working all other reflexes, helping to create a warm and loving environment for mother and baby. However, the uterus reflex may be worked during labor.

FACT

Reflexology is very helpful during labor, relaxing the muscles, allowing for increase in circulation, and providing overall relaxation. Of course, permission from the attending caregiver is needed. The laboring mom feels stronger, breathes better, and is more involved when relaxed. Reflexology supports this outcome.

Diabetes

Diabetics benefit from reflexology as peripheral circulation is encouraged during a session. Diabetes affects the circulation in the body. The supply of blood does not easily reach the nerves in the feet and hands, causing burning pain, unpleasant tingling, even lack of feeling in these extremities. If a reflexologist observes any swelling, cuts, sores, or discoloration in a diabetic receiver's feet, he or she must refer the receiver immediately to the person's medical practitioner.

ALERT!

Often receivers put off seeking medical attention, not wanting to make a big deal of their condition. Professional reflexologists make it a practice to follow up any suggested referral. They ask the receiver to give an updated report from the medical provider as they offer support and encouragement.

Dilated Varicose Veins

Arteries carry oxygenated blood from the heart to the body. Veins carry the deoxygenated blood from the body back to the heart. Valves of the veins close, pushing the blood back toward the heart. If the valves are weak, gravity can force some of the blood back down the veins, away from the direction of the heart. The backload of blood weakens the wall of the vein, making the vein bulge and stretch.

Most varicose veins form pouches that hold the backed-up blood. The veins closer to the skin are more apt to have this weakened condition, which makes varicose veins visible. Varicose veins actually look worse than they are. Because these veins cannot carry the blood back to the heart, the blood will find another alternate vein to continue the work.

The alternate veins attempt to carry most of the blood out of the pouches back to the heart. These veins are smaller, designed to carry lesser amounts of blood. Bulges and pouches may form in these veins as well. Varicose veins are generally bluish in color, at times bulging on the surface of the skin.

The great saphenous vein that runs from the foot to the pelvic region is often the affected vein. If this is the case, the reflexologist may observe a rippled, lumpy bulging vein, running from the ankle up the leg toward the groin. If a vein is bulging in such a manner, the reflexologist will not finger or thumb walk up the leg. It is best to avoid elevated veins, working the rest of the foot, but staying away from these dilated pathways.

Severe Swelling

Swelling of tissue is generally caused by excess fluid that has not been effectively dealt with by the blood and lymph vessels. The excess fluid may have a number of causes. Some swelling can be caused by kidney or liver dysfunction, a blockage in the circulatory system, or an infection.

Any of these conditions would be determined and treated by a medical provider. This swelling may present itself with a pitted surface— as the surface is pressed, it does not spring back. The swelling may be very severe, accompanied by hot or cool temperature, either indicating a systemic condition. Reflexology would not be used under these circumstances unless and until a doctor permitted such treatment.

Some swelling may indicate simple fluid retention. Some people could retain fluid because they work on their feet constantly. People who stand all day, without much movement, may develop chronic swollen ankles.

Once a doctor has ruled out any underlying conditions, you can use reflexology in such situations.

ALERT!

Swelling may indicate an internal injury, such as torn ligaments, resulting in a sprain, strain, or fracture. Do not work on an ankle or foot that is swollen and painful. This is an immediate referral to the primary care physician.

Open Sores or Cuts

Any open sores or cuts cannot be touched, for the health and safety of the receiver as well as the giver. Blisters may occur on the feet, generally from the friction of ill-fitting shoes. Blisters can be closed or open. Either way, these need to be avoided. Generally people have covered the blisters before arriving for the session. If not, keep a supply of good, strong-sticking Band-Aids to cover raw blisters.

Cuts, too, must be covered, to keep them free from bacterial infections. Strep and staph infections can infect open areas of the skin. These can in turn spread from one part of the body to another and from one person to another. Also, be aware that open sores may indicate deeper, underlying, chronic conditions, such as diabetes, or may be related to contagious skin disorders.

Contagious or Infectious Conditions

The feet may have some conditions that a reflexologist should not work on. Athlete's foot is one such condition. Athlete's foot affects athletes and many others who do not participate in sports. The transmission of this fungal infection, *tinea pedis,* may be from walking barefoot, using someone else's shoes, or from shared towels and bath mats. Whatever the cause, reflexologists do not work on an active case of athlete's foot.

Prevention is the best remedy for this condition. Basic health care, such as drying feet, especially in between the toes after bathing, is crucial as well as keeping the feet as dry as possible. Wearing white cotton athletic socks helps to prevent the warm environment needed for the growth of this fungus.

Choose shoes that can breathe, such as leather or canvas, to keep the foot well ventilated. Using a swim sneaker or flip-flop sandal at the pool or bathhouse will also help prevent transmission. To prevent an outbreak at home, change bath mats frequently.

Nail Fungus

Nail fungus generally grows in the same environment as athlete's foot. The nail may become thick and raised. A discoloration may appear with some nail fungus. Sometimes the nail is painful. You can work on these nails, though it is good practice to keep disposable gloves in your work area. Use gloves for the first part of the session if the nails are really affected. If the nails are not terribly affected, thumb walk the toe area and then wash your hands before continuing the session. If gloves were used, remove the gloves before continuing.

FACT

Always make a referral to a medical professional; do not diagnose the condition. Establishing a relationship with a local podiatrist is good practice, for those people who do not have a podiatric doctor of their own. Nail fungus has a variety of treatments, which will be decided by the medical doctor.

Plantar Warts

Plantar warts may look like a callus, but they are infectious viral conditions of the skin. The center of the wart will have tiny black or red dots, and when squeezed from the side is painful. If pushing from the top causes the pain, it is probably a callus or corn. Again, it is not your job to diagnose; leave that to the medical people. A plantar wart is a virus; therefore, you should cover this spot before working on the feet. Small round Band-Aids work well as covers, then you can thumb walk over the area.

Prevention is the best plan of action. Walking barefoot in public areas leaves the foot susceptible to the virus. The wart virus can live in any warm area: your shoes, the gym, the locker room, the swimming pool, or the bath and shower mat. Take care to prevent infection. Once a wart begins to grow on the plantar surface, it can burrow in deeply.

Poison Oak, Ivy, and Sumac

Exposure to these plants can cause an allergic contact dermatitis, which may produce itchy, fluid-filled blisters on the body. If a receiver has such blisters on the feet, ankles, or legs, do not work on the area! Explain to the receiver that until the reaction has run its course, the lesions could continue to spread. Recommend he check with his physician before returning for a reflexology session.

Soft-Tissue Infections

Whenever you have a question relating to your visual assessment of the receiver's feet, it is best to make a referral to a podiatrist. If you find bumps, blisters, scratches, cuts, sores, raw lesions, or any other irregularities that you are not sure of, you need a doctor's okay to work on those areas. Never perform reflexology if you have no knowledge of what is on the person's foot. You do not want to spread infection further, nor do you want exposure through contact.

Current Break or Sprain

A break in a bone may also be called a fracture. Bones break due to force or bone disease. Fractures may be classified by injury. The different fractures are:

- **Simple:** The break in the bone does not break the skin.
- **Compound:** The break includes tearing of soft tissue and protrusion through the skin.
- **Impacted:** The broken ends of the bones are pushed together.
- **Comminuted:** Several bones are splintered.
- **Spiral:** The bone is twisted apart.
- **Greenstick:** There are many little breaks, but the bone is not completely broken.

A reflexologist does not work on a broken bone until the attending physician gives permission. Reflexology does allow the receiver to relax, assisting in the healing; therefore, you can work on areas of the foot that are not broken or on the hands.

A sprain occurs when the joint is twisted, such as when we sprain an ankle by accidental wrenching of the foot. The muscles and connective tissue surrounding the joints become inflamed, as the blood vessels usually sustain damage. The ligaments that connect the anklebone may swell, become bruised, even become painful. Application of ice and elevation of the foot is the immediate response, with an immediate referral to a doctor.

FACT

Once the doctor has determined that there is no tear in the ligaments, reflexology can help with the swelling and pain. The entire procedure must be gentle, with slow, even movements. Generally reflexologists do not employ any turning, pulling, or chopping methods during this form of treatment.

Fever

Fever is nature's way of indicating something is out of balance within the body. Homeostasis is affected. The cause of a fever could be an infection, either bacterial or viral. However, a fever may come from a heart attack, tumor, surgery, or trauma. A fever may be a reaction to a vaccine, or a reaction to the destruction of tissues due to x-rays.

Fever comes to assist cells that have ingested toxins. The fever-producing substance, pyrogen, stimulates the hypothalamus, which in turn works to regulate body temperature. The pyrogens work to destroy the bacterial or viral toxins, assisting in the production of infection-fighting cells. The fever increases the metabolism, causing the body to fight for balance quicker and harder.

The return of homeostasis is the ideal outcome of a fever. Reflexology can assist in working with the body to speed up this process. Once the cause of the fever has been determined, reflexology can integrate with other modalities, working to create harmony.

Cancer

Cancers seem to be systemic, relating to different systems of the body. All must have medical treatment, and the inclusion of holistic treatment is on the rise. What do we really know about cancer? Research has been done to unearth some of the underlying causes of cancer. Environment may be considered as one of the causative factors. Pollutants of the air and water seem to be contributors to cancer development. Too much exposure to the ultraviolet rays of the sun may cause cancer is some people.

Some carcinogens—cancer-causing agents—may be work related. People who work around certain chemicals, asbestos, or radiation are at greater risk for cancer. Cigarette smoking is linked to cancer.

All reflexologists work to establish a healing situation with honor and respect for the recipient. Reflexology is growing as a recognized modality. It has evolved to a profession of well-educated and trained individuals all working for the common good.

Chemicals in shampoo, preservatives in foods, and chemicals used to develop certain materials used in our homes all may have carcinogens. We live in a chemical world of convenience; unfortunately, it is this very convenience that may have introduced different forms of cancer into our lives. Viruses may also cause cancer. Some chronic viral infections can lead to the development of cancer.

Whatever the causes of cancer, the disease promotes a huge amount of stress in the body. Reflexology is a gentle, effective tool used to assist in supporting and encouraging the well-being of the receiver.

Research is ongoing with regard to the treatment of cancer. Reflexology will play an active role in creating a healing environment during and after the course of medical treatment. Reflexologists use sensitive and compassionate touch in their work, integrating the reflexology techniques with the work of medical professionals. Their common goal is to aid in maintaining harmony and wholeness for the receiver. Ⓔ

Appendices

Appendix A

Reflexology
Reference Charts

Appendix B

Resources

Appendix C

Glossary

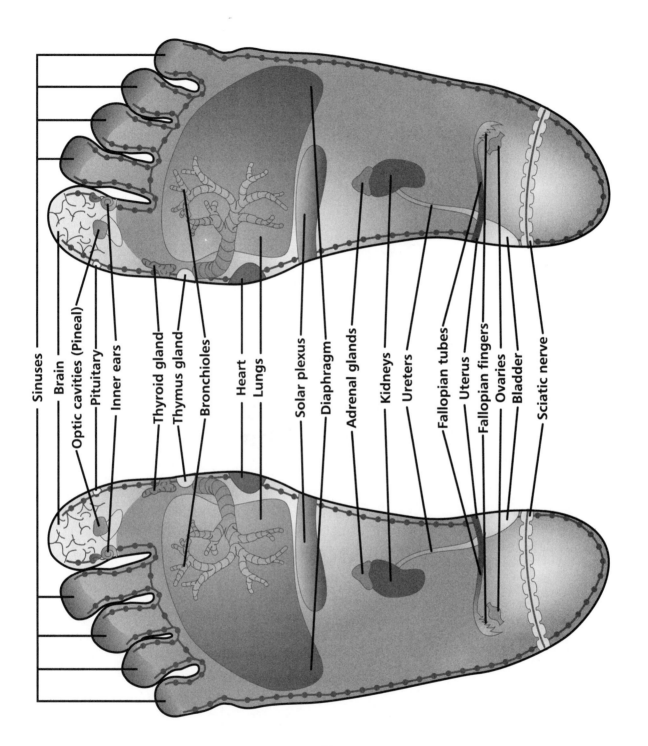

FIGURE A-1   Foot Chart 1

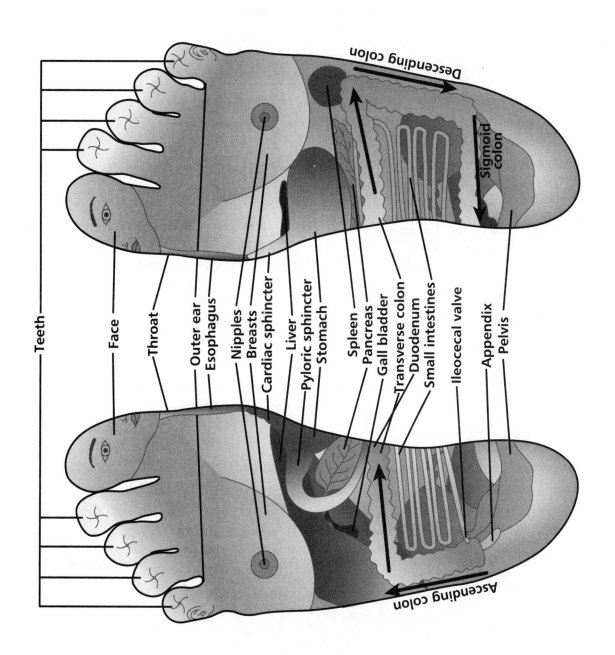

FIGURE A-2 Foot Chart 2

Inside Foot Reflexes

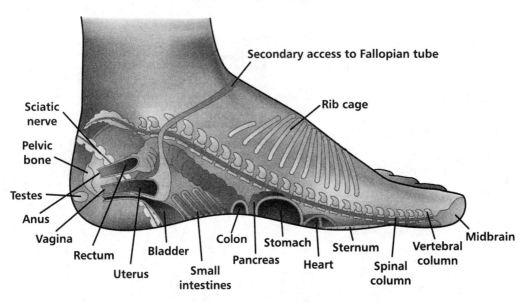

FIGURE A-3   Inside Foot Chart

Outside Foot Reflexes

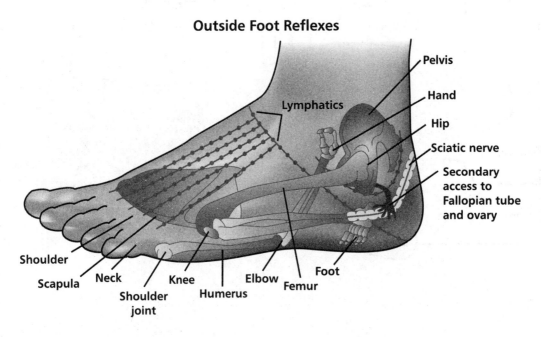

FIGURE A-4   Outside Foot Chart

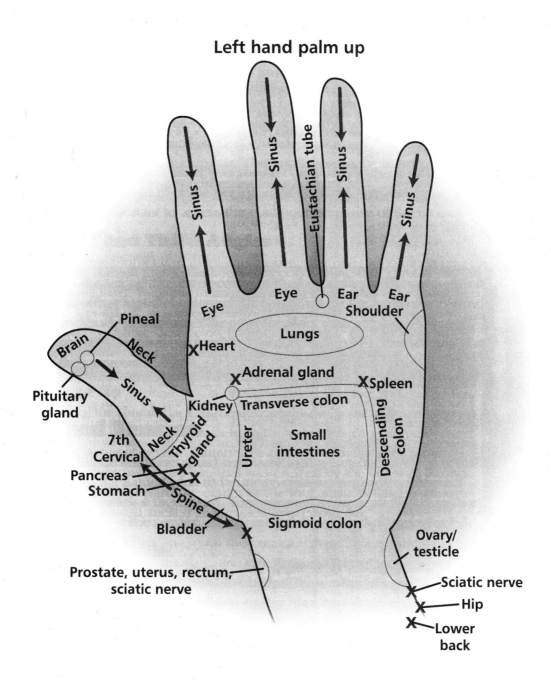

FIGURE A-5 Hand Chart

Appendix B

Resources

Books

Adamson, Suzanne and Eilish Harris. *The Reflexology Partnership.*

Bayley, Doreen E. *Reflexology Today.*

Berkson, Devaki. *The Foot Book.*

Blate, Michael. *How to Heal Yourself Using Foot Acupressure: Foot Reflexology.*

Breeding, Diane and Paul. *Success at the Last Resort.*

Brown Whichello, Denise. *Hand Reflexology.*

Brown Whichello, Denise. *Reflexology Basics.*

Brunnstrom, Signe, M.A. *Clinical Kinesiology.*

Byers, Dwight C. *Better Health with Foot Reflexology.*

Cailliet, Rene, M.D. *Foot and Ankle Pain.*

Carter, Mildred and Tammy Weber. *Body Reflexology.*

Carter, Mildred and Tammy Weber. *Hand Reflexology.*

Cash, Mel. *Pocket Atlas of the Moving Body.*

Cosway-Hayes, Joan. *Reflexology for Every Body.*

Crane, Beryl. *Reflexology: An Illustrated Guide.*

Crane, Beryl. *Reflexology: The Definitive Practitioner's Manual.*

Dougans, Inge. *The Complete Illustrated Guide to Reflexology.*

Dougans, Inge. *Reflexology: A Practical Introduction.*

Dougans, Inge and Suzanne Ellis. *The Art of Reflexology.*

Gillanders, Ann. *The Busy Person's Guide to Reflexology.*

Gillanders, Ann. *The Joy of Reflexology.*

Gordon, Richard. *Your Healing Hands.*

Grinberg, Avi. *Foot Analysis.*

Hall, Nicola M. *Reflexology.*

Hall, Nicola M. *Reflexology for Women.*

Hall, Nicola M. *Thorsons Introductory Guide to Reflexology.*

Hess, Shelley. *The Professional's Reflexology Handbook.*

Hill Ardell, Deborah. *Spiritual Reflexology: Spiritual Gifts of the Body.*

Ingham, Eunice D. *Stories the Feet Have Told Thru Reflexology.*

Issel, Christine. *Reflexology: Art, Science and History.*

Jora, Jürgen. *Foot Reflexology.*

Kaiser, Jürgen. *Hand Reflexology.*

Kaye, Anna and Don C. Matchan. *Reflexology for Good Health.*

Kluck, Michelle R. *Hands on Feet.*

Kolster, Bernard, M.D. *Reflexology.*

Kunz, Kevin and Barbara. *The Complete Guide to Foot Reflexology.*

Kunz, Kevin and Barbara. *Hand and Foot Reflexology.*

Kunz, Kevin and Barbara. *Hand Reflexology Workbook.*

Kunz, Kevin and Barbara. *The Parent's Guide to Reflexology.*

Leonard, Charles H. *Gray's Pocket Anatomy.*

Levine, Suzanne M., D.P.M. *Your Feet Don't Have to Hurt.*

Levine, Suzanne, M., D.P.M. *50 Ways to Ease Foot Pain.*

Manzanares, J., M.D. *Principles of Reflexology.*

Marquardt, Hanne. *Reflexotherapy of the Feet.*

McAllister, Russell. *Reflexology World Magazine.*

McLaughlin, Chris and Nicola M. Hall. *Secrets of Reflexology.*

McMinn, Robert M. H., Ralph T. Hutchings, and Bari M. Logan. *Foot and Ankle Anatomy.*

Mochizuki, Shogo. *Zoku Shin Do: The Art of East Asian Foot Reflexology.*

Norman, Laura, with Thomas Cowan. *Feet First.*

Oxenford, Rosalind. *Discover Reflexology.*

Oxenford, Rosalind. *Healing with Reflexology.*

Oxenford, Rosalind. *Reflexology for Health and Well-Being.*

Pritt, Dr. Donald S. and Dr. Morton Walker. *The Complete Foot Book.*

Reid, Elsa and Susanne Enzer. *Maternity Reflexology.*

Rick, Stephanie. *The Reflexology Workout.*

Roberts, Elizabeth H., D.P.M. *On Your Feet.*

Rogers, Sandi. *Anatomy Charts for Reflexology.* Teacher and student editions.

Rogers, Sandi, with Christine Issel. *Reflexognosy.*

Rude, Paul. *Souls to Soles.*

Sachs, Judith and Judith Berger. *Reflexology, The A–Z Guide to Healing with Pressure Points.*

Segal, Dr. Maybelle. *Reflexology.*

Seig, Kay W. and Sandra P. Adams. *Illustrated Essentials of Musculoskeletal Anatomy.*

Senneff, John A. *Numb Toes and Aching Soles.*

Soble, Dr. Michelle, D.P.M., P.C. *Podiatry for the Reflexologist.*

Sohnen-Moe, Cherie. *Business Mastery*, 3rd edition.

Somogyi, Imre. *Reading Toes.*

Spurzem, Dr. Wolfgang. *Foot Reflexology: Simple Self-Treatment.*

Stinnett, Leia A. *Happy Feet: A Child's Guide to Foot Reflexology.*

Stormer, Chris. *Language of the Feet.*

Stormer, Chris. *Reflexology.*

Stormer, Chris. *Reflexology, the Definitive Guide.*

Stormer, Chris. *Teach Yourself Reflexology.*

Strauss, Nathan B. *Reflexology: A Practical Guide.*

Thomas, Sherryll. *The Ear Work Book.*

Tortora, Gerard J. *Introduction to the Human Body.*

Tremaine, David, M., M.D. and Elias M. Awad, Ph.D. *The Foot & Ankle Sourcebook*, 2nd edition.

Vennells, David F. *Reflexology for Beginners.*

Wills, Pauline. *The Reflexology and Color Therapy Workbook.*

Wills, Pauline. *The Reflexology Manual.*

Wolfe, Frankie Avalon. *The Complete Idiot's Guide to Reflexology.*

Wright, Janet. *Reflexology and Acupressure.*

How-to Workshops and Courses

Academy of Natural Healing
5114 South Emporia Way
Greenwood Village, CO 80111
✆ 303-779-1094
✉ isabellehutton@yahoo.com

Academy of Reflexology & Health Therapy International
8397 East 10th Street
Indianapolis, IN 46219-5330
✆ 317-897-5111

American Academy of Reflexology
606 East Magnolia, Suite B
Burbank, CA 91501
✆ 818-841-7741

Arizona Institute of Reflexology
1660 South Alma School Road, Suite 201
Mesa, AZ 85202
✆ 480-820-3880

Australian School of Reflexology
25 Nords Wharf Road
Nords Wharf
New South Wales 2281
✉ www.reflexologyaustralia.com

Bay State Academy of Holistic Health
563 Main Street, #9
Bolton, MA 01740
✆ 978-779-7955

Beacon of Light Center
227 Royal Arms Way
Glen Burnie, MD 21061
✆ 410-760-8883

Beaumont College of Natural Medicine
MWB Business Exchange
Hinton Road
Bournemouth BH1 2EF
United Kingdom
✉ www.beaumontcollege.co.uk

British School of Reflexology
✉ www.footreflexology.com

Center for Universal Reflexology
250 Wolcott Road
Wolcott, CT 06716
✆ 203-879-3111
✉ tjenson@snet.net

Center for Universal Reflexology
800 Knibb Road
Pascoaq, RI 02859
✆ 401-765-6363
✉ footlady@aol.com

Foot Prints Wellness Center
2121 Watt, Suite D
Little Rock, AR 72227
✆ 501-225-6463

Healing Feats Holistic Health Services
7 Whitehawk Circle
Boise, ID 83716
✆ 208-343-3482

International Academy of Reflexology
1177 Sixth Street
Whitehall, PA 18052
✆ 610-403-3837

International College of Universal Reflexologies
106 SE Weir Street
Camas, WA 98607
✆ 360-335-1195

International Institute of Reflexology
P.O. Box 12642
St. Petersburg, FL 33733-2642
☎ 727-343-4811

Kunz School of Reflexology
P.O. Box 35820, Station D
Albuquerque, NM 87173-5829
☎ 800-713-6711

Laura Norman and Associates Reflexology Center
41 Park Avenue, Suite 8A
New York, NY 10016
☎ 212-532-4404

Modern Institute of Reflexology
7063 West Colfax Avenue
Lakewood, CO 80215
☎ 800-533-1837

New England Institute of Reflexology and Universal Studies
P.O. Box 1718
3203C Cranberry Highway
Onset, MA 02558
☎ 508-291-1729
✍ www.walkinbalance.com

Pacific Institute of Reflexology
535 West 10th Avenue
Vancouver, British Columbia V521K9
☎ 800-688-9748

Reflexology Academy of Southern Africa
P.O. Box 1280
Rivonia 2128, Republic of South Africa

Reflexology Seminars of New York
11173A 2nd Avenue, Suite 264
New York, NY 10021
☎ 212-517-5532

Reiki Blessings Academy
P.O. Box 2000
Byron, GA 31008-2000
☎ 478-956-8974

Sandra Day School of Health Studies
Ashley House
185A Drake Street
Rochdale Lancs OL11 1EF
United Kingdom
✍ www.sandraday.com

School of Holistic Massage & Reflexology
1040 Ogden Avenue
Downers Grove, IL 60515

Seattle Reflexology & Massage Center
419 Queen Anne Avenue North, Suite 107
Seattle, WA 98109-4518
☎ 206-284-8389

Sister Rosalind Gefre, School of Massage
149 Thompson Avenue E
West St. Paul, MN 55118
☎ 651-554-3010

Treat Your Feet School of Reflexology
93 Gage Street
Augusta, ME 04330
✍ www.treatyourfeet.com

Worldwide Associations

Reflexology Association of Australia
P.O. Box 366
Cammeray, NSW 2062, Australia

International Council of Reflexologists (ICR)
P.O. Box 78060
Westcliffe Postal Outlet
Hamilton, ON L9C7N5, Canada
☎ 905-387-8449
✍ www.icr-reflexology.org

Ontario College of Reflexology
P.O. Box 220 New Liskeard
Ontario POJ 1PO, Canada
✎ 888-OCR-FEET

Reflexology Association of British Columbia
#214-3707 Hamber Place
North Vancouver, BC, V7G2J4, Canada

Reflexology Association of Canada (RAC)
#204, 17930-105 Avenue
Edmonton, Alberta T5S2H5, Canada

China Reflexology Association
P.O. Box 2002
Beijing 100026, China

Danish Reflexologists Association
Secretariat, Overgade 14
1.tv.5000 Odense, Denmark

Association of Reflexologists
27 Old Gloucester Street
London WCIN 3XX, England

British Reflexology Association
Monks Orchard, Whitbourne
Worcester, WR6 5RB, England

Association of Finish Reflexologists
Albertinkatu 5, 00150
Helsinki, Finland

Federation Francais des Reflexologues
60 Rue de la Colonie
75013 Paris, France

Deutscher Reflexologen Verband (DRV)
Hakenfelder Str. 9A
D-13587 Berlin, Germany

Hellenic Association of Reflexologists
84 Alkionis Str. P. Faliro 17562
Athens, Greece

Rwo-Shr Health Institute International
Room 1902 Java Commercial Centre
128 Java Road
North Point, Hong Kong

Associated Reflexologists of India
X/3275 Raghubar Pura, #2 Gali #3
Gandhi Nagar, Delhi 110031, India

Indian Society for Promotion of Reflexology
D-6-B M.I.G. Flats
G-8 Area (Rajouri Garden)
Mayapuri, New Delhi-110064, India

National Register of Reflexologists (Ireland)
The Register Unit 13
Upper Mall, Terryland Retail Park
Headford Road
Galway, Ireland

Israeli Reflexologists
P.O. Box 39220
Tel Aviv 61391, Israel

Federatzione Italiana di Reflessologis del Piede
c/o MEDIA Piazza Locatelli 10
24043 Caravaggio BG, Italy

Reflexology Association of Japan
Ginza-Fuji Bldg. 4F 1-7-10 Ginza
Chuou-ku, Tokyo, 104-0061, Japan

Association of European Reflexologists
P.O. Box 9009, 1006 AA
Amsterdam, Netherlands

New Zealand Reflexology Association
P.O. Box 31 084
Auckland 9, New Zealand

Association of Reflexology (AR)
Rua de Santa Catarina, 722-3dto
4000 Oporto, Portugal

The South African Reflexology Society
P.O. Box 18850
Dalbridge, 4014, South Africa

Association Suisse D'Etude de la Reflexologie
2001 Neuchatel
Casa Postale 126, Switzerland

**The American Reflexology Certification Board
(ARCB)**
P.O. Box 740879
Arvada, CO 80006, U.S.A.
✆ 303-933-6921
✑ *www.arcb.net*

Reflexology Association of America (RAA)
4012 South Rainbow, Suite K-PMB # K585
Las Vegas, NV 89103-2059, U.S.A.
✆ 702-871-9522
✑ *www.reflexology-usa.org*

Worldwide Reflexology Associations
✑ *www.reflexology.org*

State Associations

Alabama Reflexology Association (ARA)
P.O. Box 4715
Huntsville, AL 35815

Arizona Reflexology Association (AZRA)
P.O. Box 6175
Mesa, AZ 85216-6175
✆ 520-742-1780

Foot Reflexology Awareness Association (FRAA)
P.O. Box 7622
Mission Hills, CA 91346

Reflexology Association of California (RAC)
P.O. Box 641156
Los Angeles, CA 90064
✆ 714-892-6620
✑ *www.reflexcal.org*

Associated Reflexologists of Colorado (ARC)
P.O. Box 697
Englewood, CO 80151

Georgia Reflexology Association (GRA)
2206 Huntingdon Chase
Atlanta, GA 30350

The Reflexology Association of Hawaii
465 Kapahulu Avenue, Suite 2J
Honolulu, HI 96815
✆ 808-941-2542

Reflexology Association of Illinois (RAI)
P.O. Box 5515
Buffalo Grove, IL 60089-5515

Maine Council of Reflexologists
P.O. Box 5833
Augusta, ME 04330-5833
✆ 207-967-0085
✑ *www.reflexologyofmaine.org*

Maryland Reflexology Association
9332 Shady Creek Way
Baltimore, MD 21234-3434

**New England Association of Reflexology
(NEAR)**
P.O. Box 220
Pascoag, RI 02859
P.O. Box 1718
Onset, MA 02558

Reflexology Association of New Jersey (RANJ)
1721 Prospect Ridge Boulevard
Haddon Heights, NJ 08035
✑ *www.NJreflexOLOGY.org*

**Professional Association of Reflexologists of
New Mexico**
P.O. Box 27292
Albuquerque, NM 87125-7292
✑ *ftreflex2@aol.com*

New York State Reflexology Association (NYSRA)
145 East 23rd Street, Suite 4
New York, NY 10010
212-477-2829
www.newyorkstatereflexology.org

Nevada Reflexology Organization (NRO)
P.O. Box 27108
Las Vegas, NV 89126-1108
702-615-3332
www.nvreflexology.org

North Carolina Reflexology Association
P.O. Box 6441
Hendersonville, NC 28739
828-698-8036

North Dakota Reflexology Association (NDRA)
8661 156th Avenue, NE
Drayton, ND 58225
701-454-6495

Ohio Association of Reflexologists
32945 Detroit Road
Avon, Ohio 44011-2017
440-937-5580

Pennsylvania Reflexology Association (PRA)
P.O. Box 796
Glenside, PA 19038

Washington Reflexology Association
P.O. Box 9111
Seattle, WA 98109-9111
425-891-7569

Reflexology Organization of Wisconsin (ROW)
904 Gail Place
Fort Atkinson, WI 53538

The American Reflexology Certification Board

The American Reflexology Certification Board (ARCB) is a nonprofit board that offers the voluntary national certification test. ARCB has been and continues to be a standard setting guidelines for the profession of reflexology. Most schools base their curriculum on the requirements established by this board. In conjunction with the schools, ARCB has set a continuing-education principle that allows qualified schools and instructors to offer further education in reflexology. Any reflexologist wishing to expand the knowledge of her or his practice will find information either through ARCB or through the schools and associations already listed.

The American Reflexology Certification Board (ARCB)
P.O. Box 740879
Arvada, CO 80006
303-933-6921
www.arcb.net

Glossary

abdominal cavity: The area of the body that contains the stomach, intestines (upper), liver, gallbladder, pancreas, and spleen.

abdominopelvic: The cavity in the body that contains the abdominal cavity and the pelvic cavity, without any dividing structure.

abduction: The movement of the foot away from the center or midline of the body.

acute: A condition that is immediate and severe.

adduction: The movement of the foot toward the center of the body.

adrenal gland: The endocrine glands that sit on top of each kidney. These glands produce hormones of the cortisone family as well as adrenaline.

allergies: A hypersensitivity to certain substances that may manifest in negative reactions.

ankle: The anatomical term for this bone is the *talus*.

ankle joint: This is one of the most mobile joints in the foot.

anterior: The directional term in anatomy that indicates the front of the body.

arches: We have four arches in the foot; these help to carry weight, absorb shock, and to maintain balance.

arthritis: This painful disease results in inflammation of the joints and affects mobility.

articulation: This means the point of meeting between bones; the common name for this function is *joint*.

athlete's foot: The medical terminology is *tinea pedis,* which means "fungus of the foot"; this condition may be caused by fungus or allergic reaction.

back up: This is part of the reflex technique used when a reflexologist pinpoints a reflex.

bacteria: These single-celled organisms can be essential to life or produce disease, depending upon their function.

biomechanic: This is the mechanics of movement and balance in dealing with the body.

blisters: A skin irritation generally caused by rubbing from ill-fitting shoes.

bunion: With this condition the big toe is actually pulled away from the other toes by a tendon. The anatomical name is *hallux abducto valgus,* which means the great toe is abducted (pulled away), causing a deformity.

bursa: A fluid-filled sac slipped between skin and bone to protect the body as one area moves over another.

calcaneus: This is the largest foot bone; it is the heel.

callus: Hardened layers of skin caused by pressure. The pressure comes from the way we walk or ill-fitting shoes. Generally calluses are found on the bottom of the foot.

caudal: An anatomical term of direction indicating near the spine.

chronic: A condition that lasts for a long time, showing no improvement, such as chronic pain.

claw toe: These are toes with some bones that bend up, dorsiflex, and then some bones that bend down, plantarflex.

corns: Calluses found on the top of the foot, on or in between the toes. Corns are usually caused by ill-fitting shoes.

cranial: This is an anatomical term pertaining to direction. Cranial is near the head, or skull.

cuboid: A bone of the foot that sits behind the fourth and fifth metatarsals.

cuneiforms: Bones of the foot that sit behind the first, second, and third metatarsals.

detoxify: A state when toxins leave the body.

diaphragm line: The imaginary horizontal line on the foot, denoting the separation of reflexes reflected on the chest and upper abdomen.

dislocation: The displacement of a bone from its joint, with a tearing of ligaments, tendons, and articular capsules.

distal: This is a term of direction meaning away from the point of origin, with the origin being the body.

dorsal: This is the top of the foot or top of the hand. Dorsal also means the back of the body.

dorsal metatarsal vein: The vein that returns blood to the heart, running along the top of the foot.

dorsal pedis artery: This artery brings blood to the top of the foot.

dorsiflexion: The direction of this movement is bending the foot up toward the body.

eczema: A condition of the skin, which may cause itching and scaling.

edema: A swelling generally around joints and extremities caused from fluid retention.

endocrine system: This system in the body produces the hormones that go directly into the bloodstream.

eversion: A specific ankle movement that turns the sole of the foot away from the center of the body.

extend: A movement of muscles that increases range.

fascia: A connective tissue in the body that provides protection.

fibula: The smaller bone of the lower leg.

flexor: A movement of muscles causing a bending motion.

fungus: An infection caused by yeast or mold.

gliding joint: The name of these joints refers to the movement of bones across bones; in the foot these joints deal with the tarsal bones.

gout: This form of arthritis is generally found around the first metatarsal head and is caused by an excess of uric acid in the body.

great toe: One of the anatomical terms used for the big toe.

hallux: The Latin term for the big toe.

hallux abducto valgus: This is the Latin terminology used to describe what is commonly known as a *bunion*.

hammertoe: This is the term used to name the condition of the toe that has a bone drawn up that cannot straighten; the toe bone is dorsiflexed.

heel bursitis: An inflammation of the bursa of the heel.

hinge joint: The movement of this joint is like that of a hinged door; generally the joint is used to flex and extend.

holistic: This is the body, mind, and spirit concept that reflexology practitioners ascribe to. Healing includes all these parts.

homeostasis: The anatomical term used to describe the internal balance of the body.

ingrown toenail: This is a condition in which the nail grows into the side of the foot, generally from improper cutting of the nails.

interphalangeal joint: Bends the toes at the middle.

inversion: This is an ankle movement that turns the sole of the foot in toward the center.

joints of the foot: The joints of the feet are either hinge joints or gliding joints.

lateral: The lateral direction is toward the outside of the body.

lateral column: This area of the foot is used for support.

ligament: Connective tissue that connects bones to bones.

medial: This directional term means toward the midline of the body.

medial column: The inside of the foot used for balance.

metatarsal bones: These bones connect from the base of the toes to four of the bones of the midfoot.

metatarsophalangeal joint: The MTP is the joint that bends the toes up and down.

midline: Meaning toward the centerline of the body.

muscle: These are tissues used for motion.

navicular: This bone connects between the ankle and the three cuneiform bones.

neuroma: This noncancerous tumor develops generally between the third and fourth toes where the nerves are constantly pinched, due to ill-fitting shoes.

nutrition: The proper balance of nutrients necessary to sustain homeostasis.

odor of the foot: The clinical term is *bromidrosis*. This condition is caused by a bacteria on the feet, stress, chronic disease, fatigue, or the ingestion of strong-smelling foods.

outer longitudinal arch: This outer arch of the foot carries most of the body's weight.

palmer: This is the directional term for the palm of the hand.

phalanges: Anatomical name for the toes.

plantar: The term used for the bottom of the foot.

plantar fasciitis: A painful condition on the sole of the foot; it is an inflammation due to strain on the fascia.

plantar flexion: When the foot is bent down.

plantar wart: This is a viral infection generally found on the floors of pools, gyms, locker rooms, and public bathing facilities.

pronation: This is a movement of the foot involving abduction, eversion, and dorsiflexion.

reflex: An automatic response to a stimulus. Or, a point on the feet, or hands, that reflects an area of the body.

reflexology: Applied pressure to reflex points on the hands and feet using specific finger techniques.

sprain: A forceful trauma to a joint with injury to muscles, ligaments, tendons, and nerves.

spurs: A buildup of calcium in response to stress in the fascia.

strain: An overstretching of a muscle.

subluxation: A partial dislocation of a joint.

supination: This three-plane movement involves adduction, inversion, and plantar flexion.

talus: This is what is known as the *anklebone*. Unique to this bone is the fact that there are no muscles attached to it.

tendon: This is connective tissue that connects muscle to bone.

toenails: These are protective coverings for the toes.

toxin: Anything that is poisonous to the body.

ulcers: This is a breakdown of tissue, generally an open sore, which may become infected.

varicose veins: A blockage in the veins causing a twisted, ropy, or bumpy protrusion, often on the leg.

verruca plantaris: The proper name for a plantar wart.

weak arches: Generally these are fallen arches or commonly known as *flatfeet*.

yin/yang: A Chinese concept dealing with balance.

zones: These are imaginary lines, either vertical or horizontal, that are used as guidelines in reflexology.

Index